THE
NEW GENETICS
AND THE
FUTURE OF MAN

THE
NEW GENETICS
AND THE
FUTURE OF MAN

Edited by

MICHAEL P. HAMILTON

Canon, Washington Cathedral

A book produced through the cooperation of the National Presbyterian Center, the Board of Christian Social Concerns of the United Methodist Church, and the Episcopal Cathedral of the Diocese of Washington.

WILLIAM B. EERDMANS PUBLISHING COMPANY
Grand Rapids, Michigan

CONTENTS

INTRODUCTION

All is changed, changed utterly,
A terrible beauty is born.

W. B. Yeats
Easter 1916

The utter change Yeats referred to was an attempted national revolution. That and similar political crises occupied the newspaper headlines of his day. Today—regardless of what the newspaper headlines say—the most terrible and beautiful forces shaping human events are technological rather than political. Governments come and go and human nature remains the same, but discoveries such as atomic fission or genetic engineering have a permanent effect on our social and physical well-being that makes political concerns seem unimportant by comparison.

In this book we have attempted to evaluate, from the perspective of several disciplines, new areas of medical science and practice that have genetic implications. We have tried to deal with questions such as: How can we prepare for our future in the light of the current revolutionary developments in biology? What are the medical opportunities and problems we ought to be thinking about so that decisions made in different segments of society can best serve the public welfare? If, as a result of the continuing development of industry, our daily lives are being changed, how can this latter-day beauty benefit human physical and mental health?

The book is divided into three sections: "New Beginnings in Life," "Genetic Therapy," and "Pollution and Health." In each section a scientist of publicly acknowledged prominence in his field sets forth the current state of knowledge in his discipline,

7

suggests future trends, and identifies some of the moral and social problems arising from this knowledge. The text of his essay was sent to people in three different professions to read and criticize. As a result, there is a coherent evaluation of each topic from different points of view.

The fact that the areas chosen for study deal directly or indirectly with man's heredity is important, partly because genetic changes once made are irreversible, but also because society lacks experience in making decisions about genetics. Of course, man has always influenced his own evolutionary development. When he turned from hunting to agriculture he set in motion selective factors that enabled people with certain genetically inherited characteristics to live longer and procreate more while others, less fortunately endowed, died younger and left fewer offspring. Later when men and women chose to build cities, some inhabitants suffered more than others from air and water pollution, and evolution took a new direction. While the effect of man's technology on his evolution was generally unrecognized in previous centuries, today we understand some of the connections between our environment—both natural and fabricated—and our heredity. This means we now have the opportunity and therefore, as Samuel S. Epstein argues, the responsibility to control those factors within our environment which affect our evolution.

The new technologies affecting genetics are progressing at a fast pace, and their effects in some instances amount to radical social changes. Some social commentators wonder if our traditional values and the existing forms for political decision-making are adequate to the task of using these new powers to their best advantage. They ask if we are not moving towards a discontinuity in human history. The conditions and therefore the information necessary for a reliable answer are not yet available and so readers must make their own judgments. This, to my mind, argues for more involvement by the public in the decisions being made by the Congress and by state legislatures on these vital questions. Then, even though conditions are not favorable for the best decisions to be made, the worst may be avoided.

Leon Kass criticizes the approach to technological issues of our society which generally develops techniques first and then decides whether they should be used. He argues that we should rather first discuss social goals and then consider techniques in relation to them. Dr. Kass is raising a fundamental political and philosophic issue that the reader might well keep in mind throughout the book. His concern also points to the complex relation of technology to science. A technique is usually one of many resulting from findings in a particular area of basic scientific research. Should that basic research have been blocked because some of its applications are potentially dangerous? Most basic research is undertaken without regard for its social implications. The motivation for research is the development of a theoretical structure in which each piece of new information fits into the understanding of the subject, as each piece of material contributes to the construction of a house. Hence a society that chooses to fund basic research should expect to be faced continually with new techniques that emerge without having been planned. The issue then becomes not simply that of a society choosing to develop techniques (though it may well undertake such enterprises), but that of the need for all techniques, however discovered, to be adequately evaluated prior to their adoption.

In this connection, it is important that nonscientists first learn what is being done and what is being proposed in scientific research and technology, so that they are prepared to offer intelligent criticism and contribute to political leadership in directing the future course of these fields. By the same token, scientists must be willing to give of their valuable time and energy to learn the basic ethical, social, psychological, and political implications of their work, so that their planning and style of operation will be not just a narrow intellectual one but rather will benefit from our larger cultural inheritance. The question is not whether the scientist, the politician, or the ethicist has the right to speak first, for that will be decided by which of them has new information to share. (In the case of contemporary biology and genetics it is clearly the scientists who should be heard.) The question is rather whether there is a means of communication between layman and scientist for adequate evaluation of new information. One of the purposes of this book is to further such communication.

If the contributors to this book are representative of latent public opinion regarding the controversial matters under discussion, it is clear that we as a society have yet to come to agreement on a number of important policy matters under discussion. The writers frequently disagree with each other and with the scientific exponents regarding the merits of work done and proposed. We have to do a great deal more thinking, listening, and talking to each other before public opinion can become sufficiently strong and informed to be translated into generally acceptable legislation. In the meantime a number of forces—including economic advantage acting through industrial corporations, fear of inadequate national defense, scientific curiosity, and concern for the amelioration of suffering and disease—continue to provide momentum for what remains an essentially erratic, and often narrowly conceived, course for medical research and technology. Some of the spokesmen for these forces have not been as concerned to relate their own interests to humane concerns as medical researchers generally have. This adds to the political difficulty of developing national policies, when the input to the White House, to Congress, and to state legislatures is a mixture of forces of institutional self-interest in opposition to others who have already attempted to integrate their self-interests with broader social and cultural concerns.

Faced with the obvious dangers of this scientific course, some have demanded a halt to further technological and research developments until the effect of present programs can be more fully assessed. Many who are concerned for ecological balance, for instance, have pleaded for major changes in our style of living in order to reduce pollution and compensate for depletion of natural resources. My expectation is that the momentum of technology will not be halted by such a frontal attack, but that progressive legislation and financial restraints will chip away at the evil side effects of technology. Charles Powers and Leonard Bickwit write eloquently in this vein. In the field of genetic therapy, one of the logical extensions of medical care, I would not expect a halt to research, but rather a continued surveillance of human experiments to avoid inhumane practices and, eventually, the development of guidelines for the general use of new techniques. Such a pragmatic approach, which is also advocated by W. French Anderson, frightens many. Paul Ramsey thus makes an appeal for not venturing into medical research and practice when we do not know exactly what we are doing or do not have the consent of the person or foetus involved.

However, our society has decided to risk both the known and the unknown dangers of abortion and artificial insemination because of the known advantages. I expect that our society will not object in principle to *in vitro* fertilization, cloning, and the transfer of pregnancies from one womb to another or from an *in vitro* state to a womb. But the experiments necessary to perfect such techniques may well entail ethical risks that are unacceptable to us. For instance, how can we justify experimental cloning of humans if there is the risk of a high percentage of failures? It is likely that such experiments will take place, if not in America, then in a country with different ethical standards than ours. If such experiments succeed in producing techniques that do not cause a higher incidence of abnormalities or failures than natural procreation, and if their use overcomes physiological and psychological problems in parents, I expect our society will take advantage of them. However, abuses will inevitably occur. For instance, if a husband or wife for reasons of pride chose to clone himself or herself, the psychiatric dangers of false expectations and the difficulty for the child in maneuvering through the oedipal stages would be grave. A more serious abuse could occur if a nation chose to develop a reservoir of intelligence by cloning gifted men and women for aggressive purposes, thus threatening the security of other nations. Joseph Fletcher comments on this possibility.

Some of the new techniques discussed in this book invite a reexamination of the nature of human parenthood. For centuries, we have defined parenthood in terms of biology — the genetic father and mother are the "real" parents of the child. This identification has been the basis for our common law and has been only partly qualified for adoption cases. I say "partly" because the adopted child is still legally disadvantaged in some states, as Frank Grad points out. But the inadequacy of this biological approach for the concept of parenthood is being challenged by the growing incidence of artificial insemination. For instance, who is the "real" father of a child conceived by artificial insemination, given up by the mother and finally placed with adoptive parents? More complex scenarios are feasible, as the authors of this book illustrate. Rather than attempting further legal exceptions already made necessary by adoption and A.I.D., I believe we should look for a new legal and moral definition of parenthood — a husband and wife who will accept responsibility for the care and upbringing of a baby however that baby may have been conceived or gestated. This would simplify what is becoming a chaotic legal situation and would also be consonant with the intent of the Judaeo-Christian tradition. As a corollary to this, in addition to other restraints, no experiment in developing human life should be begun unless adoptive parents are prepared to accept responsibility for the upbringing of the children so produced.

Christians believe there is a continuity in human affairs, at least seen from the perspective of God, and that man's destiny is in God's loving hands. Hence we are saved from ultimate fear of our future, whatever happens in the world. On the other hand, we remain skeptical about man's motivations, noting his continuing propensity to build Towers of Babel, and are very concerned that the effects of his selfishness and ignorance be offset. While the Christian trust in God is not something that the secular reader will share, it is hoped that this book will contribute to a common understanding of the care which our society needs to exercise in determining our genetic future.

*   *   *   *

In closing, I wish to express my thanks to many, including the Trustees of the Paddock Foundation, who originally asked me to undertake this venture and provided initial and major funding for it. I am also grateful to Dr. Lowell R. Ditzen, Director of the National Presbyterian Center, and to the Reverend Rodney Shaw of the United Methodist Board of Christian Social Concerns, who served as co-sponsors of the book and whose institutions assisted in its financing. The Very Reverend Francis B. Sayre, Jr., Dean of Washington Cathedral, with his broad vision of the scope of the ministry of this cathedral, gave me the encouragement to spend time on the project; and Dr. French Anderson, head of the Section on Human Biochemistry at the National Institutes of Health, was most helpful in giving advice on scientific matters. Nancy Montgomery, editor of *The Cathedral Age*, provided valuable assistance in editing the texts. With all this support and aid I can claim for myself only the responsibility for whatever errors and omissions occur, and this I gladly do. I have enjoyed learning about this fascinating area of man's endeavors, and I hope the reader will also find pleasure and profit from this book.

—Canon Michael Hamilton
Washington Cathedral

NEW BEGINNINGS IN LIFE

Good afternoon, ladies and gentlemen. This is your pilot speaking. We are flying at an altitude of 35,000 feet and a speed of 700 miles an hour. I have two pieces of news to report, one good and one bad. The bad news is that we are lost. The good news is that we are making very good time.

—Author unknown

* * *

One egg, one embryo, one adult—normality. But a bokanovskified egg will bud, will proliferate, will divide. From eight to ninety-six buds, and every bud will grow into a perfectly formed embryo, and every embryo into a full-sized adult. Making ninety-six human beings grow where only one grew before. Progress.

—Aldous Huxley, *Brave New World*

The oocytes were suspended in droplets consisting of fluid from their own follicle (where available), and the medium being tested for fertilization. After incubation for 1-4 hours at 37°C the oocytes were washed through two changes of the medium under test before being placed in the suspensions of spermatozoa. . . . Ejaculated spermatozoa were supplied by the husband. The spermatozoa were washed twice by gentle centrifugation in the medium under test, and made up to a final concentration of between 8×10^5 and 2×10^6 per milliliter depending on the quality of the sample. The higher numbers were used with samples of poor quality containing many inactive spermatozoa, cellular inclusions, other debris, or viscous seminal fluid. The fertilization droplets were approximately 0.05 milliliters.

—R. G. Edwards, P. C. Steptoe, and J. M. Purdy (1970). Cleavage *in vitro* of Preovulatory Human Oocytes. *Nature 227:*1307.

Now Adam knew Eve his wife, and she conceived and bore Cain, saying I have created a man with the help of the Lord.

—Genesis 4:1

CHAPTER I

NEW BEGINNINGS IN LIFE

LEON R. KASS

Struggling with the task of writing on the intriguing and awesome topic "New Beginnings in Life," I was tempted more than once to exploit the ambiguity of the title and to present, instead of what follows, an anecdotal biographical sketch with slides of my daughter, whose birth (in the natural and still customary manner) interrupted the writing of the first draft of this paper. Though I was able to resist the temptation, I feel privileged to have had the opportunity to face it. At the risk of showing my hand too early, let me add that it is my wish and concern that future generations not be denied the possibility of the same temptation.

I have been asked to outline the state of contemporary knowledge and techniques in the subject area, raise some of the

Dr. Leon R. Kass, Executive Secretary of the Committee on the Life Sciences and Social Policy of the National Research Council—National Academy of Sciences, is a biologist who was born in Chicago, Illinois, and took his undergraduate and medical degrees at the University of Chicago. He received his Ph.D. in biochemistry from Harvard University in 1967. Prior to his present employment in the National Research Council, he served as Senior Staff Fellow in the Laboratory of Molecular Biology, National Institute of Arthritis and Metabolic Diseases, in the National Institute of Health in Bethesda, Maryland. He has published a number of papers in technical journals and is presently cooperating with Daniel Callahan on a book entitled Freedom, Coercion, and the Life Sciences.

issues and questions in relationship to those techniques, and offer my opinions on the future course of events. This I will attempt to do, but not without a word of protest.

My protest is against having to begin with a discussion of techniques, of "the state of the art." The order of topics assigned to me is: first the technical, then the ethical and legal; first how to do it, then why or whether to do it. My complaint deals with our entire way of thinking about new technologies, a thinking which shapes even that new art, "Technology Assessment." We are told that new technologies are coming and that we should attend, consider, and adjust to the social consequences. This formulation treats new developments as automatic, as insensitive to human decision and choice. But only a slavish mind and a slavish society let the means dictate the ends. It is a sad fact of modern life—which I do not mean to deny by my protest—that we often seem to be tyrannized and compelled by our technique, so that the things we seek to control usurp our authority as controllers. We are often presented with pieces of technology to evaluate, even though we never planned for or deliberated about their development and introduction. It is often unavoidable, and hence in a sense appropriate, that we begin with the technical: new techniques pose difficult questions, and only then do we consider questions of ends and standards and values. But to the extent that we are or seek to be rational men, we must insist, at least in our thought and discussion, on beginning with a serious deliberation about our ends and purposes. Failure to do this casts great doubt upon, indeed nullifies, those exuberant claims of new technologians and theologists that we are well on our way to a rational understanding of and rational control over human nature and human life. It is indeed the height of irrationality triumphantly to pursue rationalized techniques while insisting that ends or purposes lie beyond rational discourse. To do so is to surrender the most important matters to the reign of our capricious wills and our fickle opinions.

I will thus make a new beginning, and begin at the beginning, with our theme, "New Beginnings in Life." Reflection on this theme can perhaps make visible early some of the larger questions against which to consider some specific technologies. Why should anyone want to provide for or perpetrate "New Beginnings in Life?" A major reason given is that in many instances, the "old"[1] beginning is not possible. Despite greatly increased abilities to diagnose and to treat the causes of infertility in recent years, some couples still remain involuntarily childless. Thus, paradoxically, while the need to limit fertility becomes ever more apparent, some scientists and physicians seem to take it as their duty to satisfy the natural desire of every couple to have a child, by natural or artificial means.

Some rather large questions arise here. Physicians have a *duty* to treat infertility by whatever means only if patients have a *right* to have children by whatever means. But the right to procreate is an ambiguous right, and certainly not an unqualified one. Whose right is it, a woman's or a couple's? Is it a right to carry and deliver (i.e., only a woman's right) or is it a right to nurture and rear? Is it a right to have your own biological child? Even if involuntary sterilization imposed by the regime would violate such a right, however defined, is it "violated" or denied by sterility not imposed from without but due to disease? Is the inability to conceive a disease, or merely a symptom of disease? If a disease, whose is it? Can a couple have a disease? If a disease, is it a disease demanding treatment wherever found? In women over seventy? In virgin girls? In men? Can these persons claim either a natural desire or right to have a child, which the new technologies might or must provide them? Those who seek to submerge the distinction between *natural* and *unnatural* means would do well to ponder these questions and reflect on what they themselves mean when they speak of "a natural desire to have children" or "a [natural] right to have children." One cannot speak of natural desires or natural rights or, indeed, about disease without some notion of the normal, the natural, the healthy.

The questions just raised deserve a careful and detailed exploration which I shall not here attempt. Yet even as posed, they suggest that both the language of rights and the language

[1]This awkward use of "old" calls attention to the subtle traps laid for us by selections of language. In a time and place where novelty and originality are considered cardinal virtues, and when faddishness has replaced tuberculosis as the scourge of the intellectual classes, one should vigorously resist the tendency to make things attractive simply by emphasizing their newness. Is the "old" way of beginning life merely *old*, simply traditional and conventional? A different cast to our discussion would result if the title were "Unnatural," "Artificial," or even "Unusual" Beginnings in Life.

of disease could lead to great difficulties in thinking about infertility. Both point to possessions or properties of single individuals, for it is an individual who bears rights and diseases. Yet infertility, as ordinarily understood, is a condition located in a marriage, in a union of two individuals. If it is a disease, it is a "social disease." Even though the pathology responsible is usually found in only one of the partners, their interaction is required to make the problem manifest. To consider infertility solely from the perspective of individual rights or of a traditional medical model of disease can only serve to undermine—in thought and in practice—the bond between childbearing and the covenant of marriage.

A second reason given for seeking "New Beginnings" is that sometimes the old beginnings are thought to be undesirable or inadequate, primarily on eugenic grounds. A diverse and perhaps incompatible collection of champions are in bed together under this rationale: patient-centered physicians and genetic counselors seeking to prevent the transmission of inherited diseases to prospective children of carrier parents, species-centered pessimists eager to combat the alleged deterioration of the human gene pool, and zealous optimists eager to engineer "improvements" in the human species. The new beginnings called for include the growth of early embryos in the laboratory with selective destruction of those who do not pass genetic muster, directed mating with eugenically selected eggs, sperm, or both, and asexual replication of existing "superior" individuals. But serious questions can be raised about these ends as well. We may know which diseases we would wish not to have inflicted upon ourselves and our offspring, but are we wise enough to act upon these desires? In view of our ignorance of why certain genes survive in our populations, can we be sure that the eradication of genetic disease (or any single genetic disease) is a biologically sensible goal? The species-centered goals are even more problematic. Do we know what constitutes a deterioration or an improvement in the human gene pool? One might well argue that the crusaders against genetic deterioration are worried about the wrong genes. After all, how many architects of the Vietnam war have suffered from Down's syndrome? Who uses up more of our irreplaceable natural resources and who produces more pollution—the inmates of an institution for the retarded or the graduates of Harvard College? It is probably as indisputable as it is ignored that the world suffers more from the morally and spiritually defective than from the genetically defective. But, emancipated from our tradition, we now believe not only that virtue can't be taught but that it does not even exist, except as a word in some ancient books. Thus, our best minds dedicate themselves instead to what they can learn how to do, designing virtuous genes.

Perhaps this is too harsh a judgment. Certainly, our genetic inheritance is entrusted to us for safekeeping and not for abuse or neglect. Perhaps a case could be made for the desirability and wisdom of certain negative or even positive eugenic goals. Still, as in the treatment of infertility, we shall also have to consider which means, if any, can be justified in the service of any reasonable goals.

Thirdly, there are scientific goals that generate "New Beginnings in Life." In other words, there is a limit to what can be learned about the nature and regulation of fertilization, embryonic development, or gene action from lives begun undisturbed in the old, natural manner. This is no doubt true. But if the goal is scientific knowledge of these processes for its own sake, there is little need to develop new beginnings in *human* life. Embryological experimentation in a wide range of mammals, employing all the new technological possibilities, would yield the basic understanding. There is at present no reason to believe that the fundamental mechanisms of differentiation differ in monkeys and in man. Until extensive animal studies show otherwise, the human experiments can only be given a technological and not a purely scientific justification.[2] These technological purposes and activities (and others, such as the use of early embryos in culture to test for mutation- or cancer-producing chemicals and drugs, or to work out techniques for genetic manipulation) may well be desirable, but they need to be so identified and distinguished from the simple quest for knowledge. To assess adequately the desirability of any specific means and to weigh properly the alternative means require a clear understanding of which ends are being served.

Finally, "New Beginnings in Life" are being sought precisely because they are new and because they can be sought. While not

[2]Indeed, it is the philanthropic foundations interested in finding new drugs for abortion or contraception who are supporting much of the work on new beginnings of *human* life. For example, the work of R. G. Edwards and his colleagues in Cambridge, England, is supported by the Ford Foundation.

praiseworthy reasons, these certainly are important reasons and all-too-human ones. Drawn by the promise of fame and glory, driven by the hot breath of competitors, men do what can be done. Biomedical scientists are no less human than anyone else.[3] Moreover, regardless of their private motives, they are encouraged to pursue the novel because of the widespread and not unjustified belief that their new findings will help to alleviate one form or another of human suffering. They are also encouraged by that curious new breed of technotheologians who, after having pronounced God dead, disclose that God's dying command was that mankind should undertake its limitless, no-holds-barred self-modification, by all feasible means. Let no one be surprised should some competent scientists respond to the call to prosecute this new holy war against human nature.

Despite the encouragement coming from outside, the major force driving toward "New Beginnings in Life" currently comes from within the scientific community, and in fact from a small number of research workers. At present there is little public pressure to perfect these technologies. Yet we can expect such pressure to appear, partly in response to buoyant claims accompanying the wide publicity given to each technical triumph along the way, partly because of the growing shortage of babies for adoption due to the growing practice of abortion on demand. Moreover, once perfected for limited use, the techniques will be desired and used on a larger scale, and for reasons other than those for which they were developed. Thus the public attitude may change rapidly from indifferent toleration to enthusiastic demand.

[3]Several scientists have explicitly warned of this problem in connection with the technologies here being considered. "Moreover, clinical irresponsibility may be fostered by the temptation to seek the glory of a first achievement. The publicity which would be attached to the first success in producing a 'test tube baby' would almost certainly push a mere heart transplantation or Moon walk off the front page of any national daily" (A. McLaren and M. G. Kerr, Egg Transplantation, *Science Journal*, June 1970, p. 56). In a letter to the editor of *The Washington Post* (Feb. 24, 1971) on the subject of human embryo experimentation, Professor James D. Watson wrote: "I think the matter is much too important to be left in the hands of the scientists whose careers might be made by the achieving of a given experiment." Professor Watson's keen appreciation of this all-too-human aspect of scientists is apparent in his book, *The Double Helix* (New York: Athenaeum, 1968).

So much then for reasons why some have called for and helped to promote "New Beginnings in Life." But what precisely is new about these new beginnings? Such life will still come from pre-existing life, no new formation from the dust of the ground is being contemplated, nothing as new—or as old—as that first genesis of life from nonliving matter is in the immediate future. What is new is nothing more radical than the divorce of the generation of new human life from human sexuality and ultimately from the confines of the human body, a separation which began with artificial insemination and which will finish with ectogenesis, the full laboratory growth of a baby from sperm to term. What is new is that sexual intercourse will no longer be needed for generating new life. This novelty leads to two others: there is a new co-progenitor (or several such), the embryologist-geneticist-physician, and there is a new home for generation, the laboratory. The mysterious and intimate processes of generation are to be moved from the darkness of the womb to the bright (fluorescent) light of the laboratory, and beyond the shadow of a single doubt.[4]

If we are not to remain in the dark about these prospects, we must also see a deeper meaning of our title. We are considering not merely new ways of beginning individual lives, but also—and this is far more important—new ways of life and new ways of viewing human life and the nature of man. A man is partly where he comes from, and the character of his life and his community will no doubt be influenced by (and will of course influence) the manner in which he comes to be.

Consider the views of life and the world reflected in the following different expressions to describe the process of generating new life. The Hebrews, impressed with the phenomenon of transmission of life from father to son, used a word we translate "begetting" or "siring." The Greeks, impressed with the springing forth of new life in the cyclical processes of generation and decay, called it *genesis*, from a root meaning "to come into being." (It was the Greek translators who gave this name to the first book of the Hebrew Bible.) The pre-modern Christian English-speaking world, impressed with the world as

---

[4]The first and perhaps best attack on this process of enlightenment was delivered by Sophocles. Do we mean to ignore what we learned from Oedipus's prideful efforts to bring into full and public light the mystery of his origins?

given by a Creator, used the term "pro-creation." We, impressed with the machine and the gross national product (our own work of creation) employ a metaphor of the factory, "re-production." And Aldous Huxley has provided "decantation" for that technology-worshipping "Brave New World" of tomorrow.

In Vitro Fertilization: State of the Art

The first technical development I shall discuss is an accomplishment recently reported from several laboratories around the world, most publicly from that of Dr. R. G. Edwards in Cambridge, England: the fertilization, in the test tube, of human egg by human sperm, and the subsequent laboratory culture of the young embryo. One of the major technical difficulties recently overcome was to obtain mature, functional eggs. Normally, eggs mature in the ovary, one during each menstrual cycle. At birth, each woman possesses her full supply of oocytes, or immature eggs. These oocytes have already completed the first stages of meiosis, the special process of cell division which results in the formation of the sex cells (eggs and sperm), each carrying half the number of chromosomes present in all the other cells of the body. The oocytes rest at this stage in their surrounding follicles; completion of meiosis and maturation does not occur until puberty. Thereafter, early in each menstrual cycle, several follicles begin to enlarge, under the influence of a reproductive hormone from the pituitary gland (follicle-stimulating hormone). A second pituitary hormone (luteinizing hormone) triggers ovulation, the release of the egg from one of the enlarged follicles, and also stimulates that egg to complete meiosis. The released and matured egg passes into the oviduct, ready for fertilization.

The difficulties in recovering these mature eggs after normal ovulation led to the search for alternative methods. The first successful *in vitro* fertilization was obtained with eggs which had been matured *in vitro* in suitable culture media, the immature oocytes having come from ovarian tissue surgically removed for clinical reasons. But, for unknown reasons, these fertilized eggs failed to develop normally on subsequent laboratory culture.

To overcome this difficulty, Edwards and his obstetrician colleague, Dr. P. C. Steptoe, have devised a surgical method, known as laparoscopy, to obtain matured eggs directly from their follicles prior to ovulation. Before the operation, women are given reproductive hormones in order to control the menstrual cycle, initiate the growth of several follicles, and induce maturation of the oocytes. Laparoscopy is performed just a few hours prior to the time of ovulation. A special vacuum collection device is inserted through a small incision made in the abdominal wall. Under direct visualization of the ovary by means of a slender telescope passed through a second abdominal incision, the thinned walls of the bulging follicles are punctured and the contents collected. As many as three or four preovulatory oocytes can be recovered from one woman.

Upon addition of sperm, fertilization occurs with a small but significant fraction of these eggs. Kept in culture medium, a majority of the fertilized eggs begin to divide. Some of these (in experiments to date, only a small fraction) reach the blastocyst stage (i.e., age of about 7-8 days), the stage at which the early embryo normally implants itself in the uterine lining. Successful implantation of laboratory-grown embryos has been reported in rabbits and in mice, but not in humans.[5] The physical transfer of the embryo into the uterine cavity poses no problem, but implantation may be difficult to achieve with regularity, since this process is poorly understood. It *is* known that the uterine lining is receptive to implantation only for a short portion of the menstrual cycle, and that only embryos at a certain stage are capable of implantation. Thus the timing of transfer is critical. The results with mice can be considered encouraging: a recent article reports that nearly half of the transferred blastocysts developed into full-term, apparently normal progeny (Mukherjee and Cohen 1970). No gross abnormalities have been noted in any of the animals born alive following blastocyst transfer. And although some researchers would prefer to learn more about the control of implantation in animals before proceeding further in the human work, others are inclined to go ahead in humans on a trial-and-error basis. In fact, Edwards and Steptoe hope to accomplish transfer and subsequent growth into a normal baby sometime in the next year or two.

This summarizes the current state of the art on new beginnings in *human* life. But there is much work being done on

[5]Chang, M. C. 1959. Fertilization of Rabbit Ova *in vitro*. *Nature 184:*466-7. Whittingham, D. C. 1968. Fertilization of Mouse Eggs *in vitro*. *Nature 220:*592-93. Mukherjee, A. B., and Cohen, M. M. 1970 Development of Normal Mice by *in vitro* Fertilization. *Nature 228:*472-3.

other mammals which will provide knowledge and techniques some day applicable to humans. Some of these developments deserve mention, although a detailed treatment is beyond the scope of this paper. Considerable progress has been made in growing older mammalian embryos in the laboratory. Dr. D. A. T. New and his colleagues in Cambridge, England, have been successful in growing rat and mice embryos bathed in blood serum medium for about one-third (the middle third) of the whole gestation period. As the embryo approaches term size, it can no longer be maintained bathed in media but requires more efficient circulation and exchange of nutriments, gases, and wastes. Various artificial pump and perfusion techniques, analogous to the artificial kidney machine, are being studied in an effort to design an artificial placenta. Finally, a longstanding barrier to *in vitro* culture, located just after the blastocyst stage, has recently fallen. Dr. Yu-Chih Hsu of Johns Hopkins University has reported the successful culture of mouse embryos from the blastocyst stage to a stage having a differentiated and beating heart.[6] Thus, from both ends and from the middle, researchers are closing in on the possibility of complete extracorporeal gestation. It should be stressed that these techniques are being pursued primarily to make possible a better understanding of the full scope of embryonic development. However, even though no scientists at present appear to be interested in going from fertilization to birth entirely in the laboratory,[7] the technology to do so is gradually being worked out, piece by piece.

Techniques to predetermine the sex of unborn children may be just around the corner. Since the sex is determined solely by the X or Y chromosome content of the sperm, techniques to physically separate X-carrying from Y-carrying sperm would make sex control possible through artificial insemination.

[6]Hsu, Y. 1971. *In vitro* Differentiation of Mouse Embryo Beyond Implantation Stage. *Federation Proceedings 30:*251 Abs. Hsu, Y. 1971. Post-blastocyst Differentiation *in vitro. Nature 231:*100-102. Sullivan, W. Embryos of Mice Are Developed to Heart-Beating Stage in Lab. *The New York Times,* April 14, 1971, p. 1.

[7]Although no scientist *appears* to be, at least one *is* interested, according to a quotation in Albert Rosenfeld's book, *The Second Genesis: The Coming Control of Life* (Englewood Cliffs, New Jersey: Prentice-Hall, 1969): " 'If I can carry a baby all the way through to birth *in vitro*,' says an American scientist who wants his anonymity protected, 'I certainly plan to do it—though obviously,' I am not going to succeed on the first attempt, or even the twentieth' " (p. 117).

Attempts to effect such a separation have all met with failure, but new efforts can be expected, partly because of recently discovered methods for detecting the Y chromosome in cells, a process which may serve as an assay for successful separation. A second method of sex control, already successfully demonstrated in rabbits, involves the sexing of embryos (prior to implantation) by cell-staining techniques or chromosome analysis.[8] Embryos of the desired sex could then be transferred to the recipient females. Though accurate, this sexing technique is not without its problems, since embryonic tissue needs to be removed for testing. In the rabbit work, only about one in five embryos sexed by these methods developed to full term, and there was at least one monstrous birth. Even if these technical difficulties are ironed out, it is doubtful that there will be many who accept the costs and inconvenience of *in vitro* fertilization or even artificial insemination to control the sex of their offspring—unless perhaps they are known carriers of a sex-linked genetic disease such as hemophilia. Less cumbersome methods, e.g., a chemical method that would selectively destroy either the X- or the Y-carrying sperm in the man's body or soon after intercourse, are possibilities but as yet unreported even in animals.

In Vitro Fertilization: Ethical Questions

At the end of a recent popular review article in *Scientific American* summarizing the work on human embryos, Drs. Edwards and Fowler offer the following conclusion: "We are well aware that this work presents challenges to a number of established social and ethical concepts. In our opinion the emphasis should be on the rewards that the work promises in fundamental knowledge and in medicine."[9] It is obvious that I do not share this conclusion, not so much because I disagree with it—which I do—but because it is as yet an unexamined conclusion drawn from doubtful premises. For one thing, we are told we *should* "emphasize" promised rewards in knowledge

[8]Gardner, R. L., and Edwards, R. G. 1968. Control of the Sex Ratio at Full Term in the Rabbit by Transferring Sexed Blastocyst. *Nature* 218:346-48.

[9]Edwards, R. G., and Fowler, R. E. 1970. Human Embryos in the Laboratory. *Scientific American 223:*45-54 (December), at p. 54.

and power at some future time at the expense of established (don't they really mean "establishment" or "conventional"?) ideas of right. This is itself a value judgment—untenable as a *general* proposition for experimentation on human subjects—whose soundness in this particular case can't be determined until the full range of ethical, social, legal, and political implications are carefully studied and understood.

Let us consider first what is probably the least controversial and likely to be the most popular use, at least initially, for *in vitro* fertilization: the provision of their own child to a sterile couple, where oviduct disease in the woman obstructs the free passage of egg and sperm, and hence also fertilization.[10]

At first glance, the intramarital use of artificial fertilization resembles, from an ethical point of view, artificial insemination by the husband (A.I.H.). The procedure simply provides for the union of the wife's egg and the husband's sperm, circumventing the pathological obstruction to that union. But there is at least this difference. There is an alternative treatment for infertility due to tubal obstruction, namely surgical reconstruction of the oviduct, which, if successful, permanently removes the cause of infertility (i.e., it treats the disease, not merely the desire to have a child). Moreover, it does so without need for manipulation of embryos. At present, the success rate for oviduct reconstruction is only fair (about 30 percent), but with effort and practice this is bound to improve. Such therapeutic surgery for women is without possible moral objections or adverse social consequences. It is therefore to be preferred over artificial fertilization, both in principle (one should use the least objectionable means to achieve the same unobjectionable end) and in practice, granted that both options are feasible and available.

A sufficient reason for this preference is found in the most important intrinsic difference between artificial insemination

10There are many infertile women so affected, crude estimates suggesting as many as 1 percent of all women. Approximately 10 percent of couples are infertile, and in more than half of these cases the cause is in the female. Blocked or abnormal oviducts account for perhaps 20 percent of the female causes of infertility. However, not all such cases—perhaps even only a minority—are suitable candidates for the intramarital use of *in vitro* fertilization. "Many women who have blocked Fallopian tubes also prove to have ovaries which are involved in generalized pelvic adhesions which make it difficult or impossible for a doctor to obtain eggs from them. For this reason only a minority of women with blocked tubes are likely to be able to provide their own eggs for fertilization" (McLaren and Kerr, p. 54).

and artificial fertilization. In the latter, fertilization and the earliest stages of embryonic development occur in the laboratory. Considerably more manipulation is involved than in artificial insemination, including manipulation of the embryo itself. There is thus a serious question concerning the safety of this manipulation; and this physiological question forms the basis of a moral objection, since the hazards are being imposed on another human being, the child-to-be, who obviously cannot consent to have such risks imposed upon him. Does the parents' desire for a child entitle them to have it by methods which carry for that child an unknown and untested risk of deformity or malformation?

How unknown are the risks? Drs. Edwards and Steptoe are reported ready to proceed with implantation if tests on the embryos can rule out the presence of genetic or other defects.[11] Apparently they are concerned about the risks but ignorant of their likelihood. In their judgment, "the normality of embryonic development and efficiency of embryo transfer cannot yet be assessed."[12] Perhaps it was a concern for possible risks to the offspring that accounts for the unexplained judgment, quite surprising in the light of his later words and deeds, rendered by Edwards in an article written only five years ago: "If rabbit and pig eggs can be fertilized after maturation in culture, presumably human eggs grown in culture could also be fertilized, *although obviously it would not be permissible to implant them in a human recipient.* We have therefore attempted to fertilize cultured human eggs *in vitro.*"[13] The last sentence indicates that Edwards had no qualms about the "permissibility" of doing the fertilizations themselves. (If taken seriously, the entire quotation displays that curious form of technocratic logic in which a course of action is deduced simply from the possibility of action: "Presumably human eggs can also be fertilized, *therefore* we have tried to fertilize them.")

In contrast to Edwards and Steptoe, Dr. Landrum Shettles at Columbia University is apparently less troubled. He does not

[11] Sullivan, W. Implant of Human Embryo Appears Near. *The New York Times,* October 29, 1970, p. 1.

[12] Edwards, R. G., Steptoe, P. C., and Purdy, J. M. 1970. Fertilization and Cleavage *in vitro* of Preovulatory Human Oocytes. *Nature* 227:1307-09, at p. 1309.

[13] Edwards, R. G. 1966. Mammalian Eggs in the Laboratory. *Scientific American 214:*73-81 (August), at p. 80. Emphasis added.

even talk about the need for such tests and appears ready to proceed, having put the burden of proof on those who might be more cautious or might raise other objections. In his latest article he states that "the grossly normal blastocyst" was not transferred to the patient for the single reason that she had recently undergone uterine surgery. He adds: "Otherwise, there was no discernible contraindication for a successful transfer *in vitro* [sic; he means *in utero*] and continued development. This is scheduled for patients with ligated or excised fallopian tubes who may want a child, with the ova obtained by culdoscopy or laparoscopy."[14] For there to be "discernible contraindications," one has first to look in order to discern them. Unhappily, very little looking has been done.

The embryo transfer experiments have been done largely in mice and in rabbits. While there have been no reports of gross deformities at birth, no systematic attempts have been made to look for defects which appear at later times or for lesser abnormalities apparent even at birth. In species more closely related to humans, e.g., in primates, successful *in vitro* fertilization has yet to be accomplished. The need to establish the risk for primates is emphasized by some researchers, including Dr. Luigi Mastroianni, chairman of obstetrics and gynecology at the University of Pennsylvania: "It is my feeling that we must be

[14]Shettles, L. B. 1971. Human Blastocyst Grown *in vitro* in Ovulation Cervical Mucus. *Nature 229:*343. These concluding remarks are strangely worded and indeed strange altogether for a scientific article, which ordinarily does not include such explicit statements of future plans in a report of completed accomplishments. This fact, along with the use of the anticipatory "scheduled" (connoting a definite date and time) rather than the more vague and usual "planned," and along with the striking one-sidedness of the list of references, strongly suggests to the ordinary reader (having no knowledge of the men other than from their writings) that a race may be on to do the first embryo transfer—or at least that credit for having been able to do it when someone else does the first one is important at least to some of the researchers in this field. This conclusion is supported by the following report of Dr. Shettles' reaction to the first published report from Edwards and his colleagues of successful *in vitro* fertilization of human eggs: "Dr. Landrum Shettles of Columbia University says he achieved *in vitro* fertilization of human eggs back in 1953 and published his series in *Ova Humanum* in 1960. 'The Cambridge group not only hasn't done anything new, they haven't even gone as far as we have' " (*Medical World News*, March 7, 1969, p. 17). If such a race is on, it is likely that the swift will throw caution to the more sober and will trust to luck that their victory in the race does not issue in a deformed or retarded child.

very sure we are able to produce normal young by this method in monkeys before we have the temerity to move ahead in the human."[15]

Can laboratory testing of the human embryos themselves, prior to transfer, provide enough information about safety? Not at present, or in the foreseeable future. Ordinary observation of the early embryo can disclose abnormalities but is too crude a measure of normality. Most genetic tests cannot be done on a given embryo without damaging it; moreover, few genetic tests are presently available. Furthermore, damages could be introduced during the transfer procedure, even after the last inspection is completed. Conceivably the manipulations may even make possible the implantation of some abnormal embryos which under natural conditions would have been spontaneously aborted.[16] And while it is true that nature often aborts those embryos with the most serious developmental defects, she does not always do so. There is at present no way of finding out whether or not the procedures of *in vitro* fertilization, culture, and transfer of human embryos will result in congenital anomalies, sterility, or mental retardation in any of the viable progeny.

If I have dwelt at length upon the problem of risks and mishaps which accompany the experimental phase of this new

[15]Cohn, V. 1971. Lab Growth of Human Embryo Raises Doubt of "Normality." *Outlook. The Washington Post*, March 21, 1971. Cohn's article quotes Dr. Mastroianni further as follows: "In our laboratory, our position is, 'Let's explore the thing thoroughly in monkeys and establish the risk.' Then we can describe that risk to a patient and obtain truly informed consent before going ahead. We must be very careful to use patients well and not be presumptuous with human lives. We must not be just biologic technicians." I would dissent from this fine statement only to suggest that both doctor and prospective parents would be "presumptuous with human lives" in proceeding unless there were known to be *no* risks. The "patient at risk"—the planned child-to-be—cannot give a "truly informed consent."

[16]A high percentage (perhaps even a majority) of fertilized eggs fail to develop normally through the early stages of embryonic development and degenerate even before a diagnosis of pregnancy is made. Some fail to implant when they reach the uterus, others undergo faulty and only transient implantation. In many cases, the failure is thought to be due to genetic and developmental abnormalities in the embryo. The likely high incidence of abnormalities in eggs fertilized *in vivo* will itself make it very difficult to establish the additional risks specifically imposed by the *in vitro* procedures.

technology, it is because it is a problem widely and remarkably ignored and because it provides a powerful moral objection to the implantation experiments. Moreover, this moral objection can and should be widely shared; it does not rest upon arguments about the will of God or about natural right. It rests instead upon that minimal principle of medical practice, *DO NO HARM*. In these prospective experiments upon the unborn, it is not enough not to know of any grave defects; one needs to know with some confidence that there will be no such defects— or at least no more than there are without the procedure. Professor Paul Ramsey, one of the few people to write on this point, has put the matter quite forcefully and, I think, correctly: "The decisive moral verdict must be that we cannot rightfully *get to know* how to do this without conducting unethical experiments upon the unborn who must be the 'mishaps' (the dead and the retarded ones) through whom we learn how."[17]

It may be objected that all new medical technologies are risky, and that the kind of ethical scrupulosity I advocate would put a halt to medical progress. But such an objection ignores an important distinction. It is one thing to accept voluntarily the risk of a dangerous procedure for yourself (or to consent on behalf of your child) if the purpose is therapeutic. Some might say this is not only permissible but obligatory, a part of one's duty to preserve his own health. It is quite a different thing deliberately to submit a hypothetical or unborn child to hazardous procedures which can in no way be considered therapeutic for him and are "therapeutic" for you only in that they "treat" your desires, albeit unobjectionable ones. (The earlier discussion of whether infertility is a disease and of the right to procreate is pertinent here. Only a strong pro-natalist position which held procreation to be an overriding duty might override these objections.) Morally, it is insufficient that your motives are good, that your ends are unobjectionable, that you do the procedure "lovingly," and even that you may be lucky in the result: You will be engaging nonetheless in an unethical experiment upon a human subject.

While on the subject of the ethics of experimentation, let me add a few comments concerning the couple. Most of the scien-

[17]Ramsey, P. *Fabricated Man* (New Haven: Yale University Press, 1970), p. 113.

tific reports on human embryo experimentation are strangely silent on the nature of the egg donors and on their understanding of what was to be done with their eggs. This is surprising considering the growing sensitivity of the scientific community to the requirement of informed consent, and especially surprising given the kind of experiment here being performed. In the report describing the first successful fertilization and cleavage of human eggs obtained via laparoscopy,[18] there are some passing references to "patients," and the one-sentence abstract of the paper only increases our confusion by its use of the word "mother": "Human oocytes have been taken from the mother before ovulation, fertilized *in vitro* and grown *in vitro* to the eight- or sixteen-celled stage in various media." If the women are indeed patients being treated for infertility, then "the mother" is surely the one thing that they are not. In the recent *Scientific American* article, there is this solitary comment: "Our patients were childless couples who hoped our research might enable them to have children."[19] We are not told, and can therefore only guess, what these women were in fact told. From the report that the women and their husbands had hopes, we can surmise that *they* considered themselves to be patients. But for the present, they are *experimental subjects*. The researchers owe us an account of how consent was obtained and what the couples were told.

Only one of the scientific articles, that describing the use of the laparoscopic surgery to recover human oocytes,[20] tells us anything more about the persons used as experimental subjects (in this case, for perfecting the laparoscopy technique),[21] and

[18]Edwards, Steptoe, and Purdy, 1307-09.

[19]Edwards and Fowler, p. 50.

[20]Steptoe, P. C., and Edwards, R. G. 1970. Laparoscopic Recovery of Preovulatory Human Oocytes After Priming of Ovaries with Gonadotrophins. *The Lancet i:*683-89 (April 4, 1970).

[21]"The volunteer patients were the women of infertile married couples numbering forty-six in all. Forty of them lived in Lancashire in the normal catchment area of the hospital, and six came from other parts of the country. We insisted that all of them were referred to us in the usual way through normal medical channels. All couples were subjected to full investigation, including laparascopic examination of the wife. The patients selected for oocyte recovery were those with peritubal lesions, tubal occlusions, absence of the tubes, 'failed' tuboplastic surgery, and male oligospermia" (from the *Material and Methods* section of the paper, *ibid.,* p. 683. The sentence on informing the patients, quoted next in the text,

about how they were informed: "The object of the investigations was fully discussed with the patients, including the possible clinical applications to relieve *their* infertility" (emphasis added). Though welcome, this statement is incomplete. It does not tell us whether the couples were also told that the much more likely possibility was that it would be future infertile women, rather than they themselves, whose infertility might be "relieved." It leaves us to wonder how the discussions were conducted, especially in the light of the following remark attributed to R. G. Edwards: "We tell women with blocked oviducts, 'Your only hope of having a child is to help us. Then maybe we can help you.'"[22] Discussions with patients must not ignore the fact that infertile couples, especially the women, are ready to consent to almost any procedure which promises them the slightest hope of conception. Therefore their consent, though necessary, will often be insufficient to justify submitting them to experimental procedures.

It is altogether too easy to exploit, even unwittingly, the desperation of a childless couple. It would be cruel to generate for them false hopes unintentionally. It would be both cruel and unethical falsely to generate hope, for example by telling women, in order to secure their participation in experiments, that they themselves, not future infertile women, might be helped to have a child. That this may already have occurred is suggested by the following extract from a news report by Patrick Massey of Reuters:

> Dr. Patrick Steptoe, who heads the team of doctors working on the experiment, disclosed on television that he had extracted an ovum from a 34-year-old housewife and fertilized it with her husband's sperm. The woman, Mrs. Sylvia Allen, . . . said *she hoped the fertilized ovum would be implanted in her womb in the next two to six weeks*, meaning that the world's first baby conceived in a test-tube could be born by the end of 1970.[23]

The implantation was never performed.

follows immediately after the end of this quoted section.). Incidentally, the article also reports that three of the forty-six women became pregnant (in the usual way) the first month following laparoscopy.

[22]*Medical World News*, April 4, 1969, p. 17. The remark was made at a scientific conference in West Berlin.

[23]Massey, P. Test-Tube Fertilization of Ovum Raises Possibility of Rented Wombs. *The Washington Post*, March 3, 1970. Emphasis added.

Much more common will be the false hopes that may be generated unless the uncertainty of the outcome is clearly understood by the couple. At this stage of technical competence, the likelihood of success can hardly be undersold. The outpouring of large numbers of volunteers for *in vitro* fertilization should make us suspicious that a proper warning has not been given them.

Let me also raise some questions concerning the experimentation done with eggs obtained from women undergoing ovarian surgery for clinical reasons. Do and should these women know what is going to be done with their eggs? To whom belong the rights governing ordinary tissue removed at surgery? Is reproductive tissue a special case? Surely, if the eggs were going to be implanted in another woman, one would think that the donor's permission should be obtained. Then what about their simple fertilization? If the woman from whom the eggs are taken has religious or other objections against *in vitro* fertilization which would lead her to refuse permission if asked, is she wronged by not being asked or informed?

So far, I have discussed the ethical questions surrounding attempts to generate a normal child by transferring a laboratory-grown human embryo into the uterus of an infertile woman. But what about all the embryos that are not so implanted? Dr. Donald Gould, editor of the British journal *The New Scientist*, has asked: "What happens to the embryos which are discarded at the end of the day—washed down the sink? There would necessarily be many. Would this amount to abortion—or to murder? We have no law to cope with this kind of situation."[24]

I don't wish to mislead anyone. At this state of the art, the largest embryo we are talking about is a blastocyst, barely visible to the naked eye. But the moral question does not turn on visibility, any more than it would in the case of murder committed by a blind man. The embryos are clearly biologically alive, even at the blastocyst stage. At some future date, techniques may permit their growth to later stages, someday even viable stages. Before that, however, the question of discarding will have to be faced. Since there is a continuity of development between the early and the later stages, I suggest we had better

[24]Shuster, A. Human Egg is Fertilized in Test Tube by Britons. *The New York Times*, February 15, 1969.

face the question now and draw whatever lines need to be drawn.

When in the course of development does a living human embryo acquire *protectable* humanity? This is a familiar question which I shall not belabor. But the situation here, though similar, is not identical to that of abortion. For one thing, we don't start with a fetus already *in utero*, which one reluctantly destroys, hopefully only for good reasons. Here, nascent lives are being deliberately created despite certain knowledge that many of them will be destroyed or discarded. Several eggs are taken for fertilization from each woman, so as not to place all baskets on one egg.[25] The fetuses killed in abortion are unwanted, usually the result of so-called accidental conception. The embryos discarded here are wanted, at least for a while; they are deliberately created, used for a time, and then deliberately destroyed. Even if there is no intrinsic wrong done at the blastocyst stage—and I am undecided on this question—there certainly would be at later stages. (Those who disagree should at least be concerned about the effects on the attitude toward and respect for human life engendered in persons who are engaged in these practices. And we should all be concerned about the consequences of successfully subduing the mystery of the origin of human life, a subject to which I shall return.)

There is a second, related difference between abortion and discarding laboratory-grown embryos. Who decides the grounds for discard? What if there is another recipient available who wishes to have the otherwise unwanted embryo? Whose embryos are they? The woman's? The couple's? The geneticist's? The obstetrician's? The Ford Foundation's? If one justifies abortion on the basis of a woman's right to decide about her family size and spacing, or even on that unbelievable ground that a woman has a paramount right to do what she wishes with her body,[26] whose rights are paramount here? Shall we say that

[25]"Several embryos will probably be grown for each couple, since it would be difficult to work with fewer. The embryos placed in the mother could be chosen for various characteristics. Choosing male or female blastocysts is one possibility. . . ." Edwards and Fowler, p. 53.

[26]Even if such a right exists, it does not govern actions involving the fetus, because the fetus is simply not a mere part of a woman's body. One need only consider whether a woman can ethically take thalidomide while pregnant to see that this is so. It is distressing that seemingly intelligent people would sincerely look upon a fetus whose heart was beating and

discarding laboratory-grown embryos is a matter solely between a doctor and his plumber?

Having discussed so far only one serious moral objection to implantation of embryos and having raised some questions about the discarding of unimplanted ones (and deliberately neglecting the ethics of creating the embryos in the first place), I suspect that I have persuaded no one not originally opposed to *in vitro* fertilization. Furthermore, the first objection may become a vanishing objection, since the experimentation will in all likelihood proceed and the problem of risks and mishaps may eventually be eliminated as the technique is perfected. The second issue will hardly get a fresh hearing in a society which has so recently converted to feticide.[27] Moreover, apart from these questions, I can find no *intrinsic* reason to reject the intramarital use of *in vitro* fertilization and implantation (at least, no reason that would not also rule out artificial insemination by the husband). But the argument does not stop here, for we must consider the likely other uses and abuses of this procedure and the more objectionable procedures which this one makes possible.

Some may object to my making an argument based upon likely or possible misuses. After all there are few if any powers, technological and nontechnological, that cannot be abused. I, too, prefer arguments from principle concerning intrinsic rightness or wrongness, arguments which abstract from the difficult task of predicting and weighing consequences, often quite remote and intangible ones. Nevertheless, we can ill afford this form of intellectual purism, especially with respect to technologies that touch the foundations of man's biological nature. No technology exists autonomously or in isolation; each arises in the context of other technologies and, more importantly, in a

which had its own EEG as indistinguishable from a tumor of the uterus, a wart on the nose, or a hamburger in the stomach.

[27]Some may object to my use of the term "feticide," but I am opposed to hiding behind euphemisms. If we are going to be brave enough to practice abortion, let us at least not be cowardly in describing it. Even if feticide were made legal everywhere, and even if it were morally justified, it would still be killing (though not necessarily murder, which is "wrongful killing"). If we must kill, let us choose to be foot soldiers in hand-to-hand combat who must be touched by the act, rather than B-52 bombardiers who may lay waste whole cities without knowing that they have killed anyone.

complex and heterogeneous world of men whose proclivity for mischief and folly we cannot in good conscience ignore. We would ourselves display such folly were we to justify the introduction of each new technology simply because some good use can be found for it.[28]

Once introduced for the purpose of treating intramarital infertility, *in vitro* fertilization could be used for any purpose. There is no reason why the embryo need be implanted in the same woman from whom the egg was obtained. An egg taken from one woman (the biological mother) could be donated to another woman (the gestational mother), either before or after fertilization. Since obtaining eggs for donation is more difficult than obtaining sperm and requires surgery on the donor, this might not seem a likely occurrence except on a small scale. However, procedures for freezing and storing eggs will permit the opening of egg-banks. These will almost certainly be established, as are sperm banks today, partly to avoid having to do repeated operations on the same women and also because there is money to be made. Indeed, enterprising financiers and scientists, with the blessings of the new technotheologians, are perhaps at present organizing under one corporate canopy, the Chaste Rational Bank and Union: The Logical Semenary.

There are enough women whose infertility is due to a failure of ovulation to make it extremely likely that the donation of eggs and embryos will be attempted and that the technique will not be confined to those intramarital cases in which it was first used. McLaren and Kerr conclude: "It should probably be accepted that clinical use of *in vitro* fertilization will rely mainly on donor eggs in a situation closely analogous to donor insemination."[29]   And why stop at couples? What about single women, widows, or lesbians? If adoption agencies now permit these women to adopt, are they likely to be denied a chance to bear and deliver?

The converse possibility will also follow, namely the use of one woman simply to incubate and deliver another woman's child. If the previous practice might lead to new business ven-

---

[28]I doubt that many readers would condone the development of chemical and biological weaponry on the ground that it is more humane to use nonlethal gas on an enemy soldier than to kill him, without first asking whether we can foreclose the further consequences of introducing such military technology.

[29]McLaren and Kerr, p. 56.

tures, advertised under "eggs for sale," this practice might lead to a new form of prostitution, advertised under "wombs for rent." Women with uterine abnormalities which preclude normal pregnancy may very well seek surrogate gestational mothers, as may women who don't want pregnancy to interfere with the skiing season. There are certainly enough poor women available to form a caste of childbearers, especially for good pay. The public is already being encouraged to accept this new form of "the oldest profession":

> A prominent British embryologist, Dr. Jack Cohen, suggested that the process of impregnation, once perfected, might lead to a system of volunteer "host" mothers, who would bear other people's children for a fee. Cohen suggested that 2000 pounds ($4,800) a birth might be a reasonable sum, especially for an actress eager for the joys of motherhood without the cares of interrupting her career or distending her figure during pregnancy.[30]

The more sentimentally minded will point out that these twin forms of foster pregnancy can be humanely and respectfully practiced. A woman may wish to donate an egg or an embryo to her sister, or may agree out of generosity to gestate a friend's embryo. It can be argued that no one should stand in the way of such acts of love.[31] But it is simply naive to think the practice would be limited to these more "innocent" cases. Moreover, there are psychological and ethical reasons for thinking that these cases may not be so innocent. What are the psychological consequences for the womb-lending sister (and the others) of giving birth to her nephew? Whose child is he? If the donor of sperm has no claim over a child born after artificial insemination, why should the donor of ova, especially if there is

[30]Massey, *loc. cit.*

[31]Even if this argument were correct, it surely cannot be correct *because* these are acts of love. The current sentimentality which endorses all acts done lovingly because they are lovingly done leads to some strange judgments. A teacher friend recently asked one student who was having difficulty appreciating the crimes of Oedipus, what she would think if she discovered that her sister was having an affair with their father. The girl replied that, although she was personally disgusted by the prospect for herself, she thought that there was probably nothing wrong with it "provided that they [sister and father] had a good relationship." It is unlikely that individuals or a whole society which is unable to find reasons (other than genetic ones) for rejecting incest will be able to sort out any of the questions raised in this paper.

a later dispute between the two women? These acts of love cannot be kept anonymous; the visible and continued presence of the progeny might well stimulate such conflict. Also, might not female relatives be under intolerable pressure to donate eggs or to lend wombs, once the first such acts of "kindness" are well publicized (just as relatives now often feel constrained to serve as transplantation donors of kidneys)? Is a person morally justified in allowing her body to be used as a "hot-house," as a human incubator? Indeed, is not a decisive objection to the extramarital use of these techniques that it requires and fosters, both in thought and in deed, the exploitation of women and their bodies?[32] The further question of the separation of procreation from sexual love and marriage will be treated later.

Use of these technologies need not be confined—nor is it likely to be confined—to the scale of individual couples making private decisions, nor to treatment of infertility. Indeed, several proposals for additional uses have already been placed before the public. As suggested in these proposals, and as I noted at the start, these techniques could serve eugenic purposes. Artificial insemination with semen from selected donors, the (positive) eugenic proposal of Herman Muller,[33] could now be supplemented by the selection of ova as well. For many people these prospects raise the fear of directed breeding programs under the dictates of a totalitarian regime. Such programs need not be coercive, since the desired donors of eggs and sperm as well as the foster mothers of the regime might be handsomely paid and highly honored. But, perhaps perversely in a time when suspicion and fear of governmental abuse of power are high and growing, I am not very worried about government-directed breeding by these methods. The eugenic advantages of this method, if there are any, are also available—more cheaply—simply by directed sexual intercourse. A regime could just as easily compel or induce this practice. While those who hold to

[32]The future may provide technological solutions to this problem of sexual inequality: transplanting uteri into men, or full extracorporeal gestation.

[33]Muller, H. J. 1961. Human Evolution by Voluntary Choice of Germ Plasm. *Science 134*:643-49. Muller, H. J. What Genetic Course Will Man Steer? In J. F. Crow and J. V. Neel, eds., *Proceedings of the Third International Congress of Human Genetics* (Baltimore: Johns Hopkins University Press, 1967).

the demonic theory of politics may think me naive, I expect that artificial fertilization and embryo culture would add very little to the already large armamentarium of those who would practice mischief and evil.

We stand in much greater danger from the well-wishers of mankind, for folly is much harder to detect than wickedness. The most serious danger from the widespread use of these techniques will stem not from desires to breed a super race, but rather from the growing campaign to prevent the birth of all defective children in the name of population control, "quality of life," and the supposed "right of every child to be born with a sound physical and mental constitution, based on a sound genotype." Thus says the retiring (but not reticent) President of the American Association for the Advancement of Science, geneticist Bentley Glass, in his presidential address: "No parents will in that future time have a right to burden society with a malformed or a mentally incompetent child."[34] These are the words not of a dictator but of a gentle biologist. Even granting the desirability of his end—optimum children of no burden to society (except from their "perfection")—consider what means it would require. This perfect condition is to be accomplished not by infanticide, not just by prenatal diagnosis and abortion of defectives, but by the laboratory growth and implantation of human embryos.

> The way is thus clear to performing what I have called "prenatal adoption," for not only might the selected embryos be implanted in the uterus of the woman who supplied the oocytes, but in that of any woman at the appropriate time of her menstrual cycle. Edwards cautiously limits the application of his developing techniques to the provision of a healthy embryo for a woman whose oviducts are blocked and prevent descent of the egg. It should be obvious that the technique can be quickly and widely extended. The embryos produced in the laboratory might come from selected genotypes, both male and female. Preservation of spermatozoa in deep frozen condition could permit a high degree of selectivity among the sperm donors, who so far have been limited to the husbands of the women donors of the oocytes. Sex determination of the embryos is possible before implantation; and embryos with abnormal chromosome constitutions can be discarded. By checking the sperm and egg donors with a battery of biochemical tests, matching of carriers of the same

[34]Glass, B. 1971. Science: Endless Horizons or Golden Age? *Science* *171*:23-29, at p. 28.

defective gene can be avoided, or the defective embryos can themselves be detected and discarded.[35]

I leave it to the reader to consider the ethical, social, legal, and
political implications of Professor Glass's proposal and to elaborate his own favorite objections. My point here is simply that
even before Edwards or Shettles opens Pandora's Box, there are
well-meaning, decent men already at work to find good uses for
its contents.[36]

A similar camel's-nose-under-the-tent argument was advanced
by opponents of artificial insemination. Ironically, some of the
same people who made light of these arguments in defending
artificial insemination are now defending the camel's neck while
again dismissing the camel's nose argument. In rebutting a
camel's nose argument against artificial insemination, one theologian wrote: "The question of test-tube babies by laboratory
parthenogenesis and artificial fertilization is another subject,
too far afield from the question under study here."[37] Too far
afield? Perhaps. But in the same ball park, no doubt. Today that
theologian will have to play in that far part of the field.
Hopefully he won't be so quick to ignore possibilities which lie
just beyond him.

It is true that the practice of artificial insemination has thus
far been confined to the treatment of infertility and has not, to
my knowledge, been malevolently, despotically, or even frivo-
lously used. But I am no longer talking about the problem of
misuse or abuse of a given technique, but rather about the fact
that one technical advance makes possible the next, in more
than one respect. The first serves as a precedent for the second,
the second for the third—not just technologically, but also in
moral arguments. At least one good humanitarian reason can be

[35]*Ibid.*, p. 28.

[36]Thus, I take no consolation from the character reference given
editorially by *Nature* ("What Comes after Fertilization," Vol. 221, p. 613,
February 15, 1969), in the issue reporting Edwards' first success at
human *in vitro* fertilization: "The fact that the techniques might one day
be developed to produce a fully grown human embryo *extra utero* should
not be a restraint to progress. The day of the test tube baby is not here
yet, and the advantages of this work are clear. *These are not perverted men
in white coats doing nasty experiments on human beings, but reasonable
scientists carrying out perfectly justifiable research*" (emphasis added).

[37]Fletcher, J. *Morals and Medicine* (Boston: Beacon Press, 1960), p.
117.

found to justify each step. Into the solemn and hallowed tent of human sexuality and procreation, the camel's nose has led the camel's neck and may someday soon, perhaps, even lead the camel's spermatozoa.

Professor James D. Watson, codiscoverer of the structure of DNA, has brought to the public his concern over one techno-logical prospect, the cloning of human beings, which the work of Edwards makes very much more possible. In his very sober and careful paper, Professor Watson concluded a discussion of the work on *in vitro* fertilization as follows:

> Some very hard decisions may soon be upon us. For it is not obvious that the vague potential of abhorrent misuse should weigh more strongly than the unhappiness which thousands of married couples feel when they are unable to have their own children. Different societies are likely to view the matter differently and it would be surprising if all come to the same conclusion. We must, therefore, assume that techniques for the *in vitro* manipulation of human eggs are likely to be general medical practice, capable of routine performance throughout the world within some ten to twenty years.
>
> The situation would then be ripe for extensive efforts, either legal or illegal, at human cloning. . . .
>
> Moreover, given the widespread development of the safe clinical procedures for handling human eggs, cloning experiments would not be prohibitively expensive. They need not be restricted to the super-powers—medium sized, if not minor countries, all now possess the resources needed for eventual success. There furthermore need not exist the coercion of a totalitarian state to provide the surrogate mothers. There already are such widespread divergences as to the sacredness of the act of human reproduction that the boring mean-inglessness of the lives of many women would be sufficient cause for their willingness to participate in such experimentation, be it legal or illegal. Thus, if the matter proceeds in its current nondirected fashion, a human being—born of clonal reproduction—most likely will appear on the earth within the next twenty to fifty years, and conceivably even sooner, if some nation actively promotes the ven-ture.[38]

[38]Watson, J. D. Potential Consequences of Experimentation with Human Eggs. Presented on January 28, 1971, before the Twelfth Meeting of the Panel on Science and Technology, Committee on Science and Astronautics, U. S. House of Representatives. An article based upon this testimony, "Moving Toward the Clonal Man: Is This What We Want?" appeared in the May, 1971, issue of *The Atlantic*, pp. 50-53.

I now turn to consider this second "New Beginning in Human Life"—the asexual reproduction of human beings, or cloning.[39]

Cloning, or Asexual Reproduction: State of the Art

In genetic terms, asexual reproduction is distinguished from sexual reproduction (whether practiced in bed or in test tubes) by two characteristics: the new individuals are, first, derived from a single parent, and second, genetically identical to that parent. Asexual reproduction occurs widely in nature and is the normal mode of reproduction of bacteria, many plants, and some lower animals. By means of a technique known as nuclear transplantation (also called nuclear transfer), experimental biologists have artificially achieved the asexual reproduction of organisms which naturally reproduce only sexually (so far, frogs, salamanders, and fruit flies).[40] The procedure is conceptually simple. The nucleus of a mature but unfertilized egg is removed (by microsurgery or by irradiation) and replaced by a nucleus obtained from a specialized somatic cell of an adult organism (e.g., an intestinal cell or a skin cell). For reasons which are not yet understood, the egg with its transplanted nucleus develops as if it had been fertilized and, barring complications, may give rise to a normal adult organism. Since almost all the hereditary material (DNA) of a cell is contained within its nucleus, the renucleated egg and the individual into which it develops are genetically identical to the organism which was the source of the transferred nucleus. Thus, the origin of the new individual is not the chance union of egg and sperm, with the generation of a new genetic constitution or

[39]I have elsewhere written an essay devoted entirely to the subject of cloning, "Freedom, Coercion, and Asexual Reproduction," which will appear in D. Callahan and L. R. Kass, eds., *Freedom, Coercion, and the Life Sciences.*

[40]The most extensive work has been done on frogs, in the laboratory of Dr. John Gurdon at Oxford (1962. Multiple Genetically Identical Frogs. *Heredity 53:*4-9), although the technique was first developed by Drs. Robert Briggs and Thomas King, then working at the Institute for Cancer Research in Philadelphia (1952. Transplantation of Living Nuclei into Enucleated Frogs' Eggs. *Proceedings of the National Academy of Sciences U.S.A. 38:*455-63). An easily readable review of this research is provided by Gurdon (1968. Transplanted Nuclei and Cell Differentiation. *Scientific American 219:*24-35 [Dec.]).

genotype, but rather the contrived perpetuation into another generation of an already existing genotype.

An unlimited number of identical individuals, i.e., a clone, all generated asexually from a single parent, could be produced by nuclear transplantation. An adult organism comprises many millions of cells, all genetically identical, each a potential source of a nucleus for cloning. In addition, techniques for storage and subsequent laboratory culture of animal tissues permit the preservation and propagation of cells long after the deaths of the bodies from which they were removed. There would thus be the possibility of a virtually unlimited supply of genetically identical nuclei for cloning.[41]

The extension of nuclear transplantation to mammals has not yet been achieved, although several people have been trying for a few years. The difficulties are technical; there is no *theoretical* reason to believe that clonal reproduction is not possible in mammals, including man. The technical problems when this work began included the following: (1) obtaining of mature mammalian eggs, (2) removal of the egg nucleus, (3) insertion of the donor nucleus, and (4) transfer and implantation of the renucleated egg in the uterus of a female at the right stage in her menstrual cycle. As a result of the work on *in vitro* fertilization,

---

[41]Some people prefer to reserve the use of the term "cloning" for such mass-scale replication and prefer instead to use "nuclear transfer" to describe the single instances of asexual reproduction, hoping thereby not to bring the opprobrium of the mass use upon individual cases. I find this suggestion conceptually fuzzy and etymologically problematic. "Clone" comes from the Greek word *klōn*, meaning "twig," and is related to the word *klan*, meaning "to break." It is defined (Webster's Third International Dictionary) as "the aggregate of asexually produced progeny of an individual, whether natural (as the products of repeated fission of a protozoan) or otherwise (as in the propagation of a particular plant by budding or by cuttings through many generations)." While the term *clone* does imply an aggregate, it is an aggregate which is formed not horizontally (during one generation) but vertically over time (generation after generation). Thus even the first asexually-produced offspring and his progenitor together form a clone, albeit a small one for the time being. "Nuclear transfer" is but the name of one of several possible techniques that could give rise to a clone and thus does not serve as a generic term for the genetically and humanly significant features of asexual reproduction. Moreover, the desire to avoid for the small-scale use the offensive connotation of mass production begs the question of whether the opprobrium is not equally fitting and leads towards the development of euphemism. I shall thus use "cloning" as synonymous with "asexual reproduction, artificially induced."

the first and fourth problems have been solved for rabbits and mice and will be for man as soon as Edwards or someone else succeeds. Recently, chemical methods to remove the nucleus from mammalian cells in tissue culture have been perfected. [42] These methods can probably be used to enucleate egg cells. The only serious difficulty remaining is the introduction of the diploid donor nucleus. And this difficulty may also be short-lived, since there are now very simple methods for fusing almost any two cells to produce a single cell containing the combined genetic material of both original cells. Fusion of an enucleated egg cell with a cell containing the donor nucleus might provide the method for getting the nucleus into the egg. In fact, Dr. Christopher Graham at Oxford has already succeeded in fusing mouse eggs with adult mouse cells. The fused egg divides several times but thus far has not gone on to form a blastocyst. Given the rate at which the other technical obstacles have fallen, and given the increasing number of competent people entering the field of experimental embryology, it is reasonable to expect the birth of the first cloned mammal sometime in the next few years. This will be almost certainly followed by a rush to develop cloning for other animals, especially livestock, thereby to propagate in perpetuity the champion meat or milk producers.

As the human embryo culture and implantation technologies are being perfected in parallel, the step to the first clonal man might require only a few additional years. Within our lifetime, possibly even by 1980, it may be technically feasible to clone a human being.

Among sensible men, the ability to clone a man would not be a sufficient reason for doing so. Indeed, among *sensible* men, there would be no human cloning. Nevertheless, the apologists and the titillators have been at work, and the laundry list of possible applications keeps growing, in anticipation of the perfected technology: (1) Replication of individuals of great genius or great beauty to improve the species or to make life more pleasant; (2) replication of the healthy to bypass the risk of genetic disease contained in the lottery of sexual recombination; (3) provision of large sets of genetically identical humans

[42]Ladda, R. L., and Estensen, R.D. 1970. Introduction of a Heterologous Nucleus into Enucleated Cytoplasm of Cultured Mouse L-Cells. *Proceedings of the National Academy of Sciences U.S.A.* 67:1528-33.

for scientific studies on the relative importance of nature and nurture for various aspects of human performance; (4) provision of a child to an infertile couple; (5) provision of a child with a genotype of one's own choosing—of someone famous, of a departed loved one, of one's spouse or oneself; (6) control of the sex of future children (the sex of a cloned offspring is the same as that of the adult from whom the donor nucleus was taken); (7) production of sets of identical persons to perform special occupations in peace and war (not excluding espionage); (8) production of embryonic replicas of each person, to be frozen away until needed as a source of organs for transplant to their genetically identical twin; (9) to beat the Russians and the Chinese—to prevent a "cloning gap."

Cloning—Some Ethical Questions

Some of the ethical and social questions raised in connection with *in vitro* fertilization apply also to cloning: questions of experimenting upon the unborn and discarding embryos, problems of misuse and abuse of power, questions concerning the camel and the tent. I will not repeat what has gone before, except to call special attention to the point about the ethics of experimentation. A significant number of grossly abnormal creatures have resulted from the frog experiments, and there is no reason to be more optimistic about the early attempts in humans. The twin issues of the production and disposition of defectives provide sufficient moral grounds for rebutting any first attempt to clone a man. Again, we cannot *ethically* get to know whether or not human cloning is feasible. This point is discussed at greater length by Paul Ramsey in his essay, "Shall We Clone a Man?" He asks, "In case a monstrosity—a subhuman or parahuman individual—results, shall the experiment simply be stopped and this artfully created human life killed?"[43]

But there are other questions which apply to cloning and not to the techniques discussed earlier. Among the most important are questions concerning identity and individuality. One problem can be illustrated by exploiting the ambiguity of the word "identity": The cloned person may experience serious concerns about his identity (distinctiveness) because his genotype, and

[43]Ramsey, p. 78.

hence his appearance, stands in a relationship of identity (sameness) to another human being.

The natural occurrence of identical twins in no way weakens the argument against the artificial production of identical humans; many things that occur accidentally ought not to be done deliberately.[44] In fact, the problem of identity faced by identical twins should instruct us and enable us to recognize how much greater the problem might be for someone who was the "child" (or "father") of his twin. I cannot improve upon Paul Ramsey's reflections on this subject:

> Growing up as a twin is difficult enough anyway; one's struggle for selfhood and identity must be against the very human being for whom no doubt there is also the greatest sympathy. Who then would want to be the son or daughter of his twin? To mix the parental and the twin relation might well be psychologically disastrous for the young. Or to look at it from the point of view of parents, it is an awful enough responsibility to be the parent of a son or daughter as things now are. Our children begin with a unique genetic independence of us, analogous to the personal independence that sooner or later will have to be granted them or wrested from us. For us to choose to replicate ourselves in them, to make ourselves the foreknowers and creators of every one of their genetic predispositions, might well prove to be a psychologically and personally unendurable undertaking. For an elder to teach his "infant copy" is a repellent idea not because of the strangeness of it, but because we are altogether too familiar with the problems this would exponentially make more difficult.[45]

Perhaps this issue can be pressed even farther, beyond such concerns for undesirable psychological consequences. Does it make sense to say that each person has a right not to be deliberately denied a unique genotype?[46] Is one inherently

---

[44]This self-evident proposition is for some reason not always accepted or appreciated. Resistance to it is a special case of that misguided thinking which lets what in fact happens serve as at least a precedent for what can happen, if not as a standard for what ought to happen. Yet who would justify the deliberate creation of an earthquake or the deliberate production of birth defects?

[45]Ramsey, pp. 71-72.

[46]There may be other means besides cloning which could be used to do this, for example chemical or physical manipulation which would cause a young embryo to split and give rise to multiple genetically-identical embryos. Such experiments are now being pursued in various mammalian species. If we conclude that the right in question exists, then the deliberate

injured by having been made the copy of another human being, regardless of which human being? We should not be deterred by the strangeness of these questions, a strangeness that arises largely because the problem could not have arisen before.

Central to this matter is the idea of the dignity and worth of each human being. This idea has grown out of the Judaeo-Christian tradition. At root is the notion of the special yet equal relationship of each person to the Creator. The following Judaic Midrash explicitly attributes personal uniqueness to this relationship:

> For a man stamps many coins in one mold and they are all alike;
> but the King who is king over all kings, the Holy
>> One blessed be he, stamped every man
>> in the mold of the first man,
> yet not one of them resembles his fellow.[47]

In modern Western political thought, which represents largely a secularized form of the Judaeo-Christian teaching, the principle of the dignity of the individual human being has become the root notion. From this root spring the twin trunks of the liberal democratic tradition: individual liberty and political and social equality.

The question we must ask is this: Is individual dignity undermined by a lack of genetic distinctiveness? One might argue, on the contrary, that indistinctness in appearance and capacity might produce a greater incentive to be distinct in deed and accomplishment. Certainly the latter are more germane to any measure of individual worth and self-esteem than are the former. On the other hand, our personal appearance is, at the very least, symbolic of our individuality. Differences in personal appearance, genetically determined, reinforce (if not make possible) our sense of self, and hence lend support to the feelings of individual worth we seek in ourselves and from others. Some put it more strongly and argue that a man not only *has* a body but *is* his body. By this argument, a man's distinctive countenance not only makes possible his sense of self but is in fact one with that self. Membership in a clone numbering five to ten would doubtless threaten one's sense of self;

production of identical human twins by these and all other methods must also be declared morally wrong.

[47]Glatzer, N. N. *Hammer on the Rock: A Short Midrash Reader* (New York: Schocken Books, 1962), p. 15.

membership in a clone of two might do the same. To answer the question posed above: We may *not* be entitled, in principle, to a unique genotype, but we *are* entitled not to have deliberately weakened the necessary supports for a worthy life. Genetic distinctiveness seems to me to be one such support.

A second and related problem of identity and individuality is this: The cloned individual is not simply denied genetic distinctiveness; he is saddled with a genotype that has already lived. He will not be fully a surprise to the world, and people are likely always to compare his performance in life with that of his alter ego. He may also be burdened by knowledge of his precursor's life history. Imagine living with the knowledge that the person from whom you were cloned developed schizophrenia or suffered multiple heart attacks before the age of forty. For these reasons, the cloned individual's belief in the openness of his own future may be undermined, and with it his freedom to be himself. Ignorance of what lies ahead is a source of hope to the miserable, a spur to the talented, a necessary support for a tolerable—let alone worthy—life for all.

But is the cloned individual's future really determinable or determined? After all, only his genotype has been determined; it is true that his environment will exert considerable influence on who and what he becomes. Yet isn't it likely that the "parents" will seek to manipulate and control the environment as well, in an attempt to reproduce the person who was copied? For example, if a couple decided to clone a Rubinstein,[48] is there any doubt that early in life young Artur would be deposited at the piano and encouraged to play? It would not matter to the "parents" that the environment in which the true Rubinstein blossomed can never be reproduced or even approximated. Nor would it matter that no one knows what is responsible for the development of genius, or even for the appearance of ordinary talents and traits for the sake of which other people might have elected to clone. Such ignorance would not deter

[48]Frequently mentioned candidates for cloning are musicians and mathematicians, such as Mozart, Newton, and Einstein, whose genius is presumed to have a large genetic component. But all such suggestions ignore the wishes of these men. I suspect that none of them would consent to have themselves replicated. Indeed, should we not assert as a principle that any so-called great man who *did* consent to be cloned should on that basis be disqualified, as possessing too high an opinion of himself and of his genes? Can we stand an increase in arrogance?

the "parents." Why else did they clone young Artur in the first place?

Thus, although the cloned individual's future is probably not determinable according to his "parents' " wishes, enough damge is done by leading him to believe otherwise and by their believing otherwise. His own potential will in all likelihood be stunted and his outlook warped as he is forced into a mold he neither fits nor wants. True, some parents are already guilty of the same crime, but many more are restrained by their impotence in determining the raw material. The opportunity to clone would not only remove this restraint but would openly invite and encourage more outrageous efforts to shape our children after our own desires.

Although these arguments would apply with even greater force to any large-scale efforts at human cloning, I find them sufficient to reject even the first attempts at human cloning. It cannot be repeated too often that these are human beings upon whom these eugenic or merely playful visions (shall I say hallucinations?) are to be worked.

Thus far, I have dealt separately with two technological prospects, one now upon us, the other on the horizon and fast approaching, in an effort to reason about and evaluate each piece of technology. I have been at pains to analyze the morally relevant features of each, in order to show that real and important distinctions can and should be drawn among different technologies, that not all "New Beginnings in Life" are equal, that the practice of one does not ipso facto justify the introduction of another. I am far more concerned that this approach be found reasonable and useful than that any of my specific arguments be found convincing.

Yet despite its practical utility, this piece-by-piece approach has grave deficiencies. It ignores the great wave upon which each of these techniques is but a ripple. All of the new technologies arise from and are part of the great project of modernity, the "conquest of nature for the relief of man's estate." They surpass many earlier techniques in that they seek to relieve man's estate by directly changing man himself. We must therefore raise some broader questions concerning this project that arise in connection with the technologies discussed above. Here I am more concerned that my arguments be found convincing than that they be useful.

Questions of Power

Though philosophically debatable, the Baconian principle, "Knowledge is power," is certainly correct when applied to the knowledge that has been sought under that principle. The knowledge of how to begin human life in new ways is a human power to do so. But the power rests only metaphorically with humankind; it rests in fact with particular men—geneticists, embryologists, obstetricians. The triumphant proclamation of *man's* growing power over nature obscures the troublesome reality that it is individual men who wield power. What we really mean by "man's power over Nature" is a power exercised by some men over other men with knowledge of nature as their instrument. (Here I draw heavily on the third chapter of a superb little book by C. S. Lewis, *The Abolition of Man.*)

While applicable to technology in general, these reflections are especially pertinent to the technologies of human reproduction and genetic manipulation with which men deliberately exercise power over future generations. Ultimately, as Lewis points out:

> If any one age really attains, by eugenics and scientific education, the power to make its descendants what it pleases, all men who live after it are patients of that power. They are weaker, not stronger: for though we may have put wonderful machines in their hands we have pre-ordained how they are to use them. . . . The real picture is that of one dominant age . . . which resists all previous ages most successfully and dominates all subsequent ages most irresistibly, and thus is the real master of the human species. But even within this master generation (itself an infinitesimal minority of the species) the power will be exercised by a minority smaller still. Man's conquest of Nature, if the dreams of the scientific planners are realized, means the rule of a few hundreds of men over billions upon billions of men. There neither is nor can there be any simple increase in power on Man's side. Each new power won *by* man is a power *over* man as well.[49]

Please observe that I am not dealing yet with the problem of the misuse and abuse of power. The point is rather that the power which grows is willy-nilly the power of only some men, and that the number of these powerful men tends to grow fewer and fewer as the power increases.

[49]Lewis, C. S. *The Abolition of Man* (New York: Collier-Macmillan, 1965), pp. 70-71.

But is this really true with respect to our topic? Recall that there is a new partner in these "New Beginnings in Life"—the scientist-physician. The obstetrician is no longer just the midwife, but also the sower of seed. Even in the treatment of intramarital infertility, the scientist-physician who employs *in vitro* fertilization and laboratory culture of human embryos has acquired far greater power over human life than his colleague who simply repairs the obstructed oviduct. He presides over many creations in many patients. And once he goes beyond the bounds of marriage, he is not simply the Fertilizer General but the Matchmaker as well. In the practice of artificial insemination by a donor, for the sake of preserving anonymity, a small number of physicians have already arranged for the fathering of several hundred thousand children—many of them, nepotistically, by their professional offspring, the medical students. I am not at present questioning this practice; my point is rather to illustrate how the new technologies lead to the concentration of power.[50]

Both a cause and an effect of the growing power of biomedical technologists is the growing complexity of scientific knowledge and the related fragmentation of disciplines and extreme specialization of their practitioners. Science understands and explains the world in ideas and language which the layman cannot understand. I am not speaking now about the problem of jargon. Rather I am talking about a more fundamental matter. The phenomena of nature as they present themselves to us in ordinary experience are understood by the scientist in terms of abstract concepts such as molecules and genes and ultimately in terms of mathematical formulae. This is to the layman a new Cabala but a Cabala with a difference, a Cabala that can create new life in test tubes and can send men to the moon. Small wonder that the scientists and technologists have become for many people the new priesthood.[51]

---

[50]The genetic counsellor is another practitioner whose power over new life is increasing, especially since the advent of amniocentesis and precise prenatal diagnosis. Although most counsellors believe that the final decision should rest with the parents, it is generally admitted that they can and do exercise—often at the parents' insistence—an influence on what is done.

[51]At a recent meeting, scientists were summarizing for a group of educated laymen the current state of knowledge in human genetics and the promising fields for the future. At the conclusion of a summary of studies

Because this new priesthood has promised its rewards here on earth, it faces perhaps a heavier responsibility—especially when it fails to deliver. The public has acquired high expectations for technology, from which impatience and frustration are easily bred. This point has been surprisingly overlooked, but I think this is what is meant every time someone starts a complaint, "Well, if they can put a man on the moon, why can't they. . . ?" Given this general disposition with regard to science and technology, is it not likely that the expectations of an infertile couple will be much higher for any baby given them by the rationalized, disinfected procedures of the laboratory than for a baby born in the usual way and obtained via adoption? Even with adequate warnings, it will be hard to get the science-worshipping patient to face the possibility of a disastrous outcome. Imagine the heartache and then the outcry if the child conceived *in vitro* should turn out to be hemophiliac or retarded. On this ground alone, prudence dictates caution.

The problem of the specific abuses of specific powers cannot be overlooked. However, because it is more widely appreciated, it is sufficient merely to mention the prospects of involuntary breeding programs, the cloning of tyrants, and the production of whole cadres of gammas and deltas to handle the onerous tasks of an advanced civilization, or the more modest abuses of cloning quintuplets for the circus, for five complete sets of spare organs, or for partners in crime who can always have an alibi. Nevertheless, while events which have occurred in our lifetime should warn us not to dismiss these possibilities, I think we have greater reason to be concerned about the private, well-intentioned, voluntary use of the new technologies. The major problem to be feared is not tyranny but voluntary dehumanization.

on mutation, a woman rose in the audience to ask about the meaning of one of the findings for the chance of her having an abnormal child. The answer came back that the matter was complicated, involving some function of "one over the square root of the mean." The woman seated herself with a look of bewilderment on her face, but said, shaking her head affirmatively, "Amen."

There is of course a revolt in progress against this new priesthood, but primarily because it has been selling indulgences to the Pentagon and because its blessings are not biodegradable. Very few are questioning the intellectual foundations of the modern scientific conception of the world. Indeed, even many from the old priesthood have been converted.

Questions of Dehumanization

Human procreation not only issues new human beings; it is itself a human activity (an activity of embodied men and women). The "New Beginnings in Life" discussed earlier represent in themselves a radical change in human procreation as a human activity. As already noted, the new beginnings occur in a new locus, the laboratory, and involve a new partner, the scientist. Moreover, the techniques that at first serve merely to provide a child to a childless couple will soon be used to exert control over the quality of the child. A new image of human procreation has been conceived, and a new "scientific" obstetrics will usher it into existence. As one obstetrician put it at a recent conference: "The business of obstetrics is to produce *optimum* babies." The price to be paid for the optimum baby is the transfer of procreation from the home to the laboratory and its coincident transformation into manufacture. Increasing control over the product is purchased by the increasing depersonalization of the process. In this continuum, artificial insemination represented the first step. Perhaps for some techniques used for some purposes, e.g., artificial insemination by the husband to circumvent infertility, the benefits outweigh the costs. But let us not say that there are no costs. The complete depersonalization of procreation (possible with the development of an artificial placenta), and its surrender to the demands of the calculating will, will in itself be seriously dehumanizing no matter how "optimum" the product.

Human procreation is human partly because it is not simply an activity of our rational wills. Men and women are embodied as well as desiring and calculating creatures. It is for the gods to create in thought and by fiat ("Let the earth bring forth . . . "). And some future race of demigods (or demi-men) may obtain its successors from the local fertilization and decanting station. But *human* procreation is begetting. It is a more complete human activity precisely because it engages us bodily and spiritually as well as rationally. Is there possibly some wisdom in that mystery of nature which joins the pleasure of sex, the communication of love, and the desire for children in the very activity by which we continue the chain of human existence? Is biological parenthood a built-in "device" selected to promote adequate caring for posterity? Before we embark on "New Beginnings in Life" we should consider the meaning of the union between sex, love, and procreation and the meaning and consequences of its cleavage.

My point is almost certain to be misunderstood. I am not suggesting that one can be truly human only by engaging in procreation. I think there is a clear need for curtailing procreation, and I have no objections to the use of any contraceptive devices. I am not suggesting that there is something inhuman about adopting children instead of getting them through the pelvis, nor do I think that the most distinctively human activities center in the groin. My point is simply this: There are more and less human ways of bringing a child into the world. I am arguing that the laboratory production of human beings is no longer *human* procreation.

There will be some who object to my calling the "New Beginnings in Life" forms of manufacture. I mean "manufacture" in a quite literal sense: *hand-made.* It matters not whether we are talking about small- or large-scale manufacture. With *in vitro* fertilization, the natural process of generating becomes the artificial process of making. In the case of cloning, the artistry is taken one step further. Not only is the process *in hand*, but the total genetic blueprint of the cloned offspring is selected and determined by the human artisan. To be sure, subsequent development must still follow natural processes, and no so-called laws of nature have been or can be violated. What has been violated, even if only slightly, is the distinction between the natural and the artificial, and, at its very root, the nature of man himself. For man is the watershed which divides the world into those things that belong to nature and those that are made by men. To lay one's hands on human generation is to take a major step toward making man himself simply another of the man-made things. Thus human nature becomes simply the last part of nature to succumb to the modern technological project, a project that has already turned all the rest of nature into raw material at human disposal, to be homogenized by our rationalized technique according to the fleeting artistic conventions of the day.

If the depersonalization of the process of reproduction and its separation from human sexuality dehumanize the activity that brings new life, and if the manufacture of human life threatens its humanness, these together add up to yet another assault on the existence of marriage and the human family. Sex is now comfortably at home outside marriage, and child-rearing is progressively being turned over to other institutions—the state, the schools, the mass media, the child-care centers. Transfer of procreation to the laboratory undermines the justification and support that biological parenthood gives to monogamous marriage. Cloning adds an additional, more specific, and more fundamental threat: The technique renders males obsolete. Human eggs, nuclei, and (for the time being) uteri are all it requires. All three can be supplied by women.

Curiously, both those who welcome and those who fear the technologies for "New Beginnings in Life" agree that they will pose serious threats to marriage and the family. Indeed, it seems not unfair to say that one of the reasons, not always explicitly admitted, for endorsement of the new technologies in some quarters is precisely that they will help lay these institutions to rest.[52] The group of deliberate family-wreckers includes persons eager to remove all restraints from human sexuality, others who see the destruction of marriage as a needed step in limiting population growth, and yet others who find the modern nuclear family a stifling and harmful institution for education and child-rearing. Such persons should at least admit this to be one of their objectives as they issue their ringing praise for each new technological advance. Then at least a real debate could begin on the merits of that objective.

I will not deny that the modern nuclear family shows signs of cracking under other pressures. It may have intrinsic limitations which may make it seem, even at best, ill-fitted for modern technological society. If so, where lies the fault? It is modern technological society that has destroyed the extended family and now places great stress on what remains. Is the final solution we should accept the complete elimination of biological kinship as a foundation of social organization? Must we imitate that old lady of song who swallowed a fly?

> I know an old lady who swallowed a fly;
> I don't know why she swallowed a fly.
> I guess she'll die.
>
> * * *
>
> (many verses and many swallowings)
>
> * * *

---

[52]Francoeur, R. T. *Utopian Motherhood* (New York: Doubleday, 1970). Grossman, E. The Obsolescent Mother: A Scenario. *The Atlantic*, May, 1971, pp. 39-50.

> I know an old lady who swallowed a cow.
> I don't know how she swallowed a cow.
> She swallowed the cow to catch the goat,
> She swallowed the goat to catch the dog,
> She swallowed the dog to catch the cat,
> She swallowed the cat to catch the bird,
> She swallowed the bird to catch the spider,
> That wriggled and jiggled and tickled inside her.
> She swallowed the spider to catch the fly,
> But I don't know why she swallowed a fly.
> I guess she'll die.
>
> I know an old lady who swallowed a horse.
> She died, of course.

I have no doubts that laboratory and governmental alternatives could be devised for procreation and child-rearing. But at what cost? How much would our humanity be stunted by the totalitarian orientation that these alternatives require and foster?

The family is rapidly becoming the only institution in an increasingly impersonal world where each person is loved not for what he does or makes but simply because he is. The family is also the institution where most of us, both as children and as parents, acquire a sense of continuity with the past and a sense of commitment to the future. Without the family, most of us would have little incentive to take an interest in anything after our own deaths. It would be a just irony if programs of cloning or laboratory-controlled reproduction to improve the genetic constitutions of future generations were to undermine the very institution which teaches us concern for the future. These observations suggest to me that the elimination of the family would weaken ties to past and present and would throw us even more at the mercy of an impersonal, lonely present. The burden of proof lies with those who believe that our humanness could survive even if the biological family does not.

Finally, there may well be a dehumanizing effect on the scientist himself, and through him on all of us. On the one hand his power of mastery increases, but on the other hand his sense of mystery decreases. The men working on "New Beginnings in Life" are out to subdue one of the most magnificent mysteries, the mystery of birth and renewal. To some extent the mystery has already been subdued. Those who perform *in vitro* fertilization are in the business of initiating new life. To the extent that they feel that there is nothing unusual or awesome in what they are doing, to that extent they have already lost the sense of mystery. The same can be said of the heart surgeon who sees the heart simply as a pump, the brain surgeon who sees the brain simply as a computer, and the pathologist who sees the corpse simply as a body containing demonstrable pathology. The sense of mystery and awe I am speaking of is demonstrated by most medical students on their first encounter with a cadaver in the gross anatomy laboratory. Their uncomfortable feeling is more than squeamishness. It is a deep recognition, no matter how inarticulate, that it is the mortal remains of a human being in which they are to be digging, ultimately a recognition of the mystery of life and death. The loss of this sense of awe occurs in a matter of days or weeks; mastery drives out mystery in all but a very few.

There is, I admit, no reason in principle why the sense of mystery should be destroyed by the increase of knowledge or power. After all, no matter how much one learns about a given phenomenon, there remain things that are dark or puzzling. And indeed, for the great men of science, knowledge served to increase, not decrease, their sense of wonder. Nevertheless, for most ordinary men of science and technology, once nature is seen or transformed into material or given over to human manipulation, the mystery is gone. Awed by *nothing*, freed from all so-called superstitions and so-called atavistic beliefs, they practice their power without even knowing what price they have paid.

A good example is the fertilization, culture and discarding of human embryos in the laboratory. Consider these excerpts from an editorial in *Nature* concerning adverse public reaction in Britain to the announcement (apparently erroneous) that Drs. Edwards and Steptoe were at that time about to do the first transfer of a laboratory-grown human embryo into a woman's uterus to circumvent her infertility.

> What has all this to do with the test tube baby? In terms of scientific fact, almost nothing at all. The test tube baby, as this phrase is usually understood, refers to the growing of a human embryo to full term outside the body and the chief obstacle to this feat (not that anybody has proclaimed it as a goal) is the formidable problem of maintaining the embryo after the stage at which it would normally implant in the uterus. The Oldham procedure concerns only the pre-implantation embryo which, except in the trivial sense that

fertilization is carried out *in vitro*, can hardly be equated with the test tube baby. Moreover, it is difficult to see that the wastage of embryos occasioned by the procedure raises moral problems any knottier than those to do with IUCD, a device that probably prevents the embryo from implanting in the womb. What then was all the fuss about? . . .

A curious feature of the public debate is that the letter-writing segment of the public, at least, seemed to believe that human life was about to be created from nothing in the test tube. For example, a correspondent in The Times voiced the fear that: "The ability of scientists to develop the technique of creating life in a test tube is so serious that I feel human beings should be given the opportunity to express their views on whether or not this line of research should be pursued. . . . (sic) Personally I find the idea of creating life at man's will terrifying." These are indeed dark and atavistic fears which have been nurtured, perhaps, by the views of Dr. Edmund Leach that scientists have usurped the creative powers and should assume the moral responsibilities formerly attributed to gods. Whatever the merit of Dr. Leach's thesis, those who are engaged in research that is at all liable to be misinterpreted will doubtless take the present episode as a warning of the misunderstandings that can arise, particularly if the true facts are not readily available from authoritative sources. There is always the danger that lack of information or misinformation may convert legitimate public concern about new knowledge into a paranoia that impedes research.[53]

The moral is clear. Research, the supreme value, is to be protected from the dark "atavistic" fears of an ignorant public by giving out only the "true facts."

The first paragraph of the excerpt contains the hard, cold technical facts, presented "scientifically" by the scientist-editor of *Nature*. That editor finds it "curious" that the public had a somewhat different view of what was done; he erroneously attributes this difference to the public's lack of the "true facts." However, the source of the difference is not the lack of information, but a different interpretation; the real reason for the difference is that the editor lacks, whereas the correspondent in *The Times* still possesses, the sense of mystery and awe concerning the initiation of new life. The editor is correct in distinguishing *in vitro* fertilization from full extracorporeal gestation and correct in analogizing the question of disposal of

---

[53](Editorial) 1970. Premature Birth of Test Tube Baby. *Nature* *225*:886.

embryos to the question concerning the IUCD (but not in thus disposing of the question). But by calling "trivial" the fact that fertilization and early embryonic development have occurred *in vitro*, he displays his own impoverishment. I do not insist that the embryo created is a human life worthy of protection, but it surely is alive, it surely is potentially human, and it surely got its start through technological manipulation. To look upon these embryos as anything less than potential human life is simply mistaken and misleading.[54] To the extent that we view as knowable only those aspects of nature which are reducible to material for manipulation, to that extent we surrender our human and humanizing ability to perceive and sense the mysteries of nature.

"Humanization": Man as Self-Creator

Among those who would take strong exception to my remarks on dehumanization are those who argue that the new biomedical technologies, including those which make possible "New Beginnings in Life," provide the means for human self-modification and improvement. They see man as imperfect, unfinished, but endowed with creative powers to complete and perfect himself. Included in this group are scientists such as Robert Sinsheimer:

> For the first time in all time a living creature understands its origin and can undertake to design its future. Even in the ancient myths man was constrained by his essence. He could not rise above his nature to chart his destiny. Today we can envision that chance—and its dark companion of awesome choice and responsibility. . . . We are an historic innovation. We can be the agent of transition to a wholly new path of evolution. This is a cosmic event.[55]

[54]Either the embryo is living and prehuman (or human) or it is a thing. If the former, then the discarding of embryos (even barely visible embryos) is a moral issue. If the latter, then *in vitro* fertilization is unquestionably a form of manufacture, and fabrication must be taken as a moral issue. One or the other moral issue must be faced.

[55]Sinsheimer, R. L. 1968. The Prospect of Designed Genetic Change. Paper presented at Symposium on "Genetic Technology: Some Public Considerations," AAAS meeting in Dallas, December, 1968, pp. 1, 15. Reprinted in *Engineering and Science Magazine*, California Institute of Technology, April, 1969.

Some theologians, such as Karl Rahner, agree:

> Freedom enables man to determine himself irrevocably, to be for all eternity what he himself has chosen to make himself.[56]

We note in passing that the theologians have done the scientists one better. Most scientists generally talk about what we are now able or free to do, about technique and its possible uses. At most, some take the fatalistic view that "what can be done, will be done." But the theologians-turned-technocrats[57] sanctify the new freedoms: "What can be done, should be done." Man, with the dead God as his copilot, is to fly off into the wild blue yonder of limitless self-modification.

The notion of man as an open, self-modifying system, as a "freedom-event," to use one of Rahner's formulations, is problematic, to say the least. The idea of man as that creature who is free to create himself is purely formal, not to say empty. It provides no boundaries that would indicate when what was subhuman became truly human, or when what was at first human became less than human. Moreover, the freedom to change one's nature includes the freedom to destroy (by genetic manipulation or brain modification) one's nature, including the

---

[56]Rahner, K. 1968. Experiment: Man. *Theology Digest* 16:57-69, at p. 61. For an excellent critique of Rahner's and similar views, see chapter three of Ramsey, pp. 139-142 *et seq.*

[57]They remind me of that wonderfully durable Vicar of Bray, immortalized in a song of the same name, who survived in his role under six monarchs, each of a different religious or political persuasion. His motto: "That whatsoever King may reign, still I'll be the Vicar of Bray, sir." Not wishing to be left alone holding the Cross, they scramble past each other to embrace the Double Helix. Their instinct of self-preservation may be sound, but it is difficult to understand why they still insist on being called theologians.

I am neither a theologian nor a student of religion. My arguments have not been drawn from specifically religious principles nor from speculations concerning God's will. Nevertheless I am well aware of the debt I owe—a debt that we all owe—to the ideas and moral teachings of the great religious traditions which have informed our civilization and on which we are nourished, wittingly or not. Only those men stripped of noble sentiment and good sense, men for whom the truth comes only in differential equations or on semi-log paper, will deny that great truth and wisdom can be and often are conveyed in what is for them, at best, myth and story. It is irrational to ignore what reasonableness these stories contain. That so-called theologians should promote such irrationality is both a symptom and a cause of our present illness.

capacity and desire for freedom. It is, literally, a freedom which can end all freedom. And it provides no standards by which to measure whether the changes made are in fact improvements. Evolution simply means change; to measure progress requires a standard which this view cannot supply and indeed would not supply if it could.

The "New Beginnings in Life" may be the "transition to a wholly new path of evolution." It may, therefore, mark the end of *human* life as we and all other humans have known it. It is possible that the nonhuman life which may take our place will be superior,[58] but I think it most unlikely and certainly not demonstrable. In either case, we are ourselves human beings; therefore, we have a proprietary interest in our survival, and our survival *as human beings*. This is a difficult enough task without having to confront the prospect of a continual utopian re-making of our biological nature, using all-powerful means but having no end in view.

A Matter of Wisdom

Earlier I raised the question of whether we have sufficient wisdom to embark upon "New Beginnings in Life," on an individual scale or in the mass. By now it should be clear that the answer must be a resounding "No." To have developed such massive powers to the point of introduction with so little deliberation over the desirability of their use can hardly be regarded as evidence of wisdom. And to deny that questions of desirability, of better and worse, can be the subject of rational deliberation, to deny that rationality might dictate that there are some things we can do that we must never do—in short, to deny the need for wisdom—can only be regarded as the height of folly. Let us simply look at what we have done in our conquest of nonhuman nature. We find there no grounds for optimism as we now consider offers to turn our technology loose on human nature. In the absence of standards to guide and restrain the use of this awesome power, we can only dehumanize man as we have despoiled our planet. Knowledge of the needed standards requires a wisdom we do not possess and, what is worse, do not even seek.

[58]To repeat, an objective standard would be required for such a judgment. This neither evolutionism nor self-creationism can supply.

In consequence of the inevitably "utopian" scale of modern technology, the salutary gap between everyday and ultimate issues,
between occasions for prudence and common decency and occasions
for illuminated wisdom, is steadily closing. Living constantly now in
the shadow of unwanted, automatic utopianism, we are constantly
now confronted with issues that require ultimate wisdom—an impossible situation for man in general, because he does not possess
that wisdom, and for contemporary man in particular, because he
denies the existence of its object: transcendent truth and absolute
value, beyond the relativities of expediency and subjective prejudice.
We need wisdom most when we believe in it least.[59]

But we have an alternative. In the absence of that "ultimate
wisdom," we can be wise enough to know that we are not wise
enough. When we lack sufficient wisdom to do, wisdom consists
in not doing. Restraint, caution, abstention, delay are what this
second-best wisdom dictates with respect to "New Beginnings in
Life." It remains for another time to discuss the practical
implications of this conclusion: how to establish reasonable
procedures for monitoring, reviewing, regulating the new technologies; how to deal with the undesirable consequences of
their proper use; how to forestall or prevent the introduction of
the worst innovations; how to achieve effective international
control so that one nation's folly does not lead the world into
degradation.

Fortunately, there are no compelling reasons to proceed,
certainly not rapidly, with these "New Beginnings in Life."
Though it saddens the life of many couples, infertility is hardly
one of our major social problems. Moreover, there are other
means of circumventing it that are free of the enormous moral
and social problems discussed earlier. At a time when we desperately need to limit population growth, it may be a questionable
sentimentality which seeks to provide every couple with its own
biological child rather than continue the practice of adoption.
But it would be a foolish sentimentality to unleash the technologies for "New Beginnings in Life" for this purpose, especially when there are no means to limit or control their use. The
same arguments apply, with equal if not greater force, to the
use of these technologies for the eradication of genetic disease.

[59]Jonas, H. Contemporary Problems in Ethics from a Jewish Perspective. *Journal of Central Conference of American Rabbis*, January, 1968, p.
36. Reprinted in Daniel Jeremy Silver, ed., *Judaism and Ethics* (New York
City: Ktav Publishing Company, 1970).

We probably do not know enough about the genetics of man, despite our well-meaning desires to prevent genetic disease, to practice eugenic abortion (e.g., following amniocentesis). We certainly don't know enough to escalate our tinkering by the eugenic use of "New Beginnings in Life."

I am aware that mine is at least on first glance not the most compassionate view, although it may very well turn out to be so in the long run. I am aware that some who now suffer will not get relief, should my view prevail. Nevertheless we must measure the cost—I do not mean the financial cost—of seeking to eradicate that suffering by any and all means. In measuring that cost, we must of course evaluate each technological step in its own terms, but we can ill afford to ignore its place in the longer journey. For, defensible step by defensible step, we can willingly walk to our own degradation. The road to Brave New World is paved with sentimentality—yes, with love and charity. Have we enough sense to turn back?

CHAPTER II

NEW BEGINNINGS IN LIFE

A Lawyer's Response

FRANK P. GRAD

The "new biology" will make it possible within a few decades to inseminate a human ovum in a bottle and to grow it to full term in its artificial womb, or to implant it at some stage of its development into the uterus of its genetic mother (or into the uterus of another mature woman) to be carried to birth. The new biology is also making rapid strides in the direction of "asexual" reproduction, or cloning, by the development of a method to obtain a genetic "twin" of a person by transplanta-

Frank P. Grad is Professor of Law at Columbia Law School and director of the Legislative Drafting Research Fund of Columbia University. Mr. Grad graduated magna cum laude from Brooklyn College in 1947 and received his LL.B. from Columbia Law School in 1949. Most of his professional career has been in Columbia University, where he has taught since 1955. He practiced law in New York City, and has contributed widely to law reviews and professional journals. He has done major legislative research in such fields as correction law, state constitutional law, public health law, housing law, and environmental law. He is also interested in medical ethics and contributed an article entitled, "Legislative Responses to the New Biology: Limits and Possibilities," to the UCLA Law Review *in 1968. His books include* Public Health Law Manual *(New York: American Public Health Association, 1970),* Alcoholism and the Law *(Dobbs Ferry, New York: Oceana Publications, 1971), and* Environmental Law: Sources and Problems *(New York: Matthew Bender, 1971).*

tion of a specialized cell of an adult organism into a denucleated and unfertilized egg. Other scientific wonders, including multiple cloning, predetermination of sex, predetermination of genetic traits through the manipulation of chromosomal materials, and electrochemical manipulation of behavior through interference with the processes of the human brain, are also upon us. All of these developments open vast and fantastic vistas—most of them frightening. Although I do not share Dr. Kass's great scientific expertise, I share many of his concerns. My conclusions as to legal and ethical consequences, however, differ from his in many significant respects.

The social, and therefore ethical and legal, issues raised fall into several related categories, which may be distinguished for the purposes of this analysis. First, there is the problem of the protection of the fetus, the possibility—or probability—that in the course of investigation and research some fetuses will develop into monstrosities and will be killed, or that some blastocysts will be disposed of because they are not needed or for some other reason. The problem has generally been subsumed under the somewhat emotionally freighted phrase, "the sanctity of life."

Second, there is the question of the range of the impact of new modes of fertilization, gestation, and birth on the structure of the family and consequently on social structure in general.

Third, there is the problem of the choices to be made—and of who is to make them—with respect to the selection of desirable genotypes, assuming that the new biology will indeed make such choices readily available. What kind of people shall we breed?

Fourth is the general problem of whether formal controls, formulated by law or by other social mechanisms, can be devised to deal with all the other issues.

Protection of the Fetus: the "Sanctity of Life"

A great deal of inexact and emotion-laden comment in this field in recent years has centered not only on new biological developments but also on recent liberalization of abortion laws and on the "rights" of the unborn.[1] The termination of the

[1]Byrn, *Demythologizing Abortion Reform,* 14 CATHOLIC LAWYER 180 (1968); Caron, *New York Abortion Law — A Critique,* 14 CATHOLIC

process of gestation—whether *in utero* or *in vitro*—has been called "feticide"[2] or even worse. As a matter of law—whether immediately after insemination or in the ninth month—a fetus is *not* a person,[3] the killing of a fetus, whether by abortion or otherwise, is *not* homicide,[4] and the fetus as such does *not* have any legal rights.[5] A fetus is not a person—at most it is an inchoate person with inchoate rights that do not become legally significant until birth makes it into a person. A fetus has no claim to its father's estate, though birth may give the child such a claim.[6] A fetus has no claim for accidental injury suffered while *in utero*, though the child will have such a claim once it is born.[7] A fetus, some recent lawsuits have suggested, may in-

LAWYER 199 (1968). Also see N. ST. JOHN-STEVAS, LIFE, DEATH AND THE LAW 43-49 (1961).

[2]See L. R. Kass, above, p. 35. Dr. Kass makes it clear that he is opposed to "feticide," whether it consists of abortion or of disposing of an unwanted blastocyst. He appears to equate "feticide" with "infanticide," which it clearly is not. Infanticide is homicide, as a matter of law. Illegal abortion is a punishable crime, but it is nowhere punishable as a "homicide" of the fetus. Dr. Kass indicates that he opposes the New York legislation that grants any woman who wants it the right to have an abortion legally. I strongly support that legislation. This basic difference in orientation—a "hidden agenda" of the debate—deserves to be articulated.

[3]*Kwaterski* v. *State Farm Mut. Auto Ins. Co.*, 148 N.W.2d 107 (Wis. 1967); *Powers* v. *City of Troy*, 156 N.W.2d 530 (Mich. 1968); *Kelley* v. *Gregory*, 125 N.Y.S.2d 669 (Sup. Ct. 1953); cited in Brodie, *The New Biology and the Prenatal Child*, A. J. OF FAMILY LAW 391, 392 (1970).

[4]Criminal abortion and intentional homicide are entirely separate crimes. Criminal abortion is generally punished by prison terms up to five years, while intentional homicide—murder—is a capital crime, generally punishable by life imprisonment or even by capital punishment.

[5]A fetus has no legal personality. It cannot sue or be sued, nor is it possible to appoint a guardian for a fetus. The one case sometimes cited to the contrary, *Hoener* v. *Bertinato*, 67 N.J. Super. 517, 171 A.2d 140 (1961), involved obtaining a court order to grant custody of a child *upon its birth* to the state social welfare department, so that the infant, expected to be born with Rh-negative blood, could be transfused, against the wish and religious beliefs of his parents, immediately *after* birth. The court order to transfer control was effective *after* birth. Had the baby been stillborn, it would have been of no effect.

[6]Even a child conceived, yet unborn, prior to his father's death has legal claims only after he is born. See ATKISON ON WILLS, §36.

[7]The first case in the United States that involved prenatal tort rights was *Dietrich* v. *Northampton*, 138 Mass. 14 (1884), an action for wrongful death. The denial of recovery in that case, in an opinion by Mr. Justice Holmes, was extended to all prenatal injuries in many jurisdictions; no case

deed have an inchoate right *not* to be born, a right that may be asserted by the child after its birth, if the child must suffer a predictable deformity and if the mother's request for abortion was denied.[8]

Of course, experimentation on the materials of human reproduction may be regarded as "human experimentation" subject to whatever legal controls may exist. Yet these controls are applicable only to a limited degree. Scientific investigation and experimentation in this area should, of course, be subject to peer group review whenever such review is required by federal regulation applicable to federally sponsored research or to research involving the experimental use of new drugs.[9] Indeed, the requirement that the known risks in such experimentation be balanced against the potential benefits should also apply.[10] But the main requirement for human experimentation is that of "informed consent" by the subject.[11] There are no special difficulties or ambiguities in obtaining the consent of the woman whose ova are used, of the man whose sperm are used to fertilize them, or of the woman into whose uterus the fertilized ovum is implanted. But it is difficult to obtain the consent of the fetus, particularly since a fetus has never been regarded as

before *Bonbrest* v. *Kotz*, 65 F.Supp. 138 (D.D.C. 1946), permitted recovery. Since that decision, an increasing trend on the part of state jurisdictions to permit recoveries for prenatal injuries has developed. See, *e.g.*, *Amann* v. *Faidy*, 415 Ill. 422, 114 N.E.2d 412 (1953); *Woods* v. *Lancet*, 303 N.Y. 349, 102 N.E.2d 691 (1951); *Williams* v. *Marion Rapid Transit, Inc.*, 152 Ohio St. 114, 87 N.E.2d 334 (1949).

[8]*E.g.*, *Gleitman* v. *Cosgrove*, 49 N.J. 22, 227 A.2d 689 (1967); Annot., *Tort Liability for Wrongfully Causing One to Be Born*, 22 A.L.R.3d 1441 (1968); cited in Brodie, *The New Biology and the Prenatal Child*, A. J. OF FAMILY LAW 391, 396-97 (1970).

[9]See, *e.g.*, Manual of New Drug Regulation, Code of Federal Regulations—Part 130. See also E. Confrey, *P.H.S. Grant-Supported Research with Human Subjects*, Public Health Reports vol. 83 (1968); W. Curran, *Governmental Regulation of the Use of Human Subjects in Medical Research*, 98 DAEDALUS 571 (1968).

[10]See Nuremberg Military Tribunal, *The Nuremberg Code* (1946), and World Medical Association, *Declaration of Helsinki* (1964).

[11]Grad, *Regulation of Clinical Research by the State*, 169 ANNALS OF N. Y. ACADEMY OF SCIENCES 533 (1970); Ladimer, *Ethical and Legal Aspects of Medical Research on Human Beings*, 3 J. PUB. L. 467 (1953); Mulford, *Experimentation on Human Beings*, 20 STANFORD L. REV. 99 (1967); Ratnoff & Smith, *Human Laboratory Animals: Martyrs for Medicine*, 36 FORDHAM L. REV. 673 (1968); Ruebhausen, *Experiments with Human Subjects*, 23 THE RECORD 92 (1968).

having any legal rights, except inchoate ones, in the first place. In experimentation involving children it is usually sufficient that the legal guardian, normally the parent, give his consent. We might require the potential "parent" to consent on behalf of the fetus, but since he is a willing participant in the procedure, such consent would not provide meaningful protection.

The law thus provides no real support for the ethical notion of the "sanctity of life" as applied to the blastocyst or even to the fetus in later stages of development. In the main, the law concerns itself with the protection of sentient human beings. I believe in the sanctity of life, or better still in the sanctity of the human being—once there is life and there *is* a human being. I am disturbed by the rather cheap (because inconsequential) concern in high places for the sanctity of the life of the yet unborn[12] and the relative lack of concern for the sanctity of the life of the sentient and living. We need not look even to the destruction of life in bloody wars, present and past, but simply to the casual manner in which we make judgments that kill thousands every year. Perhaps the destruction of blastocysts will seem less serious if we remember that the use of the automobile condemns some fifty thousand persons to death each year, that pollution-producing technology kills and maims thousands each year, that certain economic decisions may condemn thousands each year to starvation, and that—to give a less conspicuous example—every time we build a structure more than twenty stories high we condemn a number of workmen to death, and the number we condemn in this casual fashion rises in direct proportion to the height of the building.

It has been asserted that biological experimentation on human genetic materials is dehumanizing because it turns living matter into a thing, because it turns life into an object. While such experimentation is objectionable on other grounds (to be discussed below), the so-called objectification of living matter has been overstated. I don't know whether a blastocyst is a "thing," but I know that it is not a person, not a human being (and, like Dr. Kass, I don't know *when* the fetus turns into a living person, except at birth). Granted, it has the potential to grow into a living human being. But is anything that has that potential entitled to our full concern and protection? Does the unfertilized ovum deserve this protection, or the sperm prior to

[12]"Nixon Abortion Statement," *N. Y. Times*, April 4, 1971, p. 28.

fertilization? Why do they deserve protection a minute *after* fertilization and not a minute before? If they do, then we have arrived at the position of our Roman Catholic friends—a position which has at least the great merit of consistency—that equates contraception and abortion in the name of the sanctity of life.[13]

There would be little cause to worry about the protection of the fetus in experimental situations—particularly if such experimentation is opposed on other grounds—were it not for the immediate application of the argument to current concerns over legal abortion. Population control is becoming essential,[14] and contraception is indubitably the most effective and desirable method to accomplish it. But, overpopulation aside, our concern for the sanctity of life and for the human being ought to persuade us that no child should be born into this world carrying the terrible burden of rejection. The baby *in vitro* at least will be wanted. While there is no absolute *legal* right of control over one's body (there are, after all, legal prohibitions against suicide, intentional maiming and self-mutilation), concern for the child *after* birth suggests that it should be the mother's choice whether or not she wants to bear. It would be unfortunate if liberalized attitudes on abortion were to suffer a reversal because of concern for waste of human genetic materials in the course of scientific experimentation.[15]

Impact on Family and Society Structure

Recent developments in the direction of mastery of the genetic code, clonal gestation, multiple identical births, and gestation *in vitro* have been compared, in their potential for good and evil, to the harnessing of nuclear energy. But the potential impact of biological developments is more far-reaching, because nuclear energy—for peaceful or destructive purposes—can be used by any social or political system without

---

[13]*E.g.*, "Text of Pope Paul's Encyclical Reaffirming the Prohibition Against Birth Control," *N. Y. Times*, July 30, 1968, pp. 20-21.

[14]COUNCIL ON ENVIRONMENTAL QUALITY, ENVIRONMENTAL QUALITY, pp. 234-35 (Second Annual Report, 1971).

[15]For evidences of a liberalizing trend worldwide, see Roemer, *Abortion Law: The Approaches of Different Nations*, 57 AM. J. OF PUBLIC HEALTH 1906 (1967).

affecting the system itself, while biological developments are likely to have a major impact on family structure and consequently the social and political structure as a whole. There is no immediate need for panic, however. Huxley's *Brave New World* is not yet upon us, and the fact that cloning of human beings, gestation *in vitro*, and ovarian implantation may be possible in the near future does not mean that these techniques will be so readily available as to have an immediate social impact. It took many years and billions of dollars to progress from splitting the atom to the atom bomb to the nuclear power reactor. It will doubtless take a long time and cost a great deal of money to grow the first bottle baby or to clone the first child. Assuming that ultimate success is certain, the years between experiment and usable technology will provide an opportunity for some social adjustment and for the development of legal controls, created in the light of the actual problems as they arise. As long as the technology remains complex and costly, the impact is likely to be limited.

It is clear, however, that the availability of new biologic techniques and their potential for eugenic controls—both positive and negative—may have a deep impact on family structure, on the relation of the family to the state, and on the decision-making and planning processes of the government. It is unlikely that a society can simultaneously maintain both freedom of the person and an effective, i.e., compulsory, eugenic program. Even if a eugenic program were only voluntary, would not the individual's choice of a mate and of whether to procreate fall subject to some official persuasion as to what eugenic practices or standards are desirable? I fully share Dr. Kass's concern for the manner in which eugenic controls are likely to be managed. The possibility of governmental "Eugenic Control Boards" to prescribe desirable mating or fertilizing combinations, to breed soldiers for war and poets for peace, is a nightmare.[16] Yet if we assume that biological engineering will eventually achieve an inexpensive cloning process or an easy, cheap way of growing babies in bottles, the nightmare becomes prophecy. Even the well-intentioned negative eugenic controls present problems. We

---

[16]For a more detailed discussion of the regulatory problems likely to be presented by full scientific capacity for "positive eugenics," see Grad, *Legislative Responses to the New Biology: Limits and Possibilities*, 15 U.C.L.A. L. REV. 480, 490-93 (1968).

have some rather bad laws on the books that authorize the sterilization of certain defectives, criminally insane, and other supposedly congenitally deficient persons.[17] Will we extend these laws to prevent a genius with a club foot from having children?

The nuclear family has been weakened and is under attack. We do not as yet have a substitute for it, and the prospect of a society consisting of free-floating individuals, grown *in vitro*, without family attachments past or future, is difficult to visualize—just as is a race of Amazons, reproducing itself asexually. The prospect of a specialized female class of childbearers to serve as hosts for fetuses not genetically theirs, is also shocking. It revives the image of the wet-nurse, a lower-class woman who served as the feeding station for the baby of her upper-class sister anxious to keep her figure, but carries it a large step farther.

None of the ovarian implantations would raise essentially new legal problems with respect to the recipient of the implant. The usual requirements of consent and of the use of professional skills (to avoid malpractice suits) would apply.[18] But all of the new techniques would raise substantial questions relating to family relationships, rights to support, rights to inheritance, and the like. As a society we have not yet resolved analogous— and much less serious—problems in the context of long-established techniques of artificial insemination with the semen of a donor (A.I.D.).[19] The use of a donor's semen to aid a couple

[17]See, *e.g.*, IDAHO CODE ANN. §§ 66-802 - 803 (1947); IOWA CODE ANN. §§ 145.2, 145.9 (Supp. 1971); M.C.L.A. §§ 720.301-720.310 (1968).

[18]Cady, *Medical Malpractice: What About Experimentation?* in CLINICAL INVESTIGATION IN MEDICINE: LEGAL, ETHICAL AND MORAL ASPECTS 170 (Ladimer & Newman eds. 1963); CURRAN & SHAPIRO, LAW, MEDICINE AND FORENSIC SCIENCE, pp. 529-81 (1970).

[19]The unresolved legal problems created by A.I.D. have given rise to much scholarly comment. See, *e.g.*, Bartholomew, *Legal Implications of Artificial Insemination*, 21 MODERN L. REV. 236 (1958); Gutmacher, *Artificial Insemination*, 18 DE PAUL L. REV. 566 (1969); Hennesey, *Artificial Insemination*, 10 CANADIAN BAR J. 514 (1960); Dienes, *Artificial Donor Insemination: Perspectives on Legal and Social Change*, 54 IOWA L. REV. 253 (1968); Hager, *Artificial Insemination: Some Practical Considerations for Effective Counselling*, 39 N.C. L. REV. 217 (1961); Holloway, *Artificial Insemination: An Examination of the Legal*

childless by reason of the husband's infertility has been express-ly legalized very recently in only four states in the United States,[20] and the law has generally followed considerably be-hind genetics. There are a few cases on the subject involving a subsequent divorce of the couple, and in almost every instance the husband who is not the biological father of the child—though he may love him and treat him as his own—has been challenged with regard to his visitation rights, or, on the other hand, has sought to escape his obligation of support.[21] The same consequence is likely to follow if a woman bears a child following the implant of a blastocyst developed from her hus-band's semen and another woman's ovum. There is, indeed, the legal specter of the child who, though born into a family, is legally an orphan because he has no genetic ties either to the mother who bore him or to her husband. This raises a good question — what is a family? Is it primarily a biological unit composed of a fertile male, a fertile female, and children who are genetically theirs? Or is it an essentially consensual unit, wherein a man and a woman who are married to each other agree to have and raise children, to regard themselves and the

Aspects, 43 A.B.A.J. 1089 (1957); Klayman, *Therapeutic Impregnation: Prognosis of a Lawyer — Diagnosis of a Legislature,* 39 U. OF CINCIN-NATI L. REV. 291 (1970); Smith, *Through a Test Tube Darkly: Artificial Insemination and the Law,* 67 MICH. L. REV. 127 (1968); Verkauf, *Artificial Insemination: Progress, Polemics, and Confusion — An Appraisal of Current Medico-Legal Status,* 3 HOUSTON L. REV. 277 (1966); *Symposium — Artificial Insemination,* 7 SYRACUSE L. REV. 96 (1955); Comment, *Parent and Child: Legal Effect of Artificial Insemination,* 19 OKLA. L. REV. 448 (1966); Note, *Artificial Insemination: A New Scien-tific Achievement Gives Rise to a Need for New Legislation in Texas,* 23 SOUTHWESTERN L. J. 575 (1969); Note, *A Legislative Approach to Artificial Insemination,* 53 CORN. L. REV. 497 (1968).

[20]10 OKLA. STAT. § § 551-553 (Supp. 1970-71); GA. CODE ANN. § § 74-101.1 (Supp. 1970); ANN. CAL. CODE CC § 216 (Supp. 1971); KANS. STAT. ANN. 523-128 (Supp. 1970). The first reference to A.I.D. in any Anglo-American legislation occurred in the New York City Sanitary Code—now NEW YORK CITY HEALTH CODE, art. 21. First enacted in 1947, the provision regulated donors of semen, but did not legitimate the consequences of the procedure.

[21]*People* v. *Sorensen,* 254 Adv. Cal. App. 869, 62 Cal. Reptr. 462 (1967) affirmed 66 Cal. Reptr. 7, 437 P.2d 445 (1968); *Anonymous* v. *Anonymous,* 41 Misc.2d 886, 246 N.Y.S.2d 835 (Sup. Ct. 1964); *Gursky* v. *Gursky,* 39 Misc.2d 1083, 242 N.Y.S.2d 406 (1963); *People* v. *Dennett,* 15 Misc.2d 260, 184 N.Y.S.2d 178 (Sup. Ct. 1958); *Strnad* v. *Strnad,* 190 Misc. 786, 78 N.Y.S.2d 390 (Sup. Ct. 1948).

children as a family, and to give each other the comforts of material and emotional support, regardless of any genetic nexus?

In the context of artificial insemination there has been considerable question—applicable also, it would seem, to the situation of ovarian implants—of the legal status of the physician who performs it. If A.I.D. is illegal—if, indeed, it is considered adulterous—then the physician who performs it is guilty of battery, and the consent of neither the wife nor the husband will protect him. The issue of adultery is one which has fascinated a great many commentators.[22]

My own view is that we ought to grow up and get away from the ancient dynastic concept of the purity of the bloodline. We ought to legitimate the procedure, not for the sake of the physician or the parent but for the sake of the child, who really has no responsibility for the mode of his procreation and deserves the protection of legitimate birth. By the same token, if we really want to encourage childless couples to adopt children rather than have them by artificial insemination or any of the newer means, we ought to remove substantial disabilities that adopted children still suffer in many states, for instance, with relation to their rights of inheritance.

Wholesale reliance on gestation *in vitro* or on cloned reproduction is likely to end both our present family structure and our democratic institutions. Fortunately, that is a distant possibility. For the more immediate future, it should be possible to formulate legal rules that will assure children—by whatever means conceived and born—of their rights to protection by the family that brought about their creation.

Positive Eugenics and the Social Control of Choice

If new biological techniques of insemination or cloning remain difficult and hence expensive, their application is likely to remain relatively limited. Although the psychological problem of a clone and the ethical problem implicit in the selection of a

[22]The comments received their impetus from the opinion in the English case of *Orford* v. *Orford*, 58 D.L.R. 251 in which the court managed to define adultery as "the voluntary surrender to another person of the reproductive powers or facilities of the guilty person. . . ." The case, holding A.I.D. adulterous, was followed in *Dornboos* v. *Dornboos*, No. 54 - S - 14981 (Super. Ct. Cook County, Ill. Dec. 13, 1954).

genotype will always be present and should not be minimized, the possibility that a few individuals may be born or created by these new methods need not create overwhelming problems for society.

All this will change entirely, however, should the new techniques eventually become so routine, safe, and inexpensive that they may be applied in a wholesale manner. The prospect is beguiling, for it implies the possibility of creating a new society of human beings free from genetic defects and chock-full of desirable genetic traits, a society in which the balance of genotypes will no longer be left to chance and the vagaries of human mating patterns.[23] For the first time man would be able to choose the direction of human destiny by selecting and balancing the genotypes of each succeeding generation.

Our real problem is that, having sought such control in vain for so long, we don't know how to use it now that it is about to be given to us.

It is not necessary here to rehearse the utopian nightmare of Huxley's *Brave New World*, which gains greater plausibility as a projection of the future with each advance in the "new biology." Note, too, that in spite of its frightening totalitarian elements, the society Huxley describes is a functioning one. The Alpha Pluses who run it have already learned how to balance the population and know which genotypes the society needs in order to assure that all the jobs to be done are done by specimens best equipped, and not overequipped, to do them. Huxley's society is in this way far ahead of us, for we really don't know what to do with the choice. We don't know what percentage of the population ought to be of genius quality or how many poets we must have to keep literature alive. We don't know how many beautiful women—or men—we need to keep beauty alive and yet not make it a bore. We don't know how many aggressive soldiers we need; and we don't even know how to constitute any kind of governmental agency capable of formulating the criteria to make the choice.[24]

[23]For a variety of views on the subject, see *Symposium — Comments on Genetic Evolution*, 90 DAEDALUS 451 (1961).

[24]On the difficulty of policy-making involving major scientific or technological factors, see, *e.g.*, C. P. SNOW, SCIENCE AND GOVERNMENT (1961) and THE TWO CULTURES AND THE SCIENTIFIC REVOLUTION (1959); Brooks, *The Scientific Adviser*, in SCIENTIST AND NATIONAL POLICY-MAKING 73 (R. Gilpin & C. Wright, eds.

Possibly, many individual family choices would balance out in some haphazard fashion, so that only minimal governmental controls would be necessary. There is no assurance of this, however. And it is likely that once one nation decided to impose rigid genetic controls others would follow suit, and some at least would begin to make choices which those with greater ethical scruples would condemn.

We have no working mechanisms as a society for making major, life-and-death decisions. Some we make by default, as in the case of new technologies that inevitably cost thousands of lives. Some such decisions we leave to the military, as in the case of wartime destruction of civilian populations. And some such decisions we muddle through, as we do in selecting recipients for scarce medical resources such as kidney or heart transplants.[25] We have no operative criteria to evaluate persons in terms of their social utility or their replaceability in the social apparatus. Most of us are repelled by the notion that we should look at human beings in this mechanistic way. Yet we may be forced to make such evaluations and choices, as new scientific and technological developments present us with more and more options. To refuse to make a choice is itself a choice, and in this case is likely to be the choice of chaos.

Establishment of Formal Controls: The Role of the Law

It would be a fine exercise in speculative legal thought to project how the laws of the family, of marriage and divorce, of inheritance, of criminal responsibility, and of other areas will need to be legislatively adapted to the social problems that will accompany new biological developments.[26] We might even start

1964); Sayre, *Scientist and American Science Policy*, in SCIENTIST AND NATIONAL POLICY-MAKING 97 (R. Gilpin & C. Wright, eds. 1964).

[25]Sanders and Dukeminier, Jr., *Medical Advance and Legal Lag: Hemodialysis and Kidney Transplants*, 15 U.C.L.A. L. REV. 357 (1968); Vestal, Taber & Shoemaker, *Medico-Legal Aspects of Tissue Homotransplantation*, 18 U. DET. L. J. 171 (1955).

[26]For one partially facetious attempt to tackle the "rule against perpetuities" in the light of cryobiology, see Schuyler, *The New Biology and the Rule Against Perpetuities*, 15 U.C.L.A. L. REV. 420 (1968). On the issue generally, see Grad, *Legislative Responses to the New Biology: Limits and Possibilities*, 15 U.C.L.A. L. REV. 480 (1968).

to formulate the outlines of a legal code to systematize the selection of genotypes. All of this would be entirely premature, however, because we simply do not know what the problems will be. We cannot legislate, or even think of legislating, until we know a great deal more. A technology that allows a very wealthy individual to pay for the cloning of a baby will present legal problems vastly different from those of a technology that permits inexpensive mass production of babies in bottles.

If the future is so frightening and so fraught with moral and ethical hazards, why can't we use the law to put a stop to it right now? Why can't we simply prohibit certain kinds of biological and genetic experimentation, since we seem so sure that no good can come of it?

We could draft such a law, though we would indubitably face difficulties in delimiting the prohibited area of research. We could probably manage to pass the law and get it enacted. But it would be a useless law and an undesirable one.

To prohibit certain kinds of scientific investigation would be useless because never in the history of science has any such prohibition succeeded for very long, and it is not likely to do so now. We are not really going to put scientists who violate the law behind bars. As a practical matter, the requirements of the law could probably be evaded; and if the law became really burdensome, scientists would simply do their work in other countries with no such prohibitions. Such a prohibitory law, incidentally, would be a matter for state rather than federal legislation and would have to be passed by each state separately in order to be effective nationally.[27]

A prohibitory law of this kind would also be wholly undesirable. While seeming to uphold ethical values relating to the future of humanity as truly human and the "sanctity of life," it would violate values of just as great importance: freedom of inquiry and the freedom of human beings to be truly human in their pursuit of knowledge.

There are other possible means of control. One is simply to stop funding the requisite research, probably as undesirable a

[27]Such prohibitory legislation is likely to be an exercise of the *state's* plenary police power to protect the health, safety and welfare of the people. It would be difficult to subsume under any of the delegated powers of the federal Congress. For a more detailed discussion of this point, see Grad, *supra* note 26 at 485-86.

way of dealing with the problem as is prohibitory legislation. Another is to inculcate proper ethical concerns in the scientific community. It is always easy to recommend more education and more self-restraint. Instant morality is an inexpensive, not to say cheap, remedy. But the needed change is not so quick or easy. Recent investigations into the ethical concerns of medical and biological researchers indicate that medical schools and similar educational institutions devote hardly any time to teaching the legal and ethical limitations on human experimentation. Moreover, there is strong evidence that experimenters who have never been exposed to any systematic exposition of ethical constraints on human research are more likely to go ahead with clinical experimentation even when the risks are very great in proportion to the potential benefits.[28] Evidence is clear, too, that peer group review by other physicians and scientists increases the scientist's concern for the human subject. Perhaps the best solution to the problems of genetic experimentation lies in greater emphasis on the ethical training of scientists and in routinely subjecting biological experimentation to peer review.

We cannot hope to rely on exclusively legal remedies to these ethical problems, and it is questionable whether it is a proper role of the law to support a particular ethic. If past experience is any guide, knowledge will be sought whether it is forbidden or not. There is a story in Genesis that supports this point.

[28]Barber, and others, *Experimenting with Humans: Problems and Processes of Social Control in the Bio-Medical Research Community* (The Research Group on Human Experimentation, Barnard College, mimeo. 1971).

CHAPTER III

NEW BEGINNINGS IN LIFE
A Theologian's Response
JOSEPH FLETCHER

We are dealing with ethics and the laboratory reproduction of human tissue, either sexually by *in vitro* fertilization or asexually by methods such as cloning or replication from a single body cell. I am surprised to discover that the moral justification for negative eugenics, or *corrective* genetic intervention for therapeutic reasons, is almost as much at issue as is the question of whether positive eugenics, or *constructive* genetic intervention, is defensible. I shall argue that *both* are justifiable.

The substance of Dr. Kass's argument about *in vitro* fertilization is that genetic research and treatment by embryologists, gynecologists, fetologists, and obstetricians ought to be stopped

Joseph Fletcher, professor in medical ethics at the University of Virginia, received his B.D. from Berkeley Divinity School in 1929 and his S.T.D. from London University in 1939. He was dean of St. Paul's Cathedral, Cincinnati, Ohio, from 1936 until 1941, then taught at the University of Cincinnati, and was appointed social ethics professor at Episcopal Theological School in 1944. He remained there until 1970 and is now professor emeritus of that seminary. Dr. Fletcher has lectured widely in universities in this country and in Japan and Britain. He has served as director of the Institute of Pastoral Care, director of the National Council of Religion and Labor, president of the American Society of Christian Ethics, director of the Cambridge Family Society, director of the because it entails a risk of killing or even deliberate sacrifice of an embryo and a fetus—"another human being" or "living and prehuman (or human)" (p. 59, note 54). An ethic of reproduction based on this doctrine is medically impossible. It cuts the ground from under any serious advances in reproductive medicine.

I shall try to avoid the use of epithets and weighted adjectives, confining myself to generally accepted usage. It is pretty clear that Dr. Kass is a preacher and that much of his paper is more an emotional treatment than a course of analytic reasoning. It is not always clear against whom he is preaching under such labels as "theologians-turned-technocrats" who sanctify flying off "into the wild blue yonder of limitless self-modification" (p. 60). It is plain enough that he is not very trustful of human nature. Some scientists do indeed appear to wear rose-colored glasses and to contemplate things like genetic intervention rather too complacently. (Pessimists, it is said, get that way by being too long in the company of optimists, and perhaps Dr. Kass exemplifies that reaction syndrome.)

On some scores I eagerly agree with Dr. Kass. For example, it seems to me that the world suffers far more from moral than from genetic defects. And surely he is correct to contend that desirable goals do not justify every means. We will soon return to this question of means and ends, acts and consequences, but at a level that Dr. Kass has grossly neglected. And I rejoice to find him remarking rather carefully that all acts of feticide are not "murder" or unlawful killings; I trust he means morally as well as legally. I agree that merely "some" utility is not of itself enough reason to introduce a new technology; again, the princi-

~~~~~~

Massachusetts Planned Parenthood Federation, president of the Association for Voluntary Sterilization, member of the President's Committee on Business Ethics, vice-president of the Association for the Study of Abortion, director of the Euthanasia Educational Fund, and board member of the Paddock Fund. He is a frequent contributor of articles, mostly in the field of medical ethics, and his books include The Church and Industry *(London: Longmans Green and Company, 1930),* Christianity and Property *(Philadelphia: Westminster, 1948),* Morals and Medicine *(Princeton: Princeton University Press, 1954),* William Temple *(New York: Seabury, 1963),* Situation Ethics *(Westminster, 1966),* Moral Responsibility *(Westminster, 1967), and* Hello Lovers *with Thomas Wassmer, SJ (Washington: Corpus, 1970).*

ple of proportionate good should reign. It is indeed true, as he quotes C. S. Lewis: "Each new power won *by* man is a power *over* man as well."[1] Dr. Kass's discussion also suggests to me that the major danger in genetic intervention might be not tyranny but voluntary dehumanization, but my reasons for saying so may not be his.

Why do I say Dr. Kass is emotional rather than analytic? Basically I say so because of his ethical quantum leaps. The biggest is his jump across normative ethics, straight from the empirical data of microbiology (which he knows so well) to his own personal meta-ethics or meta-physics about happiness and his liking for such institutions as monogamous marriage and the nuclear family. In the reverse, he argues backward from his a priori metaphysics to a disapproval of laboratory reproduction altogether. In short, he has not set out for us a coherent normative theory or conceptual apparatus to be applied favorably or unfavorably to specific cases or classes of moral decision.

Take just one example: In his discussion of hostess gestation for an artificially fertilized ovum from a donor ("prenatal adoption") he says it is morally questionable; he calls it "womb lending" and "womb renting," and then labels it a form of prostitution. To many of us, this wish to help others unable to carry a fetus seems generous, even sacrificial. The emotional thrust of his discussion is obvious but his reasoning is neither defined nor disclosed. Even if it were, I doubt that he could justify calling the procedure prostitution.

No doubt there are the makings of an ethic in Dr. Kass's paper. For example, he speaks of "intrinsic" reasons and "natural" goods and, in one place, confesses to "prefer arguments from principle concerning intrinsic rightness or wrongness, arguments which abstract from the difficult task of predicting and weighing consequences" (p. 35). This is, I protest, exactly what he has done *in effect*, and since it is the method behind some of his conclusions (as I shall show) and the opposite of my own ethical method, it is up to me now to do what I complain about his not doing—that is, to set out my own ethical apparatus or modality and then follow it to a suitable conclusion about genetic intervention. Since Dr. Kass overtly

[1]C. S. Lewis, *The Abolition of Man* (New York: Collier-Macmillan, 1956), p. 71.

calls into question therapeutic genetics and holds that laboratory reproduction for either research purposes or cloning is wrong *as such*, it is to be expected that I shall end differently.

Leaving aside a rich but only ancillary discussion about right and wrong, let me put the starting point this way. There are those who suppose that whether it is right or good to do anything depends on the consequences of doing it. Opposed to that view, others believe that many of our actions, if not all, are right or wrong not according to their consequences but by virtue of some intrinsic rightness or wrongness in the acts themselves. This built-in moral quality is presumably known to the moral agent through intuition, guidance, revelation, or some other nonempirical means of cognition. Theirs is a meta-rational ethic. Such anti- or non-consequentialists may say, for example, that therapeutic goals are not enough to justify sterilization, *in vitro* fertilization, artificial insemination, prostaglandin abortifacients in birth control, single-cell replications in ectogenesis, or the experimental sacrifice of zygotes and embryos because such things offend against "intrinsic" goods, "rights," or "principles" such as the human status of "nascent life." The point of such a priori ethics is that ends do not justify acts, consequences are not enough to validate our conduct—in short, that a pragmatic weighing of values is not ethically sound because it is "merely" the practice of a "morality of goals." In medical terms, this means that therapeutic effectiveness cannot justify treatment procedures.

The Consequentialist Ethic

Over against this approach is the consequentialist one, seen in utilitarianism, pragmatism, and implicitly in the ethics of all biomedical research and development. Most of us reason inductively from the data of choice or option situations to decisions aimed at maximizing desirable consequences. We do not argue deductively from a priori or predetermined notions that whole *classes* of acts (such as *in vitro* fertilization or the sacrifice of test zygotes) are right or wrong to the conclusion that we ought or ought not to do anything that happens to fall in that class. For consequentialists, and I am thoroughly in their camp, what counts is results, and results are good when they contribute to human well-being.

It is not altogether clear that Dr. Kass is a nonconsequentialist, but he expresses great admiration for those who are and his manner of discussion invites that description. There is no other way to understand his saying apropos experiments with embryos: "Morally, it is insufficient that your motives are good, that your ends are unobjectionable, that you do the procedure 'lovingly' and even that you may be lucky in the result: You will be engaging nonetheless in an unethical experiment upon a human subject" (p. 30). He even quotes approvingly an anti-abortion religionist's opinion that laboratory fertilization for the sake of medical knowledge is wrong because it uses "unethical experiments upon the unborn" (p. 30).

This is clearly an anticonsequential, a priori ethic. Had he started his discussion of laboratory reproduction and positive eugenics with a clearcut methodological preface, we would not be in any doubt as to his approach.

This issue is further complicated because Dr. Kass also uses consequentialist reasoning, arguing against laboratory reproduction on pragmatic grounds. In addition to his universal negatives, he appeals to allegedly prudential considerations such as the claim that *in vitro* reproduction will result in a loss of respect for life, undermine motherhood, or lead to a tyrannical biocracy.

Consequentialists, we must not forget, are of two kinds. There are those who might balance out the good to be gained by laboratory reproduction, to use the pertinent example, and then conclude that it is or would be so frequently productive of undesirable results that *as a class or category* it ought to be disapproved. Their reason for this resort to categories might be like G. E. Moore's:[2] that they fear to trust their own judgment in apparently exceptional or atypical situations. Dr. Kass comes close to this kind of "rule utilitarianism" in much of his discussion. In contrast to these consequentialists are others who balance out the good to be gained in *each situation or case*, acting accordingly and not following generalizations about classes and categories. For the latter kind of consequentialist, whether laboratory reproduction is right or not depends upon the concrete and particular situation or network of situations— not as a matter of classes but as a matter of cases.

Therefore, sticking with our problem, to the situational con-

2G. E. Moore, *Principia Ethica* (Cambridge, England: Cambridge University Press, 1960), p. 88.

sequentialist *laboratory reproduction may be right in some cases, wrong in others.* It cannot be approved or disapproved as such. I am personally in this ethical camp. After saying that "among *sensible* men there would be no human cloning" (p. 44), Dr. Kass lists nine reasons that might be given for cloning, some corrective, some constructive. He rejects them all, but in the case of every one of these reasons I believe that it *could* be right to do what he categorically condemns.

In what kind of situation might cloning or positive eugenics be justified because the good to be gained—the proportionate good—would be great enough? When might its "utility" validate it? I must confess before proceeding that my ability to divine the future is very limited. I am no seer or forecaster, and I feel uncomfortable attempting to predict the shocks of the distant future.

Consider the cloning of humans. While Joshua Lederberg may be correct in saying that talk of cloning is "merely speculative" until more experimental work is done with animals, it is possible that such science-fiction scenarios may be useful for value analysis and ethical examination. Diderot, Shaw, Wells, Huxley and Lederberg himself have all predicted genetic engineering. These crystal ball-gazers until recently have been, like Cassandra, doubted and pooh-poohed, but now things are different.

There may be a need one day, in the human situation at large, for one or more people especially constituted genetically to survive long periods outside a bathysphere at great marine depths or outside space capsules at great heights. If the greatest good for the greatest number were served, it would be justifiable not only to specialize people by cloning or constructive genetic engineering but also to bio-engineer or bio-design parahumans or "modified" men as chimeras (part animal) or cyborg androids (part prostheses).

Ours is a Promethean situation: We cannot see clearly what the promises and dangers are although we know both exist. I would vote, for example, for cloning top-grade soldiers and scientists or for supplying them by genetic intervention if needed to offset an elitist or tyrannical power plot by other cloners—a truly frightening possibility, but imaginable. In most situations, I suspect, I would favor making and using man-machine hybrids rather than genetically engineered people to carry out dull, unrewarding, or dangerous roles required for the social welfare, such as the testing of suspected pollution areas or the investigation of threatening volcanoes.

Much of the scare-mongering indulged in by opponents of biomedical science and genetic engineering tries to link genetic control with tyranny; but this is misleading. It is said, for example, that a cloned man would be a carbon copy of his parent by phenotype as well as by genotype, as if environment and life history played no formative part in the shaping of his personality. Those opposed to such techniques often presume that society will be a dictatorship and that clonees would not be allowed to marry or reproduce from the social gene pool, nor be free to choose vocations for themselves other than the one for which they had a special constitutional capacity. But is this realistic? Is it not more an emotional outlook than a rational view of the question?

Brave New World has shown us that a slave state of the future could and probably would use genetic control. Still, Dr. Lederberg emphasizes, "it could not do so without having instituted slavery in the first place." Lederberg adds, "It is indeed true that I might fear the control of my behavior through electrical impulses directed into my brain but . . . I do not accept the implantation of the electrodes except at the point of a gun: the gun is the problem."[3] I agree. The danger of tyranny is the real danger. Genetic controls do not lead to dictatorship; if there is any cause-and-effect relation it is the other way around. Those who read *Brave New World* and *1984* and *Fahrenheit 451* forget that genetic and behavioral controls are employed only after tyranny is established. The problem of misuse is political, not biological.

I am tempted to go into details of the fascinating subject of genetic engineering and its constructive possibilities, but I have too little technical grasp of the subject. I suspect, moreover, that it is as yet more an open door than a charted path. Let me therefore try to stay well within the range of ethical discourse.

Dr. Kass strikes me as emotional and basically biased; yet I must confess that I also have reservations about the simplistic *faith* of many other scientists. I respect and share their ethic, which is primarily a love for and search for facts and truths. But many scientists have an almost blind faith that somehow the

---

[3]Joshua Lederberg, "Genetic Engineering, or The Amelioration of Genetic Defect," *The Pharos*, Jan., 1971, p. 10.

facts will always be used for good, not misused for evil. The personal and social dangers in biomedical research and development and the prospects for the use of new techniques demand the kind of overall supervision and study that Dr. Kass is engaged in for the National Research Council and justify Senator Mondale's 1968 proposal for a National Commission on Health, Science, and Society. Science deals with possibility and probability, but ethics must deal with preferability.

James D. Watson, codiscoverer with Francis Crick of the structure DNA, put it very well:

> To many people, particularly those with strong religious backgrounds, our most sensible course of action would be to de-emphasize all those forms of research which would circumvent the normal sexual reproductive process. If this step were taken, experiments on cell fusion might no longer be supported by Federal funds or tax-exempt organizations.... Even more effective would be to take steps quickly to make illegal, or to reaffirm the illegality of, any experimental work with human embryos.

Seeing this as both unlikely and undesirable, Dr. Watson expressed the hope

> that over the next decade wide-reaching discussion would occur, at the informal as well as formal legislative level, about the manifold problems which are bound to arise if test tube conception becomes a common occurrence.[4]

I have already explained why I cannot accept any blanket disapproval of positive genetic controls, any more than I can accept similar categorical condemnations of artificial insemination, ovum implantation, *in vitro* fertilization, or the laboratory sacrifice of embryonic human material. Whether any of these things is morally licit would depend, I believe, upon the particular case and the social situation. Sometimes they could be right, sometimes wrong. All depends on whether they contribute to the fulfillment of human need.

Needs and Rights

Let us focus for a minute on the question of *need*. Dr. Kass throughout his paper speaks continually of "human rights." I contend that needs take precedence over rights and that needs

[4] James D. Watson, *The Atlantic Monthly*, May, 1971, pp. 52, 53.

validate rights, not the other way around. A legalistic ethic gives first place to rights, whereas an agapistic or humanistic ethic gives first place to needs. Jurisprudence and constitutional law reveal that "rights" come into effect only after a struggle by radicals to persuade society to recognize human needs—needs that have been traditionally ignored or are only newly emerging. The right to health may be an example in today's world, or the right to breathe clean air and to swim in undegraded water.

But once a need is given the status of a right, it is sooner or later appealed to by reactionaries as a reason for not recognizing other more pressing needs. The so-called rights of property and of free association have been so used, and this is what is apt to be done with an alleged "right to be born" or a "right to life"—it will be held intrinsically valid as a claim, regardless of changing human needs. This is what Dr. Kass does when he speaks of various rights such as the possession of our own tissue, a fetus's right to be born (which he sets against another proposed right to be born mentally and physically sound), the "inherent injury" of being a copy of somebody else, and the natural right to be genetically unique.

Dr. Bentley Glass pointed out in an address in October, 1970, to the Society for Health and Human Values that values often conflict, as rights do. Preserving the molecule may be at the cell's expense, and uncontrolled cell growth can take a person's life. The individual's rights can cut across society's needs, and one nation's goals infringe on another's. Dr. Glass wisely questioned the United Nations' Bill of Human Rights for asserting the individual's "incorrigible right" to reproduce, regardless of the quality of the human lives thus procreated. Should not abortion of a seriously defective fetus be obligatory? "Cannot the substitution of a greater freedom of choice in new respects," he asked, "compensate for the restriction of some time-honored privileges?"[5]

What Is a Person?

Another ethical issue has to do with the concept of humanness and what it is to be a person. Dr. Kass says that "the laboratory production of human beings is no longer *human*

[5] Bentley Glass, "Human Heredity and Ethical Problems," unpublished ms.

procreation" (p. 54). But laboratory reproduction seems to me to be radically human and personal rather than "natural," which means genetically accidental. These concepts are ancient but vague, and as a result much of our discourse about the ethics of biomedical innovation becomes a semantic swamp. Relying on these imprecise notions, Dr. Kass calls artificial reproduction "depersonalized." On the contrary, I believe it is a highly personalized form: it is rationally willed, chosen, purposed, and controlled, as ordinary reproduction by sexual intercourse is not.

The question, "What is it to be human?" is no academic inquiry. Physicians and nurses face it thousands of times every day. It arises *in utero* when terminations of pregnancy are called for or indicated, and it arises *in terminus* when decisions have to be made about prolonging the patient's dying. When does a fetus become human, when is a dying patient no longer a person? The uncomfortable truth is that we have not put our heads together to find any meaningful, *operational* terms for such synthetic concepts. It is imperative that scientists, philosophers, sociologists, and theologians make the attempt. What makes a *human* being? To be a person must there be a minimum of cerebral-cortical function? Self-awareness and self-control? Memory? A sense of futurity, of time? A capacity for interpersonal relationship? For love? A minimum I.Q.? Could we add a desire to live? What else? And in what order are we to rank such criteria?

Let me indicate just one example of the conceptual constructs which might be adopted. Some researchers have proposed that we redefine death in terms of irreversible coma or the loss of the higher brain function (what some call "cerebral"), due perhaps to a massive injury or a cortical neoplasm. If a post-cerebral patient is no longer alive in any human or personal sense, does it not follow that a pre-cerebral embryo or fetus is not yet alive in any human sense?

In any case, what is demanded of consequentialists is a quality-of-life ethic to take the place of the traditional Western sanctity-of-life ethic. The meta-ethical and meta-rational presuppositions or first premises of the "sanctity" posture are neither verifiable nor falsifiable; moreover, they are, by their plain logical inference, opposed to empirical, humanistic medicine as well as to genetic and embryological investigation.

What is at stake is the determination of *personal* status, not human status. Biologically, both fallopian and uterine material are human; it is a species designation. The issue is whether or when a human zygote, embryo, or fetus may be terminated for reasons of consequence before it has reached *personal* form—prenatally or postnatally, according to what we decide are the hallmarks of a person. The question for situation ethics is whether or not in any particular case it is better (more good than evil) to nip a nascent human life in the bud.

Finally, let me explain what I meant at the beginning by saying that Dr. Kass has built his case against laboratory reproduction on his own personal meta-ethics or meta-physics. I mean that he starts with a subjective, nonempirical, really *religious* set of premises about human values and natural rights, about the indispensability of heterosexual intercourse for reproduction, and about marriage and the family—monogamous marriage and the nuclear family, he seems to mean—as the morally necessary context of reproduction.

These premises are similar to the dogmatic assertion by some religious opponents of abortion that even the zygote has a right to be brought to term. Such presuppositions are religious in the sense that they are faith affirmations, neither verifiable nor falsifiable. Obviously we cannot prove that any one value or set of values is given *de rerum natura*, that reality includes "rights," or that sex and reproduction are authentic only within the marriage bond. These are matters of faith or religious preference, and therefore to condemn *in vitro* fertilization or cloning on the basis of those particular faith propositions has weight only with those who share them.

Dr. Kass has pointed rather acutely to a number of possible dangers and abuses, but these considerations are consequential and prudential, and they cannot lead by force of logic to an overall repudiation of the scientific procedures under scrutiny. Neither can they validate the claim to a "right" to be born with a unique genotype or the belief that laboratory reproduction (a "second genesis") will lead to dehumanization of science and society. Such conclusions may follow logically from such metaphysical premises, but this process of reasoning excludes all nonbelievers by its first premises. Our task, if we are to avoid what Gerald Leach has called a "biocracy,"[6] is to achieve a

[6]Gerald Leach, *The Biocrats: Ethics and the New Medicine*, McGraw-Hill, 1970.

consensus built around a humanistic ethic that is not meta-rational or based on faith assumptions, but derives its cogency from shared values and reportable experience.

I am convinced that such an ethic would be consequential, not a priori; selective and situational, not categorical. That is, it would not condemn laboratory reproduction as such but would condemn it only when it appears that its means or ends are incompatible in the circumstances with human needs, as we discover them by common consent and verifiable reasoning.

CHAPTER IV

NEW BEGINNINGS IN LIFE

A Philosopher's Response

DANIEL CALLAHAN

I find Dr. Kass's paper exceedingly difficult to comment on. It may be useful for me to put forth some of the problems I feel as I think about the topic under the stimulus of that paper.

The paper made me realize, in the first place, how much of a layman I am in these matters. Not a layman in the ordinary sense. For it is true, on the one hand, that I am trained to provide ethical commentary, as a duly certified Ph.D. in philosophy. And it is true, on the other hand, that I can comprehend (more or less) the scientific data. There is very little, in other words, that I do not understand on the cognitive level; the

Daniel Callahan, director of the Institute of Society, Ethics, and the Life Sciences, a private foundation located in Hastings-on-Hudson in New York State, was born in Washington, D.C. He has studied at Yale University and Georgetown University and received his Ph.D. in 1965 from Harvard University. He served as a professor of religion at Temple University and Brown University and has taught at a number of seminaries including Union Theological Seminary.

From 1961 to 1968 he was the executive editor of Commonweal, *and he has written widely in the fields of ethics, theology, and university life. He is the author of* The Mind of the Catholic Layman *(New York: Scribner's, 1963),* Honesty in the Church *(Scribner's, 1965),* The New Church *(Scribner's, 1966),* Abortion: Law, Choice and Morality *(New York: Macmillan, 1970), and* Ethics and Population Limitation *(The Population Council, 1971).*

issues and the arguments, as stated by Dr. Kass, seem clear enough. But I am, I think, a layman in another sense. Even though I can understand *what* the scientists are doing, I am not myself a scientist. I don't share their excitement, nor am I particularly prone to enthusiasm about the vision or impetus that spurs them on. Neither is it the case, so far as I can see, that I stand to gain any personal benefit from the work they are doing. Whether my children or my children's children will benefit is problematic. In a word, the concrete aspects of the issues are remote, and I suspect that such is the case for most people. The promised benefits of *in vitro* fertilization and cloning, if they materialize, will not do any of us individually much good. The promised benefits are mainly mathematical, helpful to that statistically unknown portion of the population which either needs, or thinks it needs, or would like, the benefits. One can ordinarily feel only slight personal involvement in these problems, and that is true of scientifically educated philosophers as much as of anyone else.

But the problems themselves are not ordinary. Even if we leave aside the respect we should (ordinarily) pay the desires and work of scientists, and leave aside the benefits their work may bring for some statistical portion of the population—reasons usually sufficient to make us stand aside and allow others to achieve what they want without meddlesome comments from casual bystanders—we cannot leave aside quite so readily the long-term implications for man of the work being done on "New Beginnings in Life." Because we are part of the human community and bear some responsibility for the future of man, what is being done by our generation (even if not by us personally) becomes part of our responsibility. Thus even if it is true that most of us are laymen in these matters and that most of us will personally be neither helped nor harmed appreciably in our lifetime by what develops, we are not thereby excused from deciding or acting on the issues. Of that much Dr. Kass has convinced me. Though I do not choose his doom-laden tone and am not quite so scathing in my own denunciations of our contemporary infatuation with technology, he has convinced me of the seriousness of the issues and the need for some decisions—the difficult kind, decisions either for or against.

Precisely because the issues are so vital and the outcome so potentially fateful, none of us can afford to take refuge in the claim that he is only a layman, casually leaving the problems to some "expert" or other. If it would be morally irresponsible to do so, it would be foolish as well. There are no "experts" on such things as cloning and *in vitro* fertilization. The problems are so new, so hard, and so little limited to technical matters that none of us need feel ashamed about trying to think through and comment. Not one of us knows, or can possibly know at this point, whether the optimists or the pessimists will prove to be right in the long run. We can at most try to make reasonable guesses, use our heads and our imagination, and work the issues through as best we can. No one is disqualified from that task. And whatever else we may have learned from the twentieth century, I hope we have learned how naive and dangerous it can be simply to let things happen and then to judge events after the fact—which has too often meant trying to clean up a mess we let ourselves unthinkingly create.

There is a more pointed way of stating this line of thought. We live in a society which by and large does not interfere with science, on the one hand, or attempts, on the other, to fulfill personal individual desires and visions. Freedom is the ideal. Unfortunately the same ideal is sometimes used to bully laymen, or others not personally involved, to keep their mouths shut. Thus, men are no longer supposed to analyze women, or whites to analyze blacks, or nonscientists to analyze scientists. Everyone is supposed to be allowed to do his own thing, without interference or moralistic commentary from outsiders. The implication of this for our particular area of concern is that even those of us who do not favor "New Beginnings in Life" should leave the way open to those who do. The usual phrase thrown in the face of outsiders who comment or moralize is, "Who are *you* to say. . . ?" I believe, however, that this kind of thinking and that kind of put-down are the death of human community. For few things that one does affect himself only. Human beings live together; they always have and they always will. We are not outsiders when it comes to new beginnings in life. It is the fate of man himself we are talking about, and none of us should allow himself to be cast in the role of outsider on that.

That brings me to my second difficulty in trying to prepare a comment on Dr. Kass's paper. There is, I have come to believe, not only an ethic of politics but a politic of ethics. As I will relate shortly, I think there are some serious problems in Dr. Kass's discussion of the ethical issues. I have no doubt that in abler hands than my own some of these problems could be used to develop intriguing counterarguments against his case. It might not be necessary that these arguments be altogether persuasive. In a situation where the momentum of science, not to mention its occasional worship, is conducive to the development of new beginnings of life, Dr. Kass has an uphill fight on his hands. His viewpoint must prevail totally if it is to prevail at all. As long as there is one—just one—research team in the world carrying on its experiments, then the search for new beginnings will go forward. And if that one team succeeds, then the world is forever after blessed or cursed, depending upon one's viewpoint, by what it has done.

In that context, it is not necessary to refute Dr. Kass. His arguments need only be neutralized—and that can be accomplished simply by asking some hard and deep questions of him, questions which require that one pause at least for a few months to see if an answer can be found. But of course some of the experiments, particularly *in vitro* fertilization, may require only a few months to come to fruition. By the time someone has come to Dr. Kass's defense, countering the retorts to his view, the issue may have been decided. The course of responsible scholarly discussion—requiring months to prepare papers and more months to prepare replies to critics—is incompatible with the speed of social decision-making his paper calls for.

I came away from reading his paper, then, with the horrible sense that one can only decide about the matters he discusses by trying, hard as it is, to jump to the end of a story that is still in the writing—by deciding before all the evidence is in, before all viewpoints have been heard, and before all aspects of the problem have been fully thought out. If it is true, as Dr. Kass says, that there has been "little deliberation" about the ethical problems, ironically this observation must tell against his own position as well as against those he opposes. I suspect that he might agree with that comment. But I also suspect, from the sharpness of his attack, from the multiple considerations he brings to bear, and from his tendency to throw every imaginable objection behind his case, that he seeks as much to convert as to persuade us. The practical implication of his paper is an immediate moratorium on certain lines of investigation. More than that, if he is correct that there are no ethical ways of conducting tests on the products of *in vitro* fertilization, then the moratorium may become a permanent one. The longer we talk about the issues, presuming he is right, the longer we delay the final day of reckoning and the more time we provide for those racing to get their work done before the ethical objections stop them.

That is why I feel forced, precipitately, to try to look to the end of the story, making decisions well before everything has been thought about or can be thought about. If I am right in doing this, then something of an act of faith is required—not an irrational faith, perhaps, for it is a faith with some supporting reasons. The act of faith requires of us now, or very shortly, a simple *yes* or *no*. At that point we are forced to consult more than our reason: our emotions, passions, affections, and loathings come into play.

Critique

Dr. Kass's argument against the kind of experimentation necessary to develop new beginnings in life is straightforward. There is no way of carrying out the requisite experiments so that the safety of the embryos can be assured. On the principle, "Do no harm," and in line with widely accepted norms for experimentation upon human subjects, it is not ethical to carry out these experiments. Even if we say that embryos are not human, it is not possible to invoke the usual brief for abortion. The latter presupposes, at the very least, not only that some harm would otherwise be done to the mother's health, but that the embryos are not wanted after an accidental or unintended conception; this is not the case with the experiments leading toward the "New Beginnings."

As it stands, this is a compelling case, particularly when it is not possible to show that there are overwhelming social needs requiring the experiments in the first place. But if we are to accept this conclusion, there are some related questions which need further exploration.

At one point in his paper Dr. Kass indicates his scorn for the "so-called 'right of every child to be born with a sound physical and mental constitution, based on a sound genotype' " (p. 39). His concern is with the growing campaign to prevent the birth of all defective children. I share this concern, and share as well Dr. Kass's skepticism about invoking the "so-called 'right' " as a warrant for creating a non-right of parents to lay upon society the burden of malformed or mentally incompetent children. A social legitimization of this proposed non-right would lead, logically, to state efforts to prevent known carriers of certain genetic defects from conceiving in the first place, and if they did conceive to undergo state-enforced abortions (which, in another place, Dr. Glass has already predicted).

The only way of countering this line of reasoning would be

constitution has no right to be born. If the condition under which a certain portion of conceived human beings may be born at all is that they be born defective, they do not thereby forfeit their right to life. We will indeed have descended into the pit if we make genetic perfection a condition for the right to exist.

Nonetheless, there are some important considerations which should not be neglected here. It is dangerous to stress the right to be born without defects if this is actually a smoke screen for eugenic or population-limitation goals. There is also a case to be made for the right of those who will be born to have efforts made in their behalf to minimize or alleviate their expected defects. However, there is nothing more dubious than speaking of the rights of the unconceived; there is no subject of rights to speak of. Yet there is a legitimate sense in which one can speak of the future welfare of those yet to be conceived and born. We know, statistically, that a certain number of defective children will be born. We know, too, that there are lines of research and therapy which might, if pursued, make their lives more tolerable. Those who can, by virtue of their training, pursue such studies have a duty to do so, even though one cannot say, strictly speaking, that those yet to be conceived have a "right" to research efforts in their behalf. A duty of this kind needs to be predicated without corresponding rights, for otherwise the fate of these potential children is too much the pawn of the tastes and inclinations of researchers.

The Ethics of Consequences

Dr. Kass is quite right in preferring to make his primary case against *in vitro* fertilization and implantation on grounds of "principle concerning intrinsic rightness or wrongness" (p. 35) rather than on the grounds of harmful consequences. Nevertheless, as he points out, there is a kind of "intellectual purism" about that approach, and so he goes on to point out some of the possible harmful consequences. However, some further distinctions are needed to make a discussion of consequences helpful. In particular, it is not made clear just which consequences would be harmful per se and which would be harmful if not subjected to legal and social regulation. Would the "opening of egg-banks" (p. 36) be an intrinsically bad consequence, or would it be bad only because it would be hard to regulate legally? Would the rise of "surrogate gestational mothers" be a bad consequence in itself or because of the possibility that poor women could be exploited "to form a caste of childbearers" (p. 37)?

There are two aspects to this issue. One is the general problem of control of technology. So long as the main argument from consequences turns on the problem of establishing effective control over developments that in and of themselves need not be harmful, it is open to proponents of "New Beginnings in Life" merely to propose and support adequate legal and social safeguards. There is no reason why one could not legislate against certain kinds of potential abuses, or why laws concerning responsibility for the resulting child could not be formulated. But to what extent can we put our faith in such safeguards? Despite the stated willingness of SST advocates to be bound by elaborate regulations, Congress was not willing to take the risk that such regulations would fail. This may have been a salutary skepticism, and it provides a good precedent in the face of claims that wise legislation can take care of any potential abuse problems.

The second aspect bears on the extent to which we should think in terms of a logic of escalation. Dr. Kass contends that if we take the first steps, one thing will eventually lead to another. And it is true that the history of science and technology has shown that one thing does lead to another. Had there been no wheel there would be no tanks. Had there been no investigation of mold there would be no penicillin. The difficult question is in knowing how far anyone can reasonably be expected to look down the road; and, when that is done, knowing upon just which features of the possible landscape attention should be focused. Is it not sufficient that those pressing certain lines of technological advance respond, if they can, only to the immediate hazards their work portends? Is it fair or reasonable to ask them also to take account of, and defend themselves against,

kind of language he does, my impression is that the proponents of "New Beginnings" believe that their work is both praiseworthy and intensively human. To seek knowledge is human. To improve man's lot is human. To make things, even human beings, is human. To do what can be done is human. In a descriptive sense, the search for "New Beginnings" is uniquely human. Only man among all living beings has the capacity to conduct the search, and only man has the capacity to create visions of the good that a successful search might bring. In a word, the proponents are hardly likely to accept the charge that their work is dehumanizing. They are likely to make quite the opposite claim.

There are many confusing debates in our day, but few are as confusing as those which turn on what is really human. It has been difficult enough for zoologists, anthropologists, and biologists to determine what is descriptively human, what is and is not *homo sapiens* in our evolutionary past. It has been far harder to determine what is or ought to be normatively human. Why has this been so? Let me offer a brief list of reasons: Man is a complex being, capable of thinking, feeling, willing, relating, and shaping his environment with tools. To determine the normatively human we must find ways of ordering and relating all these different capacities in some coherent way. Man is also a historical being, shaped by his social and psychological heritage; that history must be sorted out and, on occasion, judged. Man is a creative being, capable of building cultures and of acting out his values and his aspirations, some of which will be new and different.

These are commonplace observations, but they help explain why it has never been easy to determine the normatively human. The most important characteristic for our purposes is that man is a self-interpreting animal. It is man who must interpret what it means to be human. Even interpretations that emphasize divine revelation of man's nature and destiny still require a pre-revelatory stage of human self-critique and self-understanding. Revelation will not be understood as revelation unless man already understands himself well enough to find a particular revelation plausible. Moreover, once delivered, revelation requires interpretation.

Besides this revelatory interpretation, there are any number of competing philosophical or scientific views of man. The natural law tradition, in its various manifestations, has stressed the existence of an abiding human nature that must be understood. From this understanding can come guidelines for the kind of conduct that will make man what in essence he is or is capable of becoming. At quite the opposite pole are a cluster of theories which deny either that there is an abiding human nature or that knowledge of such a nature can provide human beings with norms for living a good life. The emphasis here falls more heavily on man as a self-creator, the sole author of his meaning, values, and ends. All of these positions—though I am oversimplifying them for the sake of brevity—presuppose some capacity and need for man to be his own interpreter. The philosophical arguments arise when it is asked just what it is he is trying to interpret and for what purpose.

Dr. Kass seems to be convinced that there is an essential human nature and that it is possible for man in the process of self-interpretation—and in the process of acting—to "dehumanize" himself, to become something less than he can or should be. Yet Dr. Kass nowhere tells us just what this essence is, nor does he provide a general proposition which might serve as an overarching norm against which to measure the humanness or nonhumanness of our acts. Instead he provides us with examples of what he believes would be dehumanizing: *in vitro* fertilization, cloning, the sundering of intercourse and procreation, the demise of the monogamous family. These may be very good examples—if we had in hand a general norm of "the human" and could show how these particular actions fail to meet the norm. Otherwise, in the most profound sense, an offering of them as examples serves only to beg the question.

Begging the question may not always be a grave philosophical crime. But in this particular case the problem is serious, for the exact issue at stake is whether certain kinds of actions would be dehumanizing. It is not enough to assert that they are hoping

[several lines illegible]

others. If, in the long run, our hopes must rest on enough people having enough good impulses, however inarticulate or philosophically incomplete, then our present task is to develop the kind of thinking that will create a culture which will produce those impulses. This means that some general, comprehensive, and universal norms for "the human" must be spelled out. This Dr. Kass has not done.

Yet he is not to be blamed. It is not a one-man task; it is the kind of thing only human communities can do. Moreover, it is possible that most human beings do not conduct their moral life by recourse to general principles concerning "the human." Such principles are the linguistic artifacts of philosophers, saints, and sages, not necessarily the stuff of concrete, human decision-making. Even so, unless we have some general norm to work with, however inchoate and unfinished, we are bound to flounder.

Dr. Kass contends that a depersonalization of procreation and a complete surrender to the calculating will would be "seriously dehumanizing no matter how good the product" (p. 53). Is this because *any* act which was biologically or historically once personal leads to dehumanization if it becomes depersonalized or subject to technology? People once had servants to care for their personal needs; now machines do so. That change was not dehumanizing—quite the opposite. What kinds of acts must remain personal to be human and which can be depersonalized without leading to dehumanization? Some guidelines are needed here.

Are all acts which represent a surrender to the "calculating will" necessarily dehumanizing? A peace treaty between nations represents an act of mutually calculating wills; if it brings peace, is it not a good act? The use of contraceptives is an act of the calculating will, and a very significant surrender to that will. But the moral attraction of the surrender is premised on the benefits this will bring to procreation, child-rearing, and family life. Dr. Kass says that "human procreation is human partly because it is not simply an activity of our rational wills" (p. 53). But this statement implies that any activity which is simply an activity of the rational will is not fully human, and, more than that, that any activity in which only one of man's capacities is called into play is not fully human. All of these positions need justification, for they are not self-evidently true. Even if we agree that an activity is more completely human if it "engages us bodily and spiritually, as well as rationally" (p. 53), it does not follow that those which engage only part of our humanity are dehumanizing. The study of mathematics, or athletics, normally involves only part of our being, but neither is ordinarily considered dehumanizing. Is Dr. Kass saying that some key human acts ought to engage the whole man and will be dehumanizing if they do not—and that procreation is one of these? If so, then it needs to be shown both that there are such special and central acts and that procreation is among them.

In this respect, Dr. Kass's "distinction between the natural and the artificial" (p. 54) requires considerably more elaboration if it is to be of any use in distinguishing the good from the bad. He says for example: "To lay one's hands on human generation is to take a major step toward making man himself simply another of the man-made things" (p. 54). He assumes that there is something inherently inferior about that which is "man-made" in comparison to that which is naturally produced; and, in his use of "simply," he appears to preclude the possibility that the man-made could ever be anything but inferior. There is no special reason for assuming that, nor for assuming the further implicit proposition that if some previously natural events (e.g., procreation) came under human control, dehumanization would be the ineluctable result.

Man's relationship to culture is worth pondering in this respect. A culture is in one sense a manufactured thing, but it is "natural" to man to create cultures. Part of the nature of man is the capacity to create cultures. Moreover, there is biological and anthropological evidence that the creation of culture, and life in a culture, changes man's biological nature. Dr. Kass says that in man's interventions into procreation, "human nature becomes simply the last part of nature which is to succumb to the technological project, a project which has already turned the

be argued that the whole cultural project, especially in its reliance on technology, has gone too far, that there is now a line which should not be crossed. That is a defensible case. But that is a very different matter from implying that "human nature" has somehow, until very recently, remained free of man-made interventions and should remain free. The latter is simply not historically true. The real question is how far it is wise to go in changing human nature. Concretely, ought procreation to be included in the cultural-technological project? That it would be man-made need not count against it.

But there is something which might count against it. Dr. Kass asks whether there is "possibly some wisdom in that mystery of nature which joins the pleasure of sex, the communication of love and the desire for children . . . " (p. 53). Dr. Kass does not answer his own question, but he appears to think there is such a wisdom. If there is such a wisdom, toward what essential human ends is it directed? One could argue that in addition to preserving a randomness necessary to evolutionary adaptation, it is also directed toward the establishment of those bonds and values which serve to facilitate two human goods: first, the creation in man of a sense of obligation, without which no human community is possible; and second, the particular obligation of an irreversible commitment of adults to children. On the first point, in the parent-child relationship we see the very prototype of the concept of obligation. A child is utterly dependent upon others for his existence, and it is the parents who are responsible for that existence in the first place. Thus if anyone in the world has an obligation to preserve a child, it is his parents. The parent-child relationship is the very model of the dependence of the weaker upon the stronger, of the need for one human being to act on behalf of another. The whole ethical problem of human obligation is summed up here. To threaten this natural biological relationship would be to threaten the concept of obligation at its very roots.

On the second point, the great biological advantage of the natural parent-child relationship is that it forces a move from the general observation that children are dependent for their existence upon adults to the specific observation that particular adults are responsible for their own children. Without the bond of sexual pleasure, mutual love, and the desire for children—which together produce a concrete child out of a concrete, highly personal relationship—this irreversible commitment of specific adults to specific children would be massively endangered. The advantage of natural procreation is that it facilitates the sense of an irreversible commitment of specific adults to specific children. Its affectional and biological basis, which would be lost if there existed no "natural" parent-child relationship, gives rise to the obligation.

Dr. Kass's questions about the nature of the relationship which would obtain between scientists and their manufactured products touch on that point. No doubt it would be possible to frame legal regulations specifying who has the primary obligation to the manufactured child. One might specify by law, for instance, that any scientist who manufactures a child takes on all the obligations which now legally accrue to parents. But it is hard to see how such legislation would ever engender the responsibility felt in the natural parent-child relationship.

The word "dehumanize" must be given some concrete meaning; otherwise it simply becomes a term of mystification, open to each person's own meaning. In the issues under consideration, the concrete threat to human life is that of destroying the ground of obligation—between adults and children, between parent and child. That is the specific meaning of "dehumanize" in this context. The demise of the monogamous family is not really the central issue. It is not difficult to discern the drawbacks of the monogamous family; a plethora of critics are doing that today. The significant question is whether some conceivable alternative family or social relationship could preserve the obligations of parent toward child, of adults toward children, which has been a major contribution of the monogamous family. If such a structure of society could be implemented, then the monogamous family might be dispensed with. I have yet to see a plausible blueprint for such a social structure. All who attempt to draw one up make the same mistake: They assume that the only real issue is how to insure the physical and

for our concern must be with the behavior of most people on the whole. There seems to me no quicker way to destroy the basis of obligation than to make children nobody's obligation in particular and everybody's in general, whether "everybody" be a commune or a society.

Wisdom and Mystery

Dr. Kass lays considerable stress on the preservation of a sense of mystery about man and nature as a necessary precondition for wise decisions and actions. I must admit to something less than enthusiasm for the concept of "mystery" and for preservation of the sense of mystery as a putative source of ethical wisdom. Even if it is true that the best scientists preserve a sense of wonder and awe, that sense has provided no safeguard that they will not do harmful things. For all of its evocative power, a "sense of mystery" tells us nothing at all about what we should or should not do. To accomplish that, it becomes necessary to know what "the sense of mystery" is saying to us, and that is very hard to do. To the Druids, it said that human beings should be sacrificed to trees. To the Nazis it said that there is something mystical and transcendental in the notion of race, particularly of a super-race. I am convinced that the Druids and the Nazis got the wrong message from the "sense of mystery," but their first mistake was in relying on that sense as a test of what should be done.

It is better to rely upon our rational ability to understand the nature of things, particularly human ends and goals. Dr. Kass's use of the concept of mystery is a double-edged sword that can cut in all directions depending upon who is using it. My main objection to the notion of man as self-creator is not that it reduces our sense of mystery—too many of its adherents, including Rahner, do not see that as the outcome—but that it unnecessarily and hazardously escalates it. Everything becomes mystery, and when everything is mystery one decision becomes as good as another. Who knows, when we are suffused in mystery, what the truth or good sense of anything is? Dr. Kass complains, rightly enough, about attempts to remake man's nature with "all-powerful means but no end in view" (p. 61). But nothing he says indicates that a sense of mystery provides an immediate check to such dangers, nor that—when we do think of ends—a sense of mystery will provide us with good ends. In his hands it means that we should take care and go slow. But in other hands it means that we might as well rush along. Precisely because I believe, with Dr. Kass, that "questions of desirability, of better and worse, can be the subject of rational deliberation," I am unwilling to turn our deliberations over to anyone's sense of mystery and awe.

How are we to find wisdom concerning "New Beginnings in Life"? Dr. Kass suggests that a consideration of "what men have done in their conquest of non-human nature" (p. 61) affords "no grounds for optimism as we now consider offers to turn our technology loose on human nature" (p. 61). The implication is that man's conquest of nonhuman nature has been an unmitigated disaster, that there is no human profit or good to be discerned. I cannot share that judgment. At worst, the record shows some good conquests and some bad. At best, there is a strong balance of good over bad. Some parts of nature have perhaps been despoiled, but not nature as a whole. We have learned of late that, without wisdom, it is possible to despoil nature to the detriment of man, and we know that we need to exercise a sense of restraint. But this sense should be based on a careful examination of potential gains and losses to man, not on a pessimistic bias about human behavior.

So it is with human nature. We need standards if we are going to manipulate or intervene in human nature, and, as Dr. Kass says, that "requires a wisdom we do not possess" (p. 61). There seem to be no intrinsic reasons why we should not gain such wisdom, provided we can do so wisely and by ethical means.

Dr. Kass has made a solid case for our present inability to work out "New Beginnings in Life" in an ethical manner. But we are left with a dilemma. On the one hand, we are told that we should not act until we have the requisite wisdom to do so—which is to say that, in principle, we could act if we could

the past, man has usually acted without the necessary wisdom. Most—but not all—of his gambles have turned out well. Until one acts, talk of what is wise or unwise is speculative; to gain wisdom requires risk-taking. Perhaps, given the increased power of technology and the corresponding increase in the power of some men over other men, we should stop taking risks, especially those risks which harm others more than they affect those who devise the gambles. But that will mean a severe limitation in the possibility of becoming wiser. It will make the wisdom of the past always the norm for present action, always the standard of what is wise or unwise. The past will always triumph over the future, the known over the unknown, the safe and proved over the doubtful and unproved. This is a very fateful kind of decision, one at odds with the whole of human history and evolution.

Since all of us are the beneficiaries of the gambles of earlier generations (and of course the victims in some respects), such a program means that the possibility of our passing on some new benefits to future generations is greatly curtailed. We will be giving them less than we got. And we must gamble, too, that they will actually be better off without our chance-taking on their behalf. What would be their corresponding gain? They will be freed from dehumanizing and degrading scientific "advances"; moreover, there will be the gain that mankind will for once have tried to take its ethical norms seriously and passed that precedent on to a future generation. For if we follow Kass, agreeing that we cannot ethically gain the necessary wisdom, we will do so on the basis of some long-standing but rarely honored ethical values. Mankind has usually been very adept at finding ways to set those values aside in the name of progress, science, taste, or practical necessity. It would be a cultural milestone if for once they are not set aside. What we will lose in technological progress may well be compensated by what we will gain in ethical progress. I am willing to settle for that trade.

Gene therapy is the name applied to the attempt to treat hereditary diseases by influencing the genes directly. Several terms have been used: genetic engineering, genetic intervention, genetic surgery, and gene technology are among them. Gene therapy is only a part of a broader area which has been called genetic medicine and which involves the diagnosis, prevention, and treatment of hereditary diseases. The first attempt at gene therapy has already taken place, although the success or failure of the attempt is not yet known. Because of the explosion of knowledge in the area of genetics, other attempts at genetic therapy can be anticipated in the future. The question that can properly be asked is: What are the implications of this new power that man may obtain to manipulate his own genes? The potential uses and misuses of genetic intervention are so great

Dr. French Anderson was born in Oklahoma, studied at Harvard and at Cambridge University, England, and received his M.D. from Harvard Medical School, magna cum laude, in 1963. He served as a post-doctoral fellow of the American Cancer Society and then became research associate in the Laboratory of Biochemical Genetics at the National Heart Institute, National Institutes of Health. Since 1968 he has served as head of the Section on Human Biochemistry, Molecular Disease Branch, National Heart and Lung Institute, National Institutes of Health. He has received a number of academic honors and has published widely in scientific journals. He is presently doing research in the field of human genetic diseases.

that now is the time to examine closely what is being done and where it may lead. Society does not want to learn of the consequences of a scientific accomplishment only after great damage has already been inflicted, as was the case with nuclear power. This paper will attempt to summarize the present state of the art of genetic therapy, to speculate on the good that might come from it, and to outline some of the problems with which society as a whole must reckon.

Is There a Need for a Field of Genetic Medicine?

How significant are genetic defects in the total field of medicine? The answer is: enormously significant. Fifteen out of every one hundred newborn infants have hereditary disorders of greater or lesser severity. More than two thousand genetically distinct inherited defects have been classified. Many are mild, but a large percentage are not. Forty percent of all non-trauma deaths in children's hospitals can be attributed to diseases that are partly or wholly genetic in nature. Dr. Joshua Lederberg told the House Appropriations subcommittee hearings on the 1971 budgetary requirements for the Department of Health, Education, and Welfare:

> Today at least 25 percent of hospital beds and of all institutional places for the handicapped in this country are occupied by persons suffering some degree of genetic disease.[1]

Among diseases with a genetic basis are diabetes, cystic fibrosis, hemophilia, sickle-cell anemia, phenylketonuria (PKU), mongolism, some forms of mental retardation, and some forms of mental illness. Genetic factors are involved in such diseases as arthritis, gout, stomach ulcers, high blood pressure, schizophrenia, and certain forms of cancer. In other words, mistakes in the genetic information carried in the cells are responsible for an enormous amount of human suffering and death. It would appear that a great need exists for the field of genetic medicine.

[1]Lederberg, J. 1971. Testimony during the House Appropriations Subcommittee Hearings on the 1971 Budget Appropriations for the Departments of Labor and of Health, Education, and Welfare; 91st Congress, 2nd Session, Part 7, p. 915.

In What Form Is the Genetic Information Carried in the Cells?

Every cell in the body possesses a control center in its nucleus within which is present all the information necessary to run and reproduce the cell. This control center contains, in coded form, the blueprints for every structural component of the cell together with instructions detailing how these compo-

synthesis of an abnormal product or loss of control over the rate of reproduction, is ultimately traceable to information contained in messages dispatched from the DNA of the genes.

In order to understand and perhaps correct the abnormal states resulting from messages containing defective information, workers in the field of genetics have successfully learned to read the code language in which the messages are transcribed. The magnitude of this research problem was enormous. To make an analogy between the cell's language and the English language, it meant learning the code-letters of the cell, how the code-letters form words, how the code-words form sentences, and how the sentences form the whole language of the cell. Each code-letter is only 1/50,000,000 of an inch in diameter. Simply learning what the code-letters are was an impressive accomplishment. But actually to "break" this code so that the very language of the cells could be understood was indeed a staggering achievement.

It is now known that the genetic language of the cells is made up of the linear sequence of only four types of molecules in the DNA. These four "letters" are: adenine (abbreviated "A"), cytosine ("C"), guanine ("G") and thymine ("T"). Each of these is a specific chemical molecule composed of carbon, nitrogen, oxygen and hydrogen. "Words" are composed of three (and only three) "letters." For example, GGG is a code-word. Since four code-letters taken any three at a time result in sixty-four possible combinations, there are sixty-four genetic code-words. Each of these code-words has a special meaning. Since the cell's work is done primarily by proteins, most genes carry the information for synthesizing specific proteins. Proteins are composed of basic building blocks called amino acids, of which there are twenty. Of the sixty-four code-words, most designate one or another of the twenty amino acids (the same amino acid can be specified by more than one code-word in most cases).

Other code-words are used for punctuation. In the English language, to indicate the beginning of a new unit of information (a sentence), the first letter is capitalized. To terminate a sentence, a period is placed after the last word. In the cell, the "start" code-word is "AUG" in the messenger RNA. (Messenger RNA molecules are transcribed from the DNA of the genes and also contain four code-letters: "A," "C," "G," and "U." Uracil, "U," replaces the DNA's thymine, "T.") The "stop" word, analogous to the period, is "UAA." Therefore, a messenger from a gene might have the form:

AUG - word - word - word - . . . - word - word - UAA

The messenger specifying one of the chains of the blood protein hemoglobin might begin:

AUG-GUC-CUG-UCA-CCG-GCU— . . .

which specifies the amino acid sequence:

methionine-valine-leucine-serine-proline-alanine- . . .

Researchers now have the knowledge necessary to decipher completely the language of the cell. Progress has been so rapid, in fact, that a complete gene has now been synthesized in the test tube. This was accomplished in 1970 by Dr. H. Gobind Khorana and his colleagues at the University of Wisconsin, who hooked individual code-letters together, one at a time, in the exact order known to exist in a normally occurring gene.[2] Not only has an artificial gene been synthesized, but a natural gene has been isolated from the cell by Dr. Jonathan Beckwith and

[2]Agarwal, K. L., Buchi, H., Caruthers, M. H., Gupta, N., Khorana, H. G., Kleppe, K., Kumar, A., Ohtsuka, E., Rajbhandary, U. L., van de Sande, J. H., Sgaramella, V., Weber, H., and Yamada, T. 1970. "Total Synthesis of the Gene for an Alanine Transfer Ribonucleic Acid from Yeast." *Nature*, Vol. 227, p. 27.

his colleagues at Harvard Medical School in 1969, and has actually been observed with the electron microscope.[3] Furthermore, intact DNA molecules (containing many genes) have been reproduced in the test tube. This was accomplished in 1967 by Dr. Arthur Kornberg and his colleagues at Stanford University by isolating the proteins which are responsible for the duplication of DNA inside the cell, then utilizing these proteins in

defective gene. This, then, is the promise as well as the potential threat of the new gene therapy.

What Are the Good Uses of Gene Therapy?

The first such use is in the treatment of genetic diseases. As mentioned above, diabetes, phenylketonuria (PKU), sickle-cell anemia, hemophilia, cystic fibrosis—all are examples of hereditary diseases, conditions in which the defect is passed on from parents to offspring. From our knowledge of the genetics of mutations we can assume that the defect in chemical terms is a change in one of the code-letters in the DNA, which results in the dispatching of a message that contains an error. In sickle-cell anemia, the error is in the structure of the blood protein hemoglobin; in PKU it is in the metabolism of the amino acid phenylalanine. In fact, progress has been so rapid in applying the genetic code in this field that the exact code-word change in sickle-cell anemia can be predicted: The middle code-letter in the sixth code-word of the gene for the hemoglobin chain has changed from a thymine to an adenine. Ways of treating the

[3]Shapiro, J., Machattie, L., Eron, L., Ihler, G., Ippen, K., and Beckwith, J. 1969. "Isolation of Pure lac Operon DNA." *Nature*, Vol. 224, p. 768.

[4]Goulian, M., Kornberg, A., and Sinsheimer, R. L. 1967. "Enzymatic Synthesis of DNA. XXIV. Synthesis of Infectious Phage ϕX174 DNA." *Proceedings of the National Academy of Sciences, U.S.*, Vol. 58, p. 2321.

patient in order to overcome this genetic error are now being sought. Unfortunately, all that can be done at present for most children and adults suffering from hereditary diseases is to attempt to modify the effects produced by the disease; for example, by providing insulin injections for diabetics, or low phenylalanine diets for children with PKU. The cure for these diseases, however, is to correct or replace the inaccurate code-words in the DNA and message molecules.

A second use is in the area of viral diseases. Viruses cause a whole range of debilitating diseases such as measles, German measles, mumps, chicken pox, smallpox, poliomyelitis, influenza, mononucleosis, and the common cold. Many viruses act as outside messages which, upon entering, force the cell to translate the virus message rather than the cell's own. If the information carried by these virus messages were understood, their harmful effects might be counteracted. Two important developments have already taken place. First, the exact sequence of code-letters in certain nonpathogenic viruses has been determined. When the sequence of a virus is known, its genetic information can be determined. This work is a prelude to sequencing, or "decoding," under properly safeguarded laboratory conditions, viruses that are known to produce diseases in human beings. Second, a substance known as "interferon" has been discovered which is produced by cells and which can selectively prevent the translation of some virus messages while still allowing the cell's own messages to function normally. This is a natural defense mechanism used by the cell to protect itself against virus infections. Interferon is apparently used to induce the production of a protein which can recognize the virus as foreign genetic information. Tailor-made interferon molecules for protection against specific viruses might be synthesized artificially and then used therapeutically by man.

A third use is in the area of cancer. The process of reproduction of a cell is normally regulated by information coded in the DNA. If this normal means of regulation is lost, the cell may begin to divide rapidly and out of control; it then may become a cancer cell. The messages that direct the process of division come either from the DNA of the cell or, in some cases at least, from virus particles arriving from outside the cell. But what is the mechanism by which a cell can no longer control its growth and division? With the ability to decode messages, as well as with a detailed knowledge of the translating machinery of the cell, it might be possible to introduce a corrective gene or message, or at least to counteract the disruptive messages. Specific anti-cancer drugs might be developed to aim at the precise step or steps that convert a normal, controlled cell into a malignantly growing cancer cell. Thus drugs might be developed which act against specific cancers; they would act like rifles rather than like our present "shotgun" drugs.

reverse the aging process in older cells.

What Is Now Available for Treatment of Genetic Diseases?

Genetic medicine involves the diagnosis, prevention and treatment of hereditary diseases. Although diagnosis is relatively sophisticated today, prevention and treatment are not so far advanced. Couples can be screened prior to marriage, if they desire, for the existence of many types of genetic defects (using chromosome analysis, blood tests, x-ray examination, etc.). If a serious defect is found in both husband and wife, one, for example, that could potentially lead to the death of a child, the couple is so advised. The couple then has the option of deciding whether or not to have children. Unfortunately, all of us probably possess one or more defects in our total gene pool, many of which are not yet detectable by present-day procedures. Consequently, routine genetic screening of all couples prior to marriage is probably not practical as yet. But where the presence of a lethal defect is already suspected from family history, *i.e.*, when relatives are known to have suffered from a given disease, then genetic screening and counseling can be of direct assistance. Yet many couples do not consider genetic screening, or even want to think about it, until after the birth of a defective child. Even when both parents carry a lethal defect, children may be normal. Roughly one out of four offspring would be predicted to be completely normal and another two of the four relatively normal (assuming each parent carries only one defective gene). The parents have the option of improving the likelihood that children will be normal by means of artificial insemination of the mother with sperm from a male donor in which there is no reason to suspect the occurrence of the lethal gene.

If suspicion of a birth defect exists during pregnancy, it is now possible to obtain material from the fetus before birth and examine it for the presence of many types of genetic diseases. The process, called amniocentesis, involves the removal of a small amount of amniotic fluid from inside the mother's womb by means of a sterile needle. The fetal cells obtained in this way can be tested for possible hereditary defects by biochemical analysis of the cells grown in tissue culture. If a serious defect is discovered, the pregnancy can be terminated by a therapeutic abortion. The couple may then try again for a normal baby. Although some people have strong moral objections to such a procedure, others feel that the suffering produced for the child, the mother, and the rest of the family, by genetic defects is so great that any efforts toward prevention of defective babies is justified, including therapeutic abortion.

Once a baby is born, it is relatively easy to test for large numbers of potential defects, and techniques are now being developed for extensive screening from just one drop of blood from the newborn child.

What can be done once a defect is found in a newborn infant? In some cases, the missing gene product can be supplied to a patient who is deficient in that substance, as with anti-hemophilic factor in hemophiliacs and insulin in diabetics. In those cases in which the absence of an enzyme results in the buildup in the blood stream of a dangerous level of a given substance, two approaches are possible. First, one can try to protect the patient from exposure to the raw materials that produce the buildup. For example, since it is metabolism of phenylalanine that is defective in PKU, infants can be placed on a low phenylalanine diet. In galactosemia, a defect in one type of sugar metabolism, the patient can be given a diet deficient in galactose but adequate in other sugars. A second approach now being studied is to provide the missing enzyme to the patient in microscopic chemical "cages" that allow the enzyme to perform its function in the blood stream but protect the enzyme from being destroyed by the body.

What Would Treatment by Gene Therapy Involve?

The most satisfactory treatment for a patient suffering a genetic defect would be actual correction of the genetic material itself. In bacteria it is now a routine laboratory procedure to correct genetic defects by altering the DNA of the bacterial cell. This is accomplished in one of two ways. In one method

isolate specific human genes. Take, for example, the gene for the phenylalanine enzyme that is defective in PKU. Gene therapy would involve isolating this gene from normal human cells (grown in tissue culture) and attaching it to a nonpathogenic virus that would carry it into the cells of the PKU patient. A certain number of cells should incorporate the "good" PKU gene and might thereby overcome the effect of the patient's own "bad" PKU gene. Theoretically the carrier virus should have no effect on all the other genes in the gene pool. Therein, of course, lies the problem. It is not known, nor can it be clearly tested, what effect any virus, believed to be nonpathogenic or not, will have on the gene pool. If a virus can move the PKU gene from one place to another, might it also do the same thing with other genes, perhaps those which control the reproductive cycle of the cell? What if just one cell in the whole body lost control over its division? It might take only one cancer cell to lead (perhaps not until ten years later) to cancer. In other words, we may have the ability to manipulate genes long before we know whether it is safe to do so. The same argument can be made against almost any new therapeutic agent or procedure. The potential danger from gene intervention, however, appears to be considerably greater than that from most other new methods of treatment.

A preliminary type of gene therapy has already been attempted on human beings. In this case, the experiment appears to be justified by the tragic circumstances of the disease involved. Nonetheless, success here might encourage less justified attempts at premature gene therapy. What has already been tried involves two German sisters who are suffering from argininemia. This is a genetic defect in the synthesis of the enzyme that breaks down the amino acid arginine. Without the enzyme, arginine piles up in the blood stream, resulting in severe mental retardation, spastic paraplegia, and epileptic seizures. The two girls are hopelessly ill, and it is probable that the damage is irreversible. There is one possibility for at least slowing down the rate of degeneration in this case, however. One virus with which genetic laboratories have worked for many years appears to be totally nonpathogenic in humans, *i.e.*, it causes no harm at all. It does appear to produce at least one measurable effect, albeit a minor one: The blood arginine level is depressed in most laboratory workers who have been exposed to the virus. In other words, this apparently harmless virus may carry the gene for the enzyme arginase, a protein able to break down the amino acid arginine. This gene is apparently incorporated into a human's gene pool and appears to give him an extra dose of the enzyme (which he already has from his own genes).

Might it be possible to give the gene to the patients who are suffering from a total lack of the enzyme? The treatment simply involves exposing the two German girls to the virus and then watching their blood arginine levels to see if there is any decrease. At this time the virus has been given to the youngsters, but no word has yet been released as to whether the therapy is successful. If nothing happens, or if the patients grow worse, then the treatment will have failed. But what if their blood arginine levels return to normal? Might these children have had a completely normal life if only they had received the virus right after birth? If you were the parent of a newborn baby who was found to have argininemia and therefore to be doomed to suffer and die, would you allow your baby to be exposed to this relatively unproven technique of gene therapy? Many parents would answer, I believe, that they would not only allow it but would urge its use. In this case, with several decades of experience indicating the safety of this particular virus and absolute certainty of suffering and death without it, there seems to me to be little question about moral justification.

But what about the larger question? What about other genes, other viruses? Where does one draw the line? Suppose the technique proves itself to be totally safe and reliable. Suppose it becomes possible to insert any gene or genes one might want into human cells, including germ (reproduction) cells. Then who is to decide what are "good" uses and what are "bad" uses? Correcting a genetic defect is a "good" use. Is inserting the gene for blond hair because you like blond hair a "good" use or a "bad" use? How about a double dose of a gene responsible for size so that your son will have a better chance to be a profes-

tive intelligence, *i.e.*, mental retardation, by any one of many different single gene mutations, in the same sense that one can obtain a defective automobile by any one of many different manufacturing errors. But to improve intelligence genetically it would be necessary to make precise changes in such a way that all interrelated components would work with increased efficiency. As with improvement of automobile performance, a thorough understanding of the whole system would be an essential prerequisite for predictable success. Our present understanding of brain function, however, is still extremely rudimentary. Nonetheless, even after saying all of this, it is possible that efforts to "improve" intelligence might be attempted someday.

What Can Society Do to Protect Itself from Possible Misuses of Gene Therapy?

Many geneticists are very concerned about the question of misuses to which genetic intervention could be put. For example, Dr. Marshall W. Nirenberg, Nobel Laureate for his work in deciphering the genetic code, said in 1967:

> The point which deserves special emphasis is that man may be able to program his own cells with synthetic information long before he will be able to assess adequately the long-term consequences of such alterations, long before he will be able to formulate goals, and long before he can resolve the ethical and moral problems which will

be raised. When man becomes capable of instructing his own cells, he must refrain from doing so until he has sufficient wisdom to use this knowledge for the benefit of mankind.[5]

The rapid progress of genetic research over the past five years lends added urgency to Dr. Nirenberg's statement.

Suggestions have been made to establish a commission on genetics, composed of physicians, scientists, and concerned laymen, for the purpose of discussing and evaluating problems in genetics as they relate to medicine. Senator Walter Mondale introduced S. J. Res. 75 on March 24, 1971, which seeks to establish the National Advisory Commission on Health Science and Society along these lines. Such a commission, which would act only in an advisory capacity, might be of enormous value in providing a central and public forum for establishing goals and safeguards.

Probably the most powerful single influencing force in scientific research today is the funding policy of the federal government. The government can markedly influence the direction of research either through direct authorization for a program (like the space program) or indirectly by means of favored funding for research in specific areas (e.g., virus research in the late 1940's and early 1950's, leading to the polio and other vaccines; funding for artificial heart research beginning in the early 1960's; recently increased funding for cancer research). A commission on genetics would undoubtedly help federal funding officials make the wisest possible decisions. Of course there are many sources of research funds, and the federal government could not influence through directed funding all the research being conducted across the country.

Although an advisory commission on genetics would probably be wise and beneficial, the establishment of a regulatory commission, as some have suggested, could be most dangerous. Such a regulatory commission would have the power to dictate what genetics research could and could not be done in the country. I believe that such concentrated localization of authority could not be used wisely in the field of genetics at this time. Centralization of control in any group, no matter how distinguished, is fraught with danger. If society is unable to reach a consensus on a topic such as therapeutic abortion, how can we

[5]Nirenberg, M. W. 1967. "Will Society Be Prepared?" (editorial). *Science*, Vol. 157, p. 633.

expect any small group to reach wise and just decisions about an area as fundamental as influencing the hereditary characteristics of ourselves and our future generations? This area holds such promise for alleviating human suffering, and yet is so basic to the needs and emotions of all men, that no individual or group of individuals should take it upon themselves to make the decisions. Only the conscience of an informed society as a

though the process is an agonizing one, society is slowly coming to terms with the abortion question as well as with a multitude of other difficult sociological problems. Some have suggested that legislation be passed now either to encourage or to prevent various types of genetic research. But any type of legislation drafted now that attempted to detail specifically what should and should not be done in a field as complex as genetics would probably be premature and—in the long run—unwise.

Then what course should society take? Perhaps society's experience with heart transplantation offers a reasonable approach. Because of the number of patients suffering from irreversible heart damage, it became clear many years ago that medical research had to develop a means of providing a replacement for damaged hearts. Individual heart valves were developed, and surgical techniques were devised to install them. Patients who wanted them could get them; those who did not want them, of course, did not have to have them. Research continued on artificial hearts and immunosuppressive therapy in preparation for heart transplantation. The public knew this work was progressing. Then Dr. Christiaan Barnard demonstrated that heart transplantation was feasible. Immediately there was a burst of enthusiastic activity in which heart transplants were taking place all over the world and donor hearts were being obtained by various means (not always in an ideal way). Very soon society itself began to respond. Jokes about "fastest-knife-in-the-West" surgeons arose. A cartoon appeared showing a dozing man with a sign around his neck reading, "Sleeping; am not a heart donor candidate." The general feeling of many communities became more conservative, and this attitude was transmitted to and through the medical community. The trustees and directing boards of hundreds of hospitals across the country cautioned their surgeons to slow down or even stop their plans for heart transplantation. But certain highly skilled centers continue with the procedure, providing this treatment for those patients who want it. The country, and the world, quickly adjusted itself to this new, revolutionary procedure.

Crucial to this adjustment was public education. So, too, with gene therapy. With heart transplantation it was not particularly detrimental that society had to adjust to the sociological effects of the procedure after it was already being performed. (For example: When is a patient "dead"? When can an organ be removed for donation? On whose consent?) Not so with gene therapy. This technique is too powerful for society to be left unaware of its potential until its actual utilization.

Public education and open discussion appear to be all-important. But many of the pronouncements made in the recent past are no more than scare headlines. There is not going to be any "genetic bomb" that suddenly alters the behavior and hereditary characteristics of unsuspecting citizens. A far greater threat than gene therapy along this line is the well-established but only recently recognized effect of environmental pollution. Another piece of sensationalism is the claim that human beings could be re-engineered to produce larger heads, double stomachs, or whatever else is desired. Such "precision engineering" is clearly outside any conceivable technical capability of what we have defined as gene therapy, namely, the insertion or correction of specific genes. If society should ever decide it wants to re-engineer the human body, the most suitable procedure would be the method, tried and proven in animal husbandry, i.e., selective breeding.

Although not directly related to gene therapy, the potential for "growing" whole human beings from single cells by cloning is another area of concern for society. Dr. Kass and his respondents have dealt with this subject at length in earlier chapters, and I will only touch on it here. It is theoretically possible that millions of test tube-grown soldiers could be produced for the military advantage of a nation, although it is not likely that a regime would really go to such lengths in order to produce an "army" which would not be available for nearly twenty years. On the other hand, if such a program were started and the regime overthrown several years later, what would be done with a million five-year-old cloned humans?

Rather than cloning whole humans, however, might kidneys, hearts, livers, and other organs be "grown" for purposes of

What Are the Alternatives to Gene Therapy?

It is not an absolute necessity that research on gene therapy be continued. There are alternatives, although none is completely satisfactory. The physician is caught in a serious dilemma at present. He wants to do everything in his power to treat his individual patients, but he knows that in the long run he is causing even more suffering because he is increasing the number of defective genes in the total population. This occurs because more and more patients who would previously have died in childhood now survive to reproductive age, whereupon they may marry and have children of their own. Thus, thanks to modern medicine, natural selection is no longer working effectively to remove some types of defective genes.

The alternatives to gene therapy which are available to society are the following:

1. Stop treating serious genetic diseases, thus allowing natural selection to take control again. To refuse to treat a child who has a treatable disease is inhumane, reprehensible, and totally against the ethics of the medical profession. This, therefore, is not a real alternative.

2. Treat individuals, but attempt to control the increase of defective genes in the gene pool by means of contraception, sterilization, and restrictive marriage licenses for known carriers of defective genes. Voluntary cooperation in such a program would be ideal; but mandatory restrictions, already carried out

in certain situations, would be repulsive to many if attempted on a massive scale. And again, who would make the final decision as to which defective genes are "bad" and which are simply less than "good"?

3. Treat individuals and allow them to marry and have children. During pregnancy a determination could be made by amniocentesis, if desired by the parents, as to whether a defective fetus was conceived. If so, a therapeutic abortion could be performed. This procedure is now being carried out in a limited number of cases.

4. Continue the present research efforts to treat genetic diseases in every way other than by direct gene therapy. Society must then face the prospect that the number of defective genes in the population will increase and must be willing to care for the increasing number of defective children born. The possible extent of the problem is uncertain, since geneticists differ in their assessment of how serious to the human race this increase in defective genes might be.

Thus, alternatives to gene therapy do exist. It is society that must decide what path or paths it will follow.

I have intentionally raised more questions than I have answered. So long as the subject of gene therapy is discussed openly and critically, I am optimistic that society will be more likely to realize the good of this technique and less likely to suffer from its misuse.

I find myself in general agreement with Dr. Anderson's paper and hence, rather than responding directly to it, I would prefer in this paper to complement it. Dr. Anderson's opening description of the language of the cells is accurate and there is no need for me to add to it. I will be describing ways of managing patients with genetic disease from my perspective both as a doctor, with many years of experience as a clinician and genetics counselor, and as an investigator of genetic diseases in man.

There is one area of disagreement. Like most human and medical geneticists, I am less optimistic than Dr. Anderson

Dr. Arno G. Motulsky was born in Germany in 1923 and came to America in 1941. He received his B.S. and his M.D. from the University of Illinois Medical School in 1947. Following clinical and research training and service in the U.S. Army, he became an instructor in the Department of Medicine, University of Washington School of Medicine, Seattle, Washington, in 1953. In 1957 he studied in the Galton Laboratory, University College, London, England, under a special Commonwealth Fund Fellowship in human genetics. Since 1961 he has been professor of medicine, Department of Medicine, University of Washington, and has a joint appointment as professor of genetics. He heads the Division of Medical Genetics and is director of the Medical Genetics Training Program at the University of Washington Medical School.

He serves on a number of editorial boards, is editor of the American Journal of Human Genetics, *and has published widely in medical journals.*

regarding the possibility of successful gene therapy of most genetic diseases. Thus Dr. Anderson, a molecular biologist, says: "The ability actually to manipulate genes inside the living cell in a planned manner is rapidly approaching" (p. 113). He is correct in referring to the accelerating pace of research in the field of molecular genetics. But I believe genetic therapy is far away because, as I will explain, I see considerable conceptual difficulties in curing the majority of genetic diseases by gene therapy. Some of my pessimism in this regard is derived from the fact that I deal with patients who need treatment within the time limit of their own lives. The possibility of *safely* placing the right gene into its right place within a human chromosome (particularly in the germ tissues) in the foreseeable future seems far-fetched, in my judgment. I hope I am wrong! In the meantime we should not hold up false hopes to our patients. But there are many other ways of dealing with genetic diseases besides gene therapy. Some of these are conventional, others more novel.

I intend to describe in my paper the types and existing modes of treating and preventing genetic diseases, and some of this will go beyond the area to which Dr. Anderson addressed himself. In particular, I will explain the process of intrauterine diagnosis or amniocentesis in more detail than he has.

Management of Genetic Diseases

Infectious diseases of childhood have been markedly reduced in frequency in developed countries. The high infantile mortality of underdeveloped areas of the world is caused by various infectious organisms and no longer obtains in Western societies. Consequently, diseases caused by genetic and developmental mechanisms have become more frequent than in the past. We have no reason to assume that the absolute frequency of genetic diseases has increased in recent years, since any possible dysgenic effects of modern medicine would not have been operative long enough. The total impact of genetic diseases is difficult to assess since it is not generally agreed which diseases are genetic. Many diseases involve a subtle interaction of genetic and environmental factors, but often—as in diabetes—neither the genetic nor the extrinsic factors are well defined. Any numerical estimate of genetic disease, therefore, needs a careful definition of the meaning of "genetic disease." There is general agreement, however, that genetic factors play an important role in many types of human illness.

Types of Genetic Disease and the Outlook for Gene Therapy

Genetic diseases can be divided into the following categories:
1. Diseases caused by aberrations in number and gross struc-

embryos with such abnormalities are spontaneously aborted. In Down's syndrome (mongolism) an additional small chromosome (No. 21) is present, and the condition may be compatible with fairly long life. Gene therapy would require the removal very early in embryonic life of one of forty-seven chromosomes from a large proportion of cells at least in the brain, where the major damage is exerted. Such microsurgery of individual cells is not feasible now nor in the foreseeable future. Similar considerations regarding gene therapy would hold for other chromosome disorders. Gene therapy also appears impossible for diseases where multiple genes are operative, such as birth defects and the common diseases of middle life (e.g., hypertension). It is highly unlikely that it would be possible to get at a group of genes located on different chromosomes by direct manipulation. Autosomal dominant diseases usually affect structural proteins, and genetic therapy is theoretically conceivable but practically not likely. Replacement therapy is also very difficult in such cases, since the basic defect usually causes structural damage.

Diseases caused by deficiency of protein or enzymes (often inherited as autosomal recessive or X-linked recessives) are most accessible to genetic manipulation. The most frequently discussed strategies involve administration of normal DNA in various ways. While DNA replacement in somatic or non-germ cells poses many technical problems, it will be even more difficult to get DNA molecules to the right location in the chromosome of sperms or eggs—a requirement for genetic cure of the disease.

Existing Modes of Management of Genetic Disease

Many techniques already exist for the treatment and prevention of genetic diseases. These include:

1. Diets. In mental retardation caused by a deficiency of the enzyme phenylalanine hydroxylase (phenylketonuria or PKU), increased amounts of phenylalanine cause mental retardation. Phenylalanine restriction from birth may allow normal mental development. Other examples exist.

2. Supply of missing factors. Vitamin B_{12} deficiency or pernicious anemia can be treated by vitamin B_{12} injections. Hemophilia or antihemophilic globulin deficiency can be treated by injection of the missing protein substance.

3. Removal of excess toxic substances. Hemochromatosis is caused by excess iron in the liver, heart, and pancreas. The iron can be removed by frequent venesections. Wilson's disease is caused by copper infiltration of liver and brain. Excess copper can be removed by drugs.

4. Surgery. Splenectomy cures a hereditary type of anemia (hereditary spherocytosis) by removal of the organ that traps the abnormal red blood cells. In hereditary colonic polyposis, removal of the colon does away with the myriad of polyps which invariably become cancerous.

5. Transplantation. Genetically abnormal kidneys such as polycystic ones can be replaced by normal kidneys. In hereditary diseases affecting the blood-forming organs, such as thalassemia, transplants of normal marrow may be a useful treatment. One major block to tissue transplantation remains the difficulty of finding donors with genetically compatible tissue types.

6. Immunologic prevention. Injection of Rh globulin destroys Rh positive cells of fetal origin in mothers with Rh positive babies and prevents buildup of Rh antibodies, which cause hemolytic diseases of the newborn ("Rh babies") in the next fetus.

7. Enzyme induction. Certain enzymes can be induced by drugs. Some types of hereditary jaundice can be treated by phenobarbital, which stimulates production of the missing enzyme.

Extension of these techniques is likely to be instituted in treatment of various genetic diseases.

Modes of Management Unique to Genetic Disease

Apart from the above methods, which raise no new principles in management of genetic disease, several modes of dealing with genetic disease are based on principles different from the usual medical therapies.

risks are usually given in the form of probability statements. For instance, in autosomal dominant disease, the risk of recurrence is 50 percent. Risks less than 10 percent are considered low by most medical geneticists. The nature and chronicity of the disease and its medical, social, and emotional impact are considered in discussing risks with the family. Medical geneticists usually do not tell parents whether or not to have children but attempt to present all information in such a manner that the couple can make an informed decision. Most couples faced with risks higher than 10 percent have fewer children.

b. Prospective counseling. In the future, as it becomes possible to detect unaffected carriers of many genetic diseases, population testing for carriers is likely to be instituted. As an example, 10 percent of the black population of this country carry the sickling trait. When two carriers mate, one-fourth of their children will develop sickle-cell anemia—a severe type of anemia, associated with abdominal and joint pains, which shortens the patient's life span. Genetic counseling *after* birth of an affected child will have only a small effect on the number of total cases in the population. Since the test for the trait is simple, population testing of young people *before* marriage, followed by genetic counseling, has been recommended. Trait carriers are counseled regarding the genetic hazards of marrying another trait carrier. Prospective counseling will only be possible if it is accompanied by extensive public education.

2. *Intrauterine diagnosis and abortion*

It is possible to obtain small amounts of amniotic fluid from the uterus of women twelve to sixteen weeks pregnant. The fluid contains a few cells of fetal origin which reflect the genetic constitution of the fetus. These cells can be grown in culture and then examined by cytogenetic and biochemical tests. Cytogenetic diagnosis is well developed and allows the detection of diseases such as Down's syndrome and others caused by chromosomal abnormalities. The procedure is now used in the rare instances where a parent of a patient with Down's syndrome carries a chromosomal aberration which by itself is harmless but entails a sizeable recurrence risk (5 to 20 percent) for Down's syndrome in any additional children. Since Down's syndrome is more common among children of older mothers, it has been suggested that all pregnant women over forty years of age should have this procedure performed.

An increasing number of genetic diseases caused by enzyme abnormalities can also be diagnosed by chemical tests of the cells. The procedure becomes particularly useful for parents who have had an affected child and face a 25 percent chance of recurrence. In X-linked diseases where mothers are carriers and only males are affected (hemophilia, the Duchenne type of muscular dystrophy, and others), the procedure allows diagnosis of fetal sex by chromosomal study.

Diagnosis of an affected child, or of male sex for the X-linked disorders, is usually followed by therapeutic abortion. In the X-linked disorders, half of the aborted males would have been normal, since methods to differentiate normal from abnormal males are usually lacking. To prevent such X-linked diseases, all males are aborted.

The wide use of carrier detection by biochemical tests, followed by intrauterine diagnosis when both parents are carriers and selective abortion of affected fetuses, has much promise for the control of frequent recessive genetic diseases such as cystic fibrosis (which occurs in one in three thousand Caucasians), sickle-cell anemia (one in five hundred blacks) and Tay Sachs disease (one in five thousand Jews). Appropriate intrauterine tests for the diagnosis of fetuses affected with sickle-cell anemia or cystic fibrosis are not yet available. However, the necessary tests to detect carriers as well as affected fetuses are available in Tay Sachs disease, and extensive testing has been started on a trial basis in the Jewish population of a metropolis of the Eastern United States.

Intrauterine diagnosis is usually not offered to parents unless they are willing to have an affected fetus aborted. For parents unwilling to take that step, diagnosis of a disease in a fetus would serve no useful purpose and would only create anxiety and grief for the parents. Treatment of the affected fetus *in*

abnormal fetuses poses no real problems to many parents and their medical advisers. Decisions are best left to the parents involved.

Abortions following intrauterine diagnosis are done relatively late (seventeen to nineteen weeks) in pregnancy and are somewhat more hazardous than those done earlier. Hopefully, techniques to obtain fetal cells during early gestation will be developed. Most birth defects cannot yet be diagnosed *in utero.* Optical methods for fetal visualization of defects such as cleft lip and *spina bifida* may become available.

Future Methods of Genetic Disease Management
Other Than Gene Therapy

A variety of potentially feasible new methods depend upon current laboratory experimentation and may allow prevention or treatment of genetic disease. These methods are closer to actual introduction into medicine than is gene (DNA) therapy. These include:

1. Enzyme replacement. A missing enzyme may be administered by injection, by suspending capsules of purified enzymes in body cavities, or by percolation of the patient's blood over columns containing the enzyme.

2. Enzyme stabilization. It may become possible to stabilize unstable enzymes by chemical or physical agents.

3. *In vitro* fertilization. It is feasible to obtain human eggs by a simple laparoscopic technique. Such eggs can be fertilized

with sperm from a donor (husband or anyone else) and reintro-
duced for normal gestation. It is of interest that not only the
"egg donor" but any woman could carry such a pregnancy. This
method calls up the specter of test tube babies.

4. Cloning. Introduction of the nucleus of a frog cell into an
enucleated frog egg with normal development has already been
achieved. The frog thus created is genetically identical to the
donor from whom the original nucleus was obtained. If this
technique becomes feasible in mammals and in humans, it will
be possible to create clones of one or more genetically identical
individuals. Cloned persons would be genetically identical to the
donor. The process might be used by parents to prevent genetic
disease, but it has more far-ranging general applications which
have been discussed at length in the preceding chapters.

Conclusions

Gene therapy is a popular topic, but the reality of gene
therapy is far away. In particular, the complications arising
from using viruses to carry DNA into human cells are considerable. It is unlikely that gene therapy will become a widely used
technique in this generation. A variety of medical and surgical
techniques, not different in principle from conventional medical
therapy, already exist for the management of genetic diseases.
Other techniques such as genetic counseling and, particularly,
intrauterine diagnosis are somewhat—but not radically—
different from usual medical practices and therefore raise new
problems. Methods such as test tube fertilization may be practical in the near future, and cloning may not be very far behind.
The implications of these techniques are far different from
those of any existing treatments and should concern every
thoughtful human being.

The Law of Genetic Therapy

I hesitated for more than a moment before entitling these remarks, "The Law of Genetic Therapy," for fear that the facetiousness of that title might not be clear. In some ways, it's rather like calling a paper, "Property Law on Mars."[1] Yet since I've been invited to discuss genetics as a lawyer, it does seem

[1] Perhaps this analogy is itself no longer far-fetched enough; a couple of law professors have just written a book which could reasonably contain a

A lecturer and research associate at Yale Law School, Mr. Alexander M. Capron graduated with high honors from Swarthmore College in 1966. He then attended Yale Law School, where he served as Note and Comment Editor on the Law Journal. He has been a visiting lecturer in psychiatry and law at the University of Connecticut and law clerk to Chief Judge David L. Bazelon of the U.S. Court of Appeals for the District of Columbia. Mr. Capron is a member of the District of Columbia bar; of the Genetic Counseling-Genetic Engineering Task Force at the Institute of Society, Ethics, and the Life Sciences; and of the Task Force on Genetics and Human Reproduction at Yale Medical School. He is currently at work with Dr. Jay Katz on a report for the National Institutes of Health concerning decision-making about catastrophic diseases and their treatment, including heart and kidney transplantation, under Grant HSM-110-69-213. Grateful acknowledgement is made to the author's colleague at Yale Law School, Dr. Jay Katz, to whose wise and kind counsel the analysis of this paper owes much.

133

that "the law" belongs in the title, and its presence there prompts me at the outset to comment on the meaning which I think the term "law" has in this context. Law is usually thought of as a practical discipline, and lawyers are expected to state crisp rules about the problems on which their advice is sought. If "The Law of Genetic Therapy" raises that expectation in your breast, you will be sadly disappointed. I suspect that the "crisp rule" view of the law has its origins in the attorney-client relationship, when attorneys (perhaps to bolster their own self-assurance) impose upon their clients a simplified view of the law. Just as the physicians contributing to this volume have moved beyond the confines of the doctor-patient relationship to discuss evolving genetic theories, I feel it incumbent as a lawyer to take account of the flux and evolution of the law and to acknowledge that for every rule (crisp or otherwise) there is a counter-rule.

For our purposes, law can be viewed as the process and mechanism by which society assigns certain rights and responsibilities to its members and through which it resolves conflicts among them. Persons engaged in any particular activity, especially one as new and dynamic as medical genetics, often regard law as an enemy. Its involvement in their work, they feel, should be postponed as long as possible, for it can only lead to undue and ill-considered restrictions. As Chief Justice Burger wrote a few years ago: "Law is inherently restraint; it is a restraint on science as it is a restraint on Kings, congresses and presidents, and none of them really likes it very much."[2] This is true, however, only of law in a narrow sense, as represented perhaps by restrictive statutes or regulations. Under the broader perspective that I am suggesting, it is apparent that a geneticist, for example, need not and indeed cannot hope to operate free of the law. For even a system which permitted him to work with a free hand would represent a definite societal (or one might say *legal*) ordering, as surely as any Congressional enactment.

Having admitted an intentional ambiguity in the legal half of my title, I must confess to a similar deception as to the medical

chapter entitled, "Property Law on Mars." See S. H. Lay and H. J. Taubenfeld, *The Law Relating to Activities of Man in Space* (Chicago: University of Chicago Press, 1970).

[2] W. E. Burger, "Reflections on Law and Experimental Medicine," Vol. 15 *U.C.L.A. Law Review* pp. 436, 441 (1968).

half. Dr. Anderson has written of this field as "genetic therapy," but you have doubtless gathered from his paper that the subject still involves at least as much experimentation as it does therapy. I have no intention of drawing an unbreachable distinction between the two, but it is important to keep in mind that we are speaking not of established modes of treatment but of techniques, and even concepts, on the very frontier of medical

for providing only "soporific" discussions of genetic engineering while failing to "begin a dialogue which would educate the world's citizens and offer suggestions which our legislative bodies might consider in framing national science policies."[3] I concur with Dr. Watson; the failure of those working in a field to take the public into their confidence is not only disrespectful of democracy and detrimental to wise policy choices, but it is also a shortsighted way to protect scientific independence. Consequently, it is refreshing to hear a distinguished scientist such as Dr. Anderson go beyond the medical aspects of his field to discuss its social ramifications.

The "Good Uses" of Genetic Therapy—
A Medical or a Social Decision?

On first reading, Dr. Anderson's remarks appear to be straightforward medical comments. It seems to me, however, that at a number of points his "medical" judgments are in fact unacknowledged social policy decisions. In attempting to substantiate this position, I may seem to slip into the role of curbstone geneticist myself, but I think that appearance remains

[3]Testimony before the Panel on Science and Technology, House Committee on Science and Astronautics, 92nd Congress, 1st Session (January 28, 1971), reproduced as "Moving toward the Clonal Man," 227 *The Atlantic* 50, 52 (May 1971).

only so long as we assume that a discussion which uses medical terminology is, in fact, a *medical* discussion.

To take one example, Dr. Anderson states that the "good" uses of gene therapy include "the diagnosis, prevention, and treatment of hereditary diseases" (p. 115). Some questions can be raised about the bases on which one can determine where the line is drawn between "good" and "bad" uses of knowledge. Dr. Anderson appears to be arguing that the latter involve the social "misuses to which genetic intervention could be put" (p. 119), whereas the former—the "good" uses—are those determined by the standard medical trilogy of diagnosis, prevention, and treatment.

Treatment

Let's take those up, in reverse order, beginning with treatment. Dr. Anderson suggests that the treatment of genetic disease is uncontestably a "good" way to use gene therapy. Law can be very result-oriented, so an initial question it poses is: good treatment for what purposes? Gene therapy may have radical results not only for individual patients but for the gene pool of mankind. What goals are being sought, and who ought to have a say in fixing them? A further problem in measuring the efficacy of treatment is the question of side effects and unexpected consequences. Is one treatment to be preferred over another because it is safer, although less effective? Should we place the costs of medical errors on the persons or groups who conduct experiments, on those who knowingly choose to participate in them, on those who will benefit from the goals being sought by the experiment, or on someone else?[4] Lawyers and

---

[4]This is only one of many considerations in allocating the "costs" of medical errors. Nor is the process always aided by the present system of tort law. See, *e.g.*, Roginsky v. Richardson-Merrell, Inc., 378 F.2d 832 (2d Cir. 1967). In that case, Judge Friendly affirmed an award of compensatory damages for plaintiff's injuries caused by defendant's negligence in marketing MER/29, but reversed as to the far greater punitive damages on the grounds that sufficient negligence had not been "clearly established," a conclusion reached after a long discourse on the potentially ruinous consequences of substantial punitive awards in the "multiplicity" of MER/29 actions in courts across the country. These and other deterrent and compensatory questions are more fully discussed in I. Ladimer, "Clinical Research Insurance," Vol. 16 *Journal of Chronic Diseases* p. 1229 (1963); and G. Calabresi, "Reflections on Medical Experimentation in Humans," Vol. 98 *Daedalus* p. 387 (1969).

the courts are only now beginning to sort out the similar problems which arose from the widespread use of oral contraceptives beginning a decade ago.

Beyond the issue of what is good treatment lies the question of what one means by disease. Dr. Anderson explains how sickle-cell anemia, for instance, could be treated if we could change the middle code-letter in the sixth code-word of the

genetic disease; yet no such comment would be made if the children were born into a tribe of pygmies or a group in which polydactylism were commonplace.

Even putting aside questions of comparative normality, if health is defined as the ability to survive in the environment, a large social component is still manifest in the definition. Changes in the level of society's *scientific knowledge* change our definition of health. Today, a person with the hereditary "disease" of diabetes can live a "healthy" life although he is not "cured," but years ago, before insulin treatment was perfected, he would have been doomed to an early grave. Changes in society's *allocation of funds* also change what we mean by "health." Until recently kidney disease was inevitably fatal, but transplant and dialysis programs now allow many people with renal failure to continue to live.

The point is not simply that "health" and "disease" are relative terms, subject to marked redefinition over time and between societies. I mean to suggest a word of caution against treating the existence of disease as solely a medical matter, because we may be confronted with the question not only of whom to treat (*i.e.*, whom to alter to fit our definition of

[5]The "social" aspect of illness extends not only to diagnosis but to treatment. As a leading medical sociologist, Renee Fox, has commented: "Illness is more than a biological condition; it is also a *social role* with certain patterned characteristics and requirements." R. Fox, *Experiment Perilous* (Glencoe, Ill.: The Free Press, 1959), p. 115.

"healthy") but also of whom *not* to treat.[6] If we allow doctors alone to say who is "ill enough" to be treated, neither too well nor too ill, we will have assigned them a social (one might say legal) as well as a medical task.

A similar conflict has long existed in the area of mental health and illness. We know that for law to be an effective means for ordering human conduct, it must embody an accurate view of man. Nearly twenty years ago, the U.S. Court of Appeals for the District of Columbia concluded that the existing criterion of criminal responsibility did not reflect modern thinking about mental processes and behavioral controls. In the *Durham* case it held that a man should be acquitted on grounds of insanity "if his unlawful conduct was the product of mental disease or mental defect."[7] Judge Bazelon, author of the opinion, hoped thereby to free psychiatrists from having to speak in the moral terms of right and wrong and allow them to testify instead in the medical terminology of their own discipline.

While *Durham* in theory was intended to enrich the evidence psychiatrists could put before the jury, in practice it led medical men to testify in conclusory terms whether an accused had a "mental disease" and therefore should be excused from responsibility. The spectacle of physicians making legal determinations was all the more disturbing because there was often such a wide divergence of expert opinion about whether defendants were well or ill.[8] Sometimes the same doctors took varying views, as when in one famous instance:

> A psychiatrist made it known to the District Court that between the court session on Friday and Monday morning, St. Elizabeth's Hospital, by some process not then disclosed, altered its "official" view that sociopathic or psychopathic personality disorder was *not* a mental disease.[9]

[6]Difficulties inhere in even the so-called "medical" definition of normality. See, *e.g.*, J. B. Files, H. J. VanPeenen, and D. A. B. Lindberg, "Use of 'Normal Range' in Multiphasic Testing," Vol. 205 *Journal of the American Medical Association* p. 94 (1968).

[7]Durham v. United States, 214 F.2d 862, 874-75 (D.C. Cir. 1954).

[8]It was usually apparent that the doctors did not disagree so much in their diagnosis as in their conclusion as to whether the defendant deserved to be punished or not.

[9]Blocker v. United States, 288 F.2d 853, 860 (D.C. Cir. 1961) (*en banc*) (Burger, J., concurring in the result only).

Subsequently, in an attempt (not entirely successful) to restore the jury's role in adjudicating blameworthiness, the Court of Appeals in *McDonald*[10] set forth a legal definition of mental disease, so that psychiatric evidence would be relevant but no longer conclusive on the existence of disease.[11]

The experience with the insanity defense (and recently with

particularly high frequency among blacks, has been the focus of recent "black power" concern; as a result it is receiving more biomedical attention than in the past, and in some states bills have been proposed for mandatory sickle-cell testing for school children or persons applying for marriage licenses. If these efforts are successful and we are able to identify and treat people who have sickle-cell anemia, what will be the results? On the one hand, we will be able either to cure or to prevent the conception of persons with the homozygous form of the genetic defect (two sickle hemoglobin alleles), who now almost invariably die of the fatal anemia. On the other hand, we will eliminate the sickle-cell trait in its heterozygous form as well; yet, far from being harmful, this trait apparently provides a greater chance for survival in malarial regions. In effect, we will have diminished variety in the human gene pool and removed one of society's safeguards against the ravages of another form

[10]McDonald v. United States, 312 F.2d 847, 851 (D.C. Cir. 1962): "The jury should be told that a mental disease or defect includes any abnormal condition of the mind which substantially affects mental or emotional processes and substantially impairs behavior controls."

[11]The other part of the *Durham* insanity test (whether the defendant's act was a "product" of the mental disease) also provided fertile ground for law-making by the medical profession. To forestall that, the Court of Appeals in *Washington v. United States*, 390 F.2d 444 (D.C. Cir. 1967), ruled that psychiatrists were prohibited from testifying directly in terms of "product," "result," or "cause."

of disease. Since malaria is no longer a great scourge for mankind, this may seem inconsequential, but I think it cannot be brushed aside. Malaria itself may once again be a problem. Outbreaks have been reported among soldiers, particularly drug users, returning from Vietnam. Furthermore, malaria is only an example of one peril known to exist; attempts to "correct" genetic diseases may accidentally wipe out man's resistance to any number of other known or unknown, old or new, environmental or even hereditary perils.

Given the complex way in which nature adapts her creatures to their changing environment, we embark on a dangerous course when we decide to eliminate genetic variations which may at some point prove invaluable.[12] To decide whether a treatment program is "good," do we not need to know, for example, how difficult it is to reverse the process? Or what percentage of the population will actually decide to undergo the genetic surgery, and what inducement it will take to persuade a given number (a living "gene savings bank") voluntarily to forego treatment? In sum, society as a whole, as well as its individual members, may be ill served by the assumption that "health" and "disease" have only medical, not social, meanings and consequences.[13]

Prevention

Turning now from treatment to prevention, the second of Dr. Anderson's "good" uses of genetic therapy, we must consider how we can decide which gene types we wish to prevent and which to allow. One traditional legal mechanism is the courts. The common law approach has much to recommend itself, since it is restricted to specific situations when the issues are well defined and the opposing views are championed by advocates

[12]To parents of a child who has Down's syndrome (mongolism) or cystic fibrosis, concern with the different meanings of the word "disease" probably seems too theoretical in the face of their immediate grief. Yet some comfort perhaps lies in knowing that these conditions may have hidden strengths which our training to look for "diseases" has made us too blind to see.

[13]Similarly, in another area of genetic innovation, it can be argued that the decision to "experiment" with human cloning will not only harm the individual who is someone else's carbon copy but can also harm society by putting asexual reproduction, which implies a static genotype, in place of sexual reproduction, through which man has evolved and will continue to develop with each new combination of genomes.

committed to a particular outcome of the case. Genetic therapy may have a hard time getting into court, but one conceivable route is through an abortion case (which would combine the common and statutory law approaches). The question might be raised whether the legality of abortion on "grounds of health" should include an abortion to prevent the birth of a child with genetic defects. Such a question might arise in a suit against a

tionary judicial decision of the year."[15]

A second forum is legislatures, especially the Congress. Dr. Anderson opposes an active legislative stance on genetics, which he believes would lead to restrictive legislation or regulatory commissions. I am not entirely clear about the basis of his objections. At one point he suggests that we should not put a "concentrated localization of authority" in an "individual or group of individuals" just because we cannot "expect any small group to reach wise and just decisions" on such a fundamental topic. This suggests, as he puts it, that "Only the conscience of an informed society as a whole should make these decisions" (p. 121). Besides the Congress, no other collective body suggests itself for this role, and Dr. Anderson offers none, yet he rejects any congressional move to enact specific legislation as "premature and, in the long run, unwise" (p. 121). I disagree with this analysis on two points. First, "no legislation" does not mean "no law." It merely puts the lawmaking power in the

[14]This problem could arise even under "liberalized" laws if legal abortions are limited to the first trimester of pregnancy, since some genetic diseases cannot be detected until 18-24 weeks.

[15]Vol. 273 *New England Journal of Medicine* p. 687 (1965). A few years ago courts were asked to adopt the XYY chromosome anomaly as a new basis for "insanity acquittals." The courts' almost universal reluctance to accept this new defense has subsequently been supported by the questions raised by social as well as genetic scientists about the validity of the evidence on which it was asserted that XYY was a "criminal" chromosome combination.

hands of a particular group of individuals, namely, the physician-investigators. Second, I do not believe legislation in this area is necessarily evil.

While the law is a conservative and slowly changing institution, it is not necessarily either unresponsive or overreactive. For example, once organ (particularly heart) transplantation became a phenomenon of some public interest, legislatures across the nation moved quickly to replace their old statutes concerning organs with the Uniform Anatomical Gift Act. The earlier statutes, which derived from ecclesiastical law and from nineteenth-century attempts to discourage grave-robbing for medical school cadavers, were unresponsive to the needs of modern science. Rather than allowing physicians to proceed entirely by their own lights, each taking the risk that he might become entangled in some outmoded law, the states acted to bring the law into line with scientific knowledge and to place limits on the scope of transplantation.

Instead of relying on elected representative bodies, Dr. Anderson favors the creation by Congress of "a commission on genetics . . . which would only act in an advisory capacity" (p. 120). I have no quarrel with a scheme to give greater ventilation to the issues, through both debate among geneticists and education of the public. However, when Dr. Anderson suggests that this body could "help federal funding officials make the wisest possible decisions" (p. 120), I have a hunch he's gotten us into deeper water than he anticipated.

Like all budget determinations, decisions about how much to spend on genetics (as against other programs) and how to spend it (on research in various genetic diseases and on differing kinds of diagnosis, prevention and treatment) are merely policy choices disguised as columns of dollars-and-cents figures. Faced with a scarcity of both money and manpower, it is difficult to decide whether to engage in research and treatment of particular diseases. If only a few people suffer from a particular defect, large-scale projects dealing with it look suspiciously like collective choices to save some people while letting others perish. As Guido Calabresi has suggested, the involvement of public bodies in the health process places increasingly severe strains on our social system the closer the decision comes to choosing between particular individuals.[16]

16See generally G. Calabresi, *The Cost of Accidents* (New Haven: Yale

If we are able to agree on who should make funding decisions, other problems lurk in the decisions themselves. Arguments come to mind that were raised during the peak of heart transplantation a few years ago. Some critics of the operation argued that transplantation not only was unjustified as a therapeutic technique but represented a faulty allocation of resources as well. Since the public footed so much of the bill for

[illegible text]

to treat it. If we allocate only a certain amount for treatment, can we then require that to be eligible for treatment a patient must have taken certain precautionary measures? Specifically, this could mean a mandatory gene assay for all couples. If a basis were found for predicting a genetic defect in offspring, normal conception would have to be foregone in favor of either: (1) no children; (2) postnatal adoption; (3) prenatal adoption through artificial insemination, ovum implantation, or both; or (4) fetal diagnosis (where feasible for the defect at issue) and mandatory abortion when the defect is found. The limited treatment funds could then be used to give the maximum feasible medical care to those children (many fewer in number) born with unforeseeable defects despite their parents' compliance with the prevention requirements. Let me make clear that I am not endorsing this program; I am merely suggesting that these are the kinds of programs we must consider in order, as Dr. Anderson put it, to "assist federal funding officials to make the wisest possible decisions."

Another issue arises in situations where we can prevent the manifestations of a genetic disorder although science has been unable, as yet, to recode the genes in such a way as to prevent the disorder itself. Dr. Anderson has mentioned the low-phenylalanine diets given to children suffering from phenylketonuria

University Press, 1970), and G. Calabresi, "Reflections on Medical Experimentation in Humans," Vol. 98 *Daedalus* p. 387 (1969).

(PKU). This genetic disease affects metabolism and is "commonly associated with mental retardation, although some phenylketonuria babies grow up to be normal or bright without treatment."[17]   Although relatively few children suffer from PKU, Dr. Robert Guthrie's development a few years ago of a simple blood test and the production of a special PKU diet led to a widespread movement, supported by the American Medical Association, for PKU screening programs. As a result, children are now tested for PKU within a few days of birth in most states, and those with "positive" results are put on a low phenylalanine diet. Even aside from the issue of the "genetic deterioration" caused by the resulting increase in prevalence of the PKU genetic type in the childbearing population, this program cannot be rated an unqualified success. First, the test for detection has turned out not to be very precise. Dr. Charles W. Blumenfeld of Sacramento reported that about half of the children tested who have PKU do not show up as "positives" on the test. Meanwhile, Dr. Guthrie himself reported that about 85 percent of the presumed positives turned out to be false positives. The latter result takes on vital significance in the light of the findings of Dr. William B. Hanley of the University of Toronto that a low-phenylalanine diet may cause poor weight gain, inadequate linear growth, serious malnutrition, and, ironically, permanent intellectual impairment.[18] Here was a case in which the preventive technique may have consequences as bad as—or worse than—the disease itself.

Is this example of legislatures enacting inadequate science into law exactly what Dr. Anderson has preached against? No; this was enabling legislation to support diagnosis and prevention, not the sort of restrictive regulation he has warned against. Whatever the legislators' error, some of the blame should be laid at the door of the scientific community, which allowed a small group to push through a PKU program that had not been adequately verified by the standards usually applied by scientists. The PKU experience supports the view that society should move cautiously in following medical science's lead.

[17]J. D. Cooper, "Creative Pluralism: Medical Ombudsman," testimony on *Research in the Service of Man, Hearings on Biomedical Development, Evaluation of Existing Federal Institutions before the Subcommittee on Government Research of the Senate Committee on Government Operations,* 90th Cong., 1st Sess. 48 (1967).

[18]*Hospital Tribune* 1 (June 3, 1968).

Diagnosis

One of the disturbing aspects of the PKU affair is that the patient-subjects are newborn children, incapable of consenting to the manipulation involved. This point arises in the light of diagnosis, the third "good use" of gene therapy set forth by Dr. Anderson. As he explains, when a birth defect is suspected during pregnancy "it is now possible to obtain material from [illegible] benefit. Yet the rigor of this rule has been sullied by the difficult situations in which it has sometimes been invoked, only to be skirted.[19]

Most medical geneticists have surely given the question of whether a fetus has rights conscientious consideration before performing amniocentesis. But the treating physician's primary concern is, and must be, for the mother's well-being. When a procedure involves as much risk to another being as is involved in amniocentesis, either intentionally (through abortion) or unintentionally (as a consequence of the diagnostic manipulation), can the matter be left to an individual physician's determination? What is involved here is an extension of the question posed earlier—not only, "What is health?" but, "What is life?" When the heart transplant boom forced us a few years ago to

[19]For example, parents with a healthy child (often a twin) have persuaded courts to allow them to give consent for the transplantation of one of his kidneys into his ailing sibling, on the theory that although risks are involved (both in the operation and in being left with only one kidney) the psychological benefits outweigh them. See Strunk v. Strunk, 445 S.W. 2d 145 (Ky. 1969). Professor Curran describes three of the early, unreported Massachusetts cases. W. J. Curran, "A Problem of Consent: Kidney Transplantation in Minors," Vol. 34 *N.Y.U. Law Review* p. 891 (1959). The imbalance in the sibling situation has led at least one commentator to conclude that "children should on no account be [organ] donors." D. Daube, "Transplantation: Acceptability of Procedures and The Required Legal Sanctions," in G. E. W. Wolstenholme and Maeve O'Connor, eds., *Ethics in Medical Progress—With Special Reference to Transplantation* (Boston: Little, Brown & Co., 1966), p. 198.

face the converse question, "What is death?" we discovered, with some surprise, that there was no clear medical answer to the question and that the answers given varied according to the social goals involved (as law, in its own definitions of death, had held all along). Although we still have no universally satisfactory definition of death, there has been a general move to protect the rights (indeed, the lives) of organ donors by assuring that they have their own doctors, unconnected with the recipient. Any use of human sperm and ova, even *in vitro*, may give rise to a need to protect the embryo as "human," although the question, "What beings deserve human rights and respect?" has not been resolved by the law. Amniocentesis and *in vitro* culture of human embryos are already entering medical practice, and if we are not yet able to define life and health, we should at least provide a medical advocate for the unborn patient.[20]

A Model of Law in the Process of Gene Therapy Development—Who, How and Why?

Having touched on some of the issues which Dr. Anderson's paper raises, I would like now to sketch a legal model through which it may be possible to arrive at ways of dealing with these issues. In applying the law to questions of medical innovation we are concerned with *the people* making the decisions ("Who?"), the *procedures* they follow ("How?"), and the *standards* they employ, either expressly or implicitly ("Why?"). Discussions of law as a means of guiding and controlling human conduct eventually focus on three points: (1) Who formulates the law and on what basis? (2) Who administers the law and how do they approach their task? (3) Who reviews the legal decisions and their consequences? Looking at the development of genetic therapy, there appear to be four major participants involved at various stages in the process: the physician-investigator (geneticist), the patient-subject, the professions and the public.[21]

[20] A first step in this direction is represented in the latest revision of the Massachusetts General Hospital's *Human Studies: Guiding Principles and Procedures* (2d ed., 1970).

[21] The analysis employed herein is developed in greater detail in a casebook, *Experimentation with Human Beings*, on which the author is working with Dr. Jay Katz, to be published in June, 1972, by the Russell Sage Foundation.

The Physician-Investigator

When one examines a new area of medicine, like gene thera-py, the nexus of authority seems naturally to lie with the physician-investigators who have set out on the uncharted seas. While there is today widespread recognition of the need for

ethics, and, once he has the subject's informed consent, choice should lie with the physician-investigator.

Is this approach adequate for the problems posed by genetic manipulation? I think not. A code of ethics is too blunt an instrument. Procedurally, codes lack mechanisms for resolving competing claims; substantively, they lack the richness which statutes achieve through their greater length and their legislative history and which the common law achieves by fact-based, case-by-case articulation of rules and principles. What do codes tell an investigator about how to evaluate different types of harm to his subjects and society, or how to weigh these risks against the principle that scientists must pursue truth wherever it may lead? Can ethical principles tell an investigator whether potential injury to subjects is justified by societal interests, and if so, what those interests are? Clearly, codes cannot answer these questions or myriad others, such as whether a geneticist definitely ought (or definitely ought not) to randomize the selection of his subjects when testing new treatments. Codes speak on a higher, more abstract plane. The Declaration of Helsinki adopted by the World Medical Association in 1964, for example, instructs physicians that their work "should be pre-ceded by careful assessment of inherent risks in comparison to foreseeable benefits to the subject or to others" and that in

22Vol. 274 *New England Journal of Medicine* pp. 1354, 1360 (1966).

most cases they should not proceed "without [the subject's] free consent . . . in writing."[23]

The Patient-Subject

Although general exhortations about "free consent" do not offer investigators much concrete guidance, the principle they embody ought not to be belittled. Personal self-determination has long been a fundamental part of our concept of man as well as a basic rule in the common law of medical malpractice. Its importance was made shockingly apparent by Nazi doctors' treatment of nonconsenting prisoner-subjects. The Nuremburg Code, which emerged from the judgment that our military tribunal passed on those doctors after the war, has as its central requirement that "the voluntary consent of the human subject is absolutely essential."[24] In the period since the war, the rights of subjects and patients alike have received increased attention, and the doctrine of "informed consent" has been extended from medical therapy to experimentation as well.

Can we depend on this second legal device—informed, voluntary choice by patient-subjects—to provide adequate control over the development of genetic manipulation? Here again, I think not, although I believe my position differs from that of most critics who raise these questions.

For a subject's consent to be "informed" his decision must be based, as the California courts have declared, on all the "facts which are necessary to form the basis of an intelligent consent."[25] Yet in many circumstances the difficulties of communication and understanding make a subject's comprehension of "all the facts" problematic at best. Moreover, as Sir Austin Hill has stated, often only "illusory or uncomprehending consent" is possible because the physician-investigator cannot describe "the pros and cons of a new and unknown treatment . . . to a patient so that he does not lose confidence . . .

[23]"Declaration of Helsinki," Sections I-4 and II-3a & 3c.

[24]Vol. 2 *Trials of War Criminals before the Nuernberg Military Tribunals* (*The Medical Case*), p. 181 (Washington, D.C.: U. S. Govt. Printing Office, 1949).

[25]Salgo v. Leland Stanford, Jr. University Board of Trustees, 154 Cal. App.2d 560, 578, 317, P.2d 170, 181 (1957).

[which is] the essence of the doctor/patient relationship."[26] The more novel and advanced the technique, the more difficult the task. One legal commentator summed up the prevailing view: "The complexities of modern research often make 'informed' consent virtually impossible to achieve."[27]

The subjects of research, it is true, are unlikely to be as knowledgeable as those who perform research. However, unless

make too great an effort to communicate with their subjects and to choose subjects with more of an eye to ease of selection than to reducing the "competence gap," as Talcott Parsons puts it.[29]

Yet we need not despair of all hope for self-determination by subjects in medical innovation. When we compare the kind of choices for which we seek patient-subjects' consent with other choices which the law allows people to make for themselves, adequate informed consent appears more attainable. People make innumerable important decisions about property, marriage, education, career, and need for medical treatment. Many of these decisions are ill-advised, some are foolhardy. But we don't second-guess them, trying to psychoanalyze what people really want or what will really do them the most good; we don't turn all complicated decisions over to "the experts." We do care, of course, that as much information as possible be communicated about the choices offered. For example, we allow

[26]A. B. Hill, "Medical Ethics and Controlled Trials," Vol. 1 *British Medical Journal* pp. 1043, 1046 (1963).

[27]R. D. Mulford, "Experimentation on Human Beings," Vol. 20 *Standard Law Review* pp. 99, 106 (1967).

[28]See H. Jonas, "Philosophical Reflections on Experimenting with Human Subjects," Vol. 98 *Daedalus* pp. 219, 235 (1969).

[29]See *Proceedings of the Conference on the Ethical Aspects of Experimentation on Human Subjects* (sponsored by *Daedalus* and the National Institutes of Health) p. 37 (1967).

men to decide to go to the moon, despite the obvious risks; yet, supposing no means had been developed to get them back to earth, we would be outraged if they were not told so. If a person is given an accurate view of the risks of a certain procedure, or is told that no one knows the likely consequences, I believe we should allow him to proceed if he so chooses, even if his technical understanding of the procedure is deficient.

Besides being concerned with the *content* of what is disclosed, we may also wish to evaluate the validity of an "informed consent" in the *context* in which it is given. A distinction is sometimes drawn between the kind of consent needed from a patient in treatment and that required of a subject in research. Others have argued that there is no basis for such a distinction. A. C. Ivy has written:

> Even after the therapy of a disease is discovered, its application to the patient remains, in part, experimental. Because of the physiological variations in the response of different patients to the same therapy, the therapy of disease is, and will always be, an experimental aspect of medicine. . . . The patient is always to some extent an experimental subject of the physician. . . .[30]

Jay Katz has carried this argument one step further. He finds in physicians' collective "reluctance to examine" the ethics of medical experimentation a "conscious or unconscious realization that any resolution of the problems posed by human experimentation cannot be limited to research settings, but instead has far-reaching consequences for medical practice."[31]

It is true in a certain sense that all treatment is experimentation, and yet I believe there is a distinction between the conditions for consent in the two settings.[32] Those who make such a distinction usually set higher requirements for the consent of experimental subjects than for that of patients. Accordingly, many physicians fear that the standards developed for subjects

[30]A. C. Ivy, "The History and Ethics of the Use of Human Subjects in Medical Experiments," Vol. 108 *Science* pp. 1, 5 (1948).

[31]J. Katz, "The Education of the Physician-Investigator," Vol. 98 *Daedalus* pp. 480, 481-482 (1969).

[32]I have, rather arbitrarily, limited this discussion to experimentation and therapy and have assumed that diagnosis should be treated as part of one or the other, depending upon the extent to which it has been tested and its safety established.

will be extended to their patients, for whom physicians have traditionally been allowed to make many decisions on the ground of the patient's best interests.

Yet if we look at the contexts carefully and focus on the psychological situation of the patient or subject, it seems to me that the usual approach has it backwards. Higher requirements

[illegible faded text]

cially) and on whom he is probably dependent for his future well-being. The procedure may be offered, despite unknown risks, because more conventional methods have proved ineffective. Even when a successful but slow recovery is being made, patients offered new therapy often have eyes only for its novelty and not for its risks. Dr. Francis D. Moore has observed, "People in this country have been weaned on newspaper accounts of exciting new cures." In the field of genetics as in other fields, "patients are pressing their doctors to be the subject of innovation."[34]

How many of us, having read Dr. Anderson's account of virus-instigated changes in genes, would volunteer to have that procedure performed on us tomorrow? Yet what would our responses be if we suffered from a rare genetic anomaly? Dr. Anderson was quite right, speaking of the "relatively unproven technique of gene therapy" being used to treat argininemia:

[33]I exclude from the meaning of "experimentation" here the trivial sense in which we might say that giving aspirin to a new patient is an experiment. I include only those situations in which a doctor is concerned with the person before him not only as a patient but also as a means for discovering something about human beings and their illnesses, or for finding new ways of diagnosing and treating a disease (usually, but not always, the disease which has brought the patient to him).

[34]*Proceedings of the Conference on the Ethical Aspects of Experimentation on Human Subjects* (sponsored by *Daedalus* and the National Institutes of Health) p. 31 (1967).

"Many parents . . . would not only allow it but would urge its use" (p. 118). Certainly, part of the difference in response between healthy subjects and patient-subjects is due to the obviously greater potential benefits which the latter may derive from participation. But that does not entirely explain their far more favorable response. While, as I argued previously, we may not wish *in any particular instance* to disregard the consent of a patient whose strong desire for treatment causes him to overrate the benefits and underestimate the risks of a research technique, I believe we should nevertheless decide *as a general rule* to set higher requirements for consent and to impose additional safeguards on therapy combined with experimentation, lest investigators even unwittingly expose "consenting" patient-subjects to unreasonable risks.[35]

The Professions and the Public

Dr. Anderson's description of gene therapy makes apparent that the technique involved will be developed largely in connection with the treatment of genetically ill individuals. That being the case, we must be concerned not only with ethical codes and informed consent but also with the necessary legal safeguards. This brings us to the third and fourth sets of who's, how's, and why's that make up the legal system we are discussing: the professions and the public.

Turning to other areas of medical innovation for an understanding of the role and authority of the professions and the public provides us with some guidance but not a great deal. Professional organizations are traditionally involved in the process only to the extent that they participate in the licensing of physician-investigators and in evaluating the work they publish.[36] These functions involve only minimal control over the rudiments of medical skill and ethical conformity.

[35]The disinterested weighing of risks and benefits suggested here is not intended to imply that patients usually ought to be excluded as subjects. In some research it may be necessary to have persons manifesting a disease or defect in order to study that condition. Yet this is not always the case. For example, the ova for research on *in vitro* human development need not be obtained from infertile women; these women merely provide a more compliant subject population for the necessary laparoscopy (surgery on the egg follicles) than would normal women.

[36]On the question of professional censorship there is no unanimity of opinion. Some argue that the best sanction for unethical research is to

Of late, the professions have been more active through the "peer group review committees" required for the past five years at institutions conducting research funded by the Public Health Service.[37] Serious questions have been raised, however, about the effectiveness of this method. One criticism is that much research escapes their attention. Physicians faced with a sudden opportunity to try a new gene therapy technique might balk at

among institutions, but the sources of many rules remain unarticulated. In passing on a proposal for genetic testing and treatment of the mentally retarded, for example, should a committee weigh as a benefit the financial savings to the public in not having to support these children? Fairness suggests that if the public interest is a factor in committee decisions, it should have broadly-based community representation. Yet few of them do: on the whole, review committee membership is at least 95 percent medical.[38] Women are woefully unrepresented on review committees. Their presence is especially important for committees considering genetics, since women are not only vitally concerned with reproduction but are most often the experimental subjects for genetic research.

refuse scholarly publication, while others believe, with Justice Brandeis, that "sunlight is the best disinfectant" and it is better to print the report so as to expose the investigator to criticism by his peers. Compare British Medical Research Council, "Memorandum on Clinical Investigation" (Oct. 16, 1953), and T. F. Fox, "The Ethics of Clinical Trials," Vol. 28 *Medico-Legal Journal* pp. 132, 139 (1960), with J. Katz, "Letter to the Editor," Vol. 275 *New England Journal of Medicine* p. 790 (1966).

[37]See generally a study being conducted on the structure and processes of peer group review by Bernard Barber, John Lally, Julia Makarushka, and Daniel Sullivan, to be published by the Russell Sage Foundation in 1972.

[38]Many of these doubts also apply to the peer group review procedure instituted on March 17, 1971, by the F.D.A. for investigational new drug testing. See Vol. 36 *Federal Register* p. 5037 (1971).

Public involvement through governmental institutions has been concentrated on the federal level.[39] Since 1962 the federal government has taken a direct role in experimentation with its complex regulations for new "drugs intended solely for investigational use by experts qualified by scientific training and experience to investigate the safety and effectiveness of drugs."[40] As the techniques of genetic therapy advance to the testing stage, their sponsors will have to submit to the Department of Health, Education, and Welfare: (1) reports of pre-clinical tests; (2) statements of responsibility from investigators; and (3) reports of the results of the clinical trials, under the F.D.A.'s IND (Investigational New Drug) procedures.[41] The magnitude of the agency's task will compel it to rely on the sponsors of new drugs to police themselves. Only in exceptional cases can any close supervision be given to the methods, risks, and benefits of proposed new treatments. Usually these are reviewed only after a new drug has reached the market; when untoward results occur, then congressional investigations and major damage actions may follow.

Conclusion

In conclusion, I would like briefly to touch upon certain "political" aspects of the legal process that I think medical scientists must consider as their work takes on increasing social consequences.

First, it is absolutely necessary to be open with the public and to regard it as educable and interested, rather than lumpish

[39]There is no state statutory or case law to speak of on human experimentation. State institutions are involved only in licensing profes-sionals and in policing "informed consent" through tort actions brought in state courts. The states are now coming to play a more active role; for instance, Assemblyman Stavisky introduced into the current session of the New York Assembly "A Bill to Amend the Education Law in Relation to Scientific Research on Human Subjects, to Provide for the Advancement of Such Research through the Protection of its Subjects, and to Establish a State Board on Human Research."

[40]21 U.S.C. § 355(i) (1971).

[41]Depending on the type of genetic therapy developed, the new methods may be subject to the separate, but similar, procedures covering biologics. See Act of July 1, 1944, 42 U.S.C. § 201 et seq. (1971); Act of March 4, 1913, 21 U.S.C. § 151 et seq. (1971); and 9 C.F.R. §§103.1 to 103.3.

and bored. To do this honestly a scientist must first accept the possibility that, having heard the arguments, the public may choose wrongly. At the worst, an area of science may even be closed off from lawful investigation.

Second, there is a strong underlying sentiment against social (including genetic) "planning" in this country that cannot be entirely overcome by showing that the planners have made wise

at some point, the strain may be too great on the general conception of what is man and what machine, or what conduct is human and what pretends to the superhuman or divine. When that point comes, the scientist can expect to hear the cry that science can go no further, that mankind does not desire a chart showing the chemistry of the soul and how it can be reproduced in a test tube.[43] While few could equal its eloquence, Norman Mailer's *Of a Fire on the Moon*[44] may be representative of the profound and widespread schizophrenia of modern man. Alter-

[42]To illustrate (and this need not relate to a subject as emotional as genetics): We may wish to assure that each person has an equal chance to certain scarce medical resources. Making the resources available regardless of income and allocating them on the basis of a lottery may seem arbitrary because it would fail accurately to reflect some people's stronger desire to undergo a risky procedure in order to live. Yet if the alternative is to construct a complicated, varying price scale for the medical resource (or to use the tax structure in a similar manner), the lottery may be a more palatable choice, because the "income neutral" model involves such a patent attempt to get the right number of people to do what we (collectively) want them to.

[43]This mood is nicely evoked, and summed up, by Theodore Roszak in *The Making of a Counter Culture* (New York: Anchor Books, 1969). The responses of which he writes are in many ways novel. In the "counter culture's" reaction to all of "scientific progress," and the "establishment's" counterreaction, we may divine a phenomenon which reverses an old verity: we are witnessing the impatience of old age and the conservatism of youth.

[44]Boston: Little, Brown, 1970.

nately describing the Apollo flight in a detail that speaks of infatuation and rhapsodizing on the moon's mysteries, Mailer suggests that there exists at once in us a desire for the most "objective" scientific facts alongside a yearning to preserve the individual, subjective, and nonscientific view of man and his universe.

In sum, my caution is this: Geneticists, if they do not know it already, will learn that the contradictions of law result not really from muddle-headed lawyers but from this human dichotomy. And law, they will learn, as a vehicle for the choices of men in society, can at one moment aid science and at the next turn and cry, "Halt, and go no further! Here rules man with his conceptions of liberty, justice, and equality, and science is his subject, not his master."

Dr. Anderson proposes an advisory commission composed of "physicians, scientists and concerned laymen" (p. 120) to establish goals, safeguards, and guidelines that should govern our practical applications of biomedical knowledge. Whether this procedural recommendation is adequate to the problem analyzed may be questioned. However, the choice between an

Dr. Paul Ramsey, Paine Professor of Religion at Princeton University, is a teacher and scholar in the field of Christian ethics and social theory. A trustee of Drew University, he served as president of the American Society of Christian Ethics in 1962-63, and in 1964-65 was president of the American Theological Society. Dr. Ramsey was born in Mississippi, studied at Millsaps College, and received his B.D. and his Ph.D. from Yale University Divinity School in 1940 and 1943 respectively. Among his books are Basic Christian Ethics (New York: Scribner's, 1950), The Just War: Force and Political Responsibility (Scribner's, 1968), Deeds and Rules in Christian Ethics (Scribner's, 1967), Fabricated Man: The Ethics of Genetic Control (New Haven: Yale University Press, 1970). In 1968 and again in 1969 he held a research appointment at Georgetown Medical School, serving as the Joseph P. Kennedy, Jr., Foundation Visiting Professor of Genetic Ethics, studying the moral issues in modern medical practice. In 1969, he gave the Lyman Beecher Lectures at the School of Medicine and the Divinity School of Yale University. These were published in The Patient as Person: Explorations in Medical Ethics (Yale University Press, 1970).

157

advisory commission through which the conscience of an informed society can be expressed and a regulatory commission limiting the uses and abuses of a laissez-faire system can scarcely be made without some notion of what should or should not be done. As our philosophical or ethical standards of human good vary, so will vary our esteem for advisory or mandatory regulation of the activity of an elite group of scientists which may threaten that good.

In any case, my role as an ethicist in this study is presumably to discuss what ought to be done, whether physicians and scientists act alone, with the advice of a public commission, or under the compulsion of societal regulation.

The Meaning of "Therapy"

As a first step in the direction of an ethical analysis of possible genetic interventions, we need a clearer, more limited use of the word "therapy" than Dr. Anderson's (p. 109).

Therapy means "treatment," treatment of an existing human individual. Therefore I suggest that the term "gene therapy" be reserved for targeted genetic remedies applied to a conceptus or to an individual after birth—to one of us *in utero* or *extra utero*. For this sort of procedure genetic "surgery" is a metaphor. It is only a metaphor, although a helpful one, because it brings all such cases under accepted medical ethics governing dangerous therapeutic intervention, justified only when the consequences would be worse without the trial treatment and there is no other recourse. The ethics of therapy calls for balancing judgments as to the consequences. In gene therapy upon existing individuals, those responsible must decide with fear and trembling on behalf of the fetus or child, just as one decides for an unconscious patient. The choice made for a patient who is for any reason unable to consent or dissent should always be for the probable best treatment at least risk.

This limited use of the word "therapy" is crucial to any ethical deliberation concerning "gene therapy." Norman Rosten wrote recently:

> We have only a handful of crucial words standing between light and darkness. To blur the meaning of even one is to hasten darkness. I suggest that we keep our eyes and minds on language as we would upon our sanity.[1]

[1] *The New York Times*, Mar. 29, 1971.

"Therapy"—treatment—is one such crucial word standing between us and disaster. What we mean by the word should be kept exact.

Dr. Anderson's broad use of "therapy" seems to me to be misleading—with morally indefensible consequences. In one place, he speaks of "gene therapy" upon an as yet unconceived individual, upon germinal matter, the gametes, *i.e.*, ovum or

[text obscured]

not surgery or "therapy" or treatment. Proper terminology would place gametic manipulation alongside other methods of *preventive* genetic medicine—contraception, sterilization, specific conditions for marriage licenses, and pre-marital genetic counseling. We ought not to go to work improving the child preconceptually, deciding whether it should be one sort of conceptus or another when in fact it is not yet. Preventive genetic medicine has a number of familiar, proven options more desirable than gametic manipulation. If we want to promote responsible parenthood by means of our knowledge of genetics, if we wish to stop transmitting serious defects in human lives, the first question is not whether, assuming the child must be, we should make it of this or that genetic composition, but whether a conceptus should be conceived at all. We ought not to choose for another the hazards he must bear, while choosing at the same time to give him life in which to bear them and suffer our chosen experimentations.

In any case, in order to keep clear the decisions we are making, the manipulation of the eggs and sperm of potential parents ought not to be called "gene therapy." There is as yet no patient under treatment. If the proposed changes are to be made on the genetic makeup of a born or unborn baby or of an adult patient, that may be called treatment. Then our decision must be made by comparing the benefits and hazards for an existing human life. If, however, the changes are to be introduced in the gametes of persons not yet parents, then the

comparison must be between several means of preventing transmission of a known genetic defect. Gametic manipulation, and
the introduction of gene changes into laboratory sperm and ova
cultures, must be deemed least desirable, indeed prohibited. It is
not a proper goal of medicine to enable women to have children, and marriages to be fertile, *by any means necessary*, even
one which imposes an additional hazard upon the child not yet
conceived.

In a second respect Dr. Anderson's use of the word
"therapy" is too broad, and again we must strive to use words
precisely enough to preserve the moral wisdom impacted into
their long-established meanings. Otherwise the owl of Minerva
has already taken flight, and mankind is passing into a darkness
whose length we cannot tell. Anderson speaks of "therapeutic
abortion," using the word "therapeutic" with a meaning the
word acquired only recently in medical, moral, legal, and political discussions of abortion. Treatment is construed to include
killing the patient for his own sake in order that he may not
have a life deemed by others not to be worth living. And the
findings of amniocentesis easily meet the requirements of those
laws that allow abortion in case there is likelihood that the child
will be born seriously impaired, physically or mentally. The
so-called "fetal indications" for abortion can already, and increasingly in the future, be identified with certainty; not only a
defective fetus but a carrier as well can be detected. And we
have learned to call killing them "therapeutic." What is actually
being "treated" in genetic abortions: the patient, society's
pocketbook, or parents' desires?

Abortion is not on the agenda of this study, and yet it is on
the hidden agenda in all three of the areas under consideration.
A conceivable method of pollution control, an escape hatch for
all the failures and mishaps as we undertake to find new ways to
begin human life, the practice of abortion is also held to be
important for the genetic purgation of our species and for the
prevention of suffering from genetic diseases.

I do not deny that lives *in utero* should sometimes be treated
as a special part of the population. For example, if the genetic
or pharmacological history of a fetus' parents and the results of
amniocentesis make it highly probable that the fetus will be
born gravely defective, parents can then consent on its behalf,
and it can be part of the ethical practice of medicine to employ
hazardous procedures to cure the unborn. This is the proper

meaning of "gene therapy" or "genetic surgery." Even now, in the practice of fetology, if a fatality occurs it is more often than not the procedure and not the disease that kills, *e.g.*, in fetal blood transfusions for Rh incompatibility. It is impossible to believe, however—because it is a logical and moral contradiction—that abortion is a form of "treatment" of human life, or that adult consent to that killing on behalf of the unborn is

proposes to destroy defective lives ought not to add to that destruction the further insult of claiming the procedure to be "therapy," the care that was needed. That horrendous notion we would not apply to ourselves or to our children already born, who are suffering, genetically defective, vulnerable, and in need. Such euphemistic misuse of language only prevents us from recognizing what we are doing—removing defective lives that are said to be of no worth.

The ethical reasoning I express is no sectarian religious opinion. It is rather in accordance with the ethical criterion most generally endorsed by contemporary philosophers. The test is whether in situations that are similar in all important respects similar actions are taken. Those who justify abortion as "treatment" rest their case primarily upon the defect, the suffering which that particular killing can eliminate. Dr. Anderson refers, in evident agreement, to people who "feel that *the suffering produced for the child*, the mother, and the rest of the family, by genetic defects is so great that any efforts towards prevention of defective babies is justified including therapeutic abortion" (p. 116) (italics added). The efforts called "treatment" extend to the elimination of *the patient*. Strange treatment, that; and if it is indicated in one case it is no doubt indicated in similar cases, to prevent a like degree of suffering. Universalizing that principle, if abortion can be called "treatment" so can infanticide. If we are going to do abortions for these reasons, we must be able to prescribe killing universally as a "treatment" to be administered to other grossly defective human beings. The moral course here set will lead to that conclusion in practice if we do not recover the proper meaning of "treatment" and "therapy."

New York state law now permits abortion up to twenty-four weeks upon the private decision of a woman and her physician. Fetuses from twenty to twenty-eight weeks have 10 percent viability; this means that infanticide—the destruction of possibly viable fetuses—is permitted in that state. As a consequence, twenty-eight fetuses lived following abortion procedures in the first nine months of the operation of the new law; one lived to be adopted; and, of course, an uncounted number of viable babies have been killed. It has been reported that Cyril C. Means, Jr., professor at New York Law School and an expert on New York State's abortion law, recommended that twenty-four weeks would be a good cutoff point because of legislative precedent and because many birth defects cannot be detected until twenty weeks' gestation or later.[2]

Let us turn now to the first case of experimental gene therapy: the case of the two German sisters suffering from argininemia. According to Dr. Anderson's account (p. 118), these girls are being exposed to a virus believed to cause no harm to see whether this will decrease the arginine level in their blood. I contend that we need to know more than that the virus appears to be harmless. We must also ask what benefit can come to the patients.

From other sources I have learned that these girls are the only known cases of argininemia; it is described as a "new inborn error of metabolism." Its symptoms are spastic diplegia, epileptic seizures, and severe mental retardation, all progressive conditions believed to be untreatable. The two girls are the children of related parents who have three normal children. The older patient is about seven, and it is admitted that it is probably too late to do anything for her. For the younger sister, two years old, there is some hope that the progress of the symptoms may be stopped. The "messenger" being used in therapy is the Shope virus, believed by some scientists to be a possible cause of cancer.[3]

[2] Susan Edmiston, "A Report on the Abortion Capital of the Country," *The New York Times Magazine*, Sunday, Apr. 11, 1971, p. 44.

[3] See H. G. Terheggen, A. Schwenk, *et al.*, "Argininaemia with Argin-

In view of these facts, I cannot agree with Dr. Anderson that "the experiment appears justified because of the tragic circumstances of the disease involved" (p. 117). Precisely because of these tragic circumstances, the experiment seems to me unjustifiable. Dr. Anderson supports his position with a question: "If you were the parent of a newborn baby who was found to have argininemia and therefore to be doomed to suffer and die,

The German sisters' situation is entirely different. For the younger girl, the most that is hoped for is to arrest further progress of the disease. But for her older sister there is not even that hope. She can derive no benefit from the treatment, and its only justification appears to be its research value.

If—as seems likely in the case of the older girl at least—the dying of these children is being prolonged purely for experimental purposes, I know of no line of moral reasoning that can justify what is being done. We ought not to speak of gene "therapy" in this connection. It is rather a case of genetic *experimentation* in which men have chosen retardates and taken from them something which they cannot give, namely, free consent to prolong their dying for the sake of scrutinizing it scientifically. We ought to speak of whether or not a successful experiment—not "a successful therapy," as Dr. Anderson puts it—is taking place. This more exact use of language would help us see that a possibly immoral piece of research has been undertaken.

Of course, a dying adult can understandingly consent for his dying to be made the subject of research. Moreover, as Hans Jonas has argued, the fact that it is *his* disease that is needed for study may be a chief part of a dying patient's remaining sense

ase Deficiency," *The Lancet*, Oct. 4, 1969, pp. 748-9; Dr. Stanfield Rogers, "Skills for Genetic Engineers," *New Scientist*, Jan. 29, 1970; and Harold M. Schmeck, Jr., "Virus Is Injected into 2 Children in Effort to Alter Chemical Traits," *The New York Times*, Sept. 20, 1970.

of bodily identity. "A residue of identification is left to him that it is his own affliction by which he can contribute to the conquest of that affliction"—even though the dying should be spared "the gratuitousness of service to an unrelated cause."[4] If we should keep far from the dying the intrusion of irrelevant or unconsented investigations, then we should respect dying retardates as well. It is our ethical obligation to allow a person to die in undisturbed peace and comfort.

In this light, it is possible that the work with the German sisters can be considered treatment, not simply experimentation. If the gene change introduced by the virus in fact gives them ease and a more humane dying (even at the cost of some nonbeneficial prolongation of their dying process), then a parent may rightfully consent to it on their behalf.

Shortcomings of an Advisory Commission

Dr. Anderson's proposal for an advisory genetics commission is worth pondering. Granted that there are dangers in centralized authority and mandatory regulation, an advisory commission is a solution by no means cut to the measure of the magnitude of the problem as analyzed in the paper. Dr. Marshall W. Nirenberg was quoted as saying, "When man becomes capable of instructing his own genes, he *must refrain from doing so* until he has sufficient wisdom to use this knowledge for the benefit of mankind" (italics added). An advisory commission would not insure even that degree of constraint. The commission could, of course, affect the funding policies of the federal government. It would provide, as Dr. Anderson suggests, a "public forum" through which "goals and safeguards" could be established, through which "the conscience of an informed society as a whole" could make decisions (p. 121). None of these things, however, would alter the laissez-faire system of biomedical investigations and application enough to insure that every researcher would refrain from undertaking possible procedures until men have sufficient wisdom to know them to be right and beneficial.

One illustration Dr. Anderson uses seems to indicate that he values an advisory commission *because* it would be permissive and little prevent men from adopting techniques as they be-

---

[4]Hans Jonas, "Philosophical Reflections on Experimenting with Human Subjects," *Daedalus*, Vol. 98 (Spring, 1969), pp. 219-247.

come available. "If society is unable to reach a consensus on a topic such as therapeutic abortion," he writes, "how can we expect any small group to reach wise and just decisions about an area as fundamental as influencing the hereditary characteristics of ourselves and our future generations?" (p. 121). It is evident that Dr. Anderson expects that vague entity, "an informed society as a whole," to arrive at nonconstraining guide-

should raise the same question about the dangers in the concentrated funding of science by the National Institutes of Health and the National Science Foundation. Dr. Anderson is too much predisposed in favor of the wisdom of nonprescriptive advice. Even an advisory commission might misuse its power if its advice were heeded but proved to be unwise or dangerous.

Moreover, we need to distinguish the task of a peer committee on the one hand in insuring that the experiments conducted during genetic research are ethical from the task of deciding how genetic procedures shall be applied in medical practice. Society's stake in the latter may be so great that a regulatory commission will be needed.

Heart transplantation, Dr. Anderson believes, has suggested the "reasonable approach" we should take toward gene therapy. This is not very reassuring as to the usefulness of a merely advisory commission. Society's experience with heart transplantation began with the decision by heart surgeons that this branch of medicine needed to be developed. That specialists should determine society's stake in matters involving medical and social priorities is questionable, especially in the light of the theoretical determinism and moral permissiveness which Dr. Anderson and many others today bring to the question. "It became clear many years ago," he writes, "that medical research *had to* develop a means of providing a replacement for damaged hearts" (italics added). The world, he goes on to say, "quickly adjusted itself to this new, revolutionary procedure"

(p. 122). Is adjustment to inevitable developments what we mean by "wisdom"?

Dr. Anderson believes that genetics "holds such *promise* for alleviating human suffering" (italics added) that no body of men, no commission, no public policy should lay down mandatory regulations. I submit, however, that his own analysis of the extraordinary powers now and in the near future to be placed in man's hands supports the opposite description as well: This area holds such *dangers* of untold human suffering, dehumanization, exploitation, radical alteration of the conditions of human existence, genetic SST's and Lake Eries, that we are obligated to search out ways by which regulatory public policy can be devised. Dr. Anderson himself insists that genetic technology, unlike heart transplantations, is "too powerful for society to be left unaware of its potential until its actual utilization" (p. 122). However, he seriously underestimates the danger at one point: "There is little danger," he writes, "of single gene insertions affecting such complex polygenic attributes as behavior, musical ability, personality or intelligence in a predictable way" (p. 119). There is indeed little danger that we can predictably improve these traits. But there is real, unforeseeable, and unforeclosed danger that the treatment of ordinary, inborn genetic errors may deleteriously affect these polygenetic traits.

If no group of individuals "should take it upon themselves" to make decisions involving such danger and promise, then scientists should not. Dr. Anderson does not recognize that a commission would not take anything on itself arbitrarily; it would be charged with this public responsibility. Nor does his reference to environmental pollution as a far greater threat than gene therapy convincingly support his proposal. The prevention of environmental pollution would have required more adequate systems analysis of agricultural and manufacturing decisions, procedures for public policy formation in that area, and finally—I am afraid—regulation for the sake of the common good. If—as he says—the "Nazi physicians all too clearly demonstrated that any technique can be misused," if cloning can produce "millions of test-tube grown soldiers for the military advantage of a nation," how then does "a pragmatic approach to cloning . . . seem to be the wisest course of a society that is keeping itself informed"? In current public discussions of these genetic issues, someone from any panel or audience can be counted on to intimate ominously (without actually mentioning

Red China) that some nation is even now manufacturing superior soldiers. Anticipatory response to that possibility will not be excluded by a permissive, pragmatic approach to cloning; so genetic applications may fall under the "action-reaction" syndrome of interstate politics and be justified for these reasons.

Because men differ concerning whether certain things ought

tions to be made of genetic knowledge, not first of all in the experimentation that may continue to be pursued. Nongovernmental agencies, pluralistic systems like peer or public committees in medical research centers, could be charged with the job of determining public policy. It is not the legalities but the insurance which society should seek, by whatever necessary means.

Using one or several of the possible institutions or decision-making procedures that could be devised, society has a right and a duty to tell genetic investigators and experimenters to keep their indefinitely tampering fingers from cloning a human being, *in vitro* baby manufacture, and—in genetic counseling and the proffering of preventive genetic medical advice—gametic manipulation. How can we say that a child (who may already have inherited money from its grandfather) should be killed at the request of its parents because it is unborn, genetically ill, and in need of more than money? In any case, what society can legally permit it can legally prohibit, as we still prohibit genetic infanticide and destruction of terminal patients who are also unwanted ballast. In matters of life and death this should clearly be so; and we should judge a society to be better and more civilized the better it can deal with grave social problems, including human suffering, while ruling out death-dealing actions such as abortion or methods of treatment likely to induce injury in a conceptus, followed by abortion.

Still, within the bounds of proper treatment, within the

limits of "gene therapy" on the deleterious genes of existing lives *in utero* and *extra utero*, problems may be approaching in which an advisory public commission may be needed to help medical science set guidelines. We should consider this, even though ethical physicians consulting together should themselves be wise enough to make moral decisions when there is uncertainty concerning the consequences for the individual patient. One such case is that given by Dr. Anderson: No one knows the effects upon other genes of moving the PKU gene from one place to another. We are likely to learn how to manipulate defective genes long before we know whether it is safe in the long run to do so or whether other and later results may be worse. It is better not to say as flatly as Dr. Anderson does that "The most satisfactory treatment for a patient suffering a genetic defect would be actual correction of the genetic material itself" (p. 117). Instead, the risks involved in gene "surgery" will be kept more clearly in mind if we say that satisfactory treatment is that which is likely to restore the patient to the greatest health with least danger. As Dr. Anderson said, doctors face the same problem in introducing any new therapeutic agent or procedure; in genetic "surgery" the problem is greater by several magnitudes but not entirely novel. Assuming grave need of treatment and understanding consent on the part of patients or those who can validly consent for "incompetent" patients needing treatment, doctors can be trusted to decide whether to use gene therapy on individual patients. It is hard to see what moral insight an advisory committee could give them. Such a committee might do more harm than good if its effect were to lessen the moral responsibility of physicians. Moreover, "concerned citizens" on a genetic advisory commission today would very likely be not only informed but also scientifically minded, oriented toward medical progress, and even more inclined than doctors to regard medicine as our savior from all suffering. Such a commission might only reach the same conclusions that would have been reached in its absence. Where would be the advantage?

Unforeseen Effects

So far I have assumed that gene therapy upon individual patients is not inheritable. If only the good effects prove inheritable, that of course will be an added advantage. But this is not known. Suppose some particular case of gene therapy should set off unforeseeable gametic disturbances in the individual treated. Such a case would bring gene therapy to a morally significant degree under the category of gametic manipulation. Gametic manipulation, it is true, would not be the purpose of the treatment but one of its unintended effects; but for that very reason these effects would be unanticipated, uncalculated, and

Friedmann and Roblin conclude: "Although the ethical problems posed by gene therapy are similar in principle to those posed by other experimental medical treatments, we feel that the irreversible and heritable nature of gene therapy means that the tolerable margin of risk and uncertainty in such therapy is reduced."[5] I suggest that we may have to go further and say that, in cases involving both genetic therapy and gametic manipulation, the unknown and unforeclosed risks to future generations may outweigh any benefit that might be secured for the individual patient. In a matter of such grave importance, "no discernible risk" is not adequate protection. We need to know that there are no risks—a requirement which inheritable gene therapy is not apt to meet. These prospects bring to mind the wisdom and moral responsibility enshrined in the traditional religious teaching that our procreative capacities are not, like other parts of our bodies, to be mastered and managed for our own sakes alone but rather are powers we hold in stewardship for future generations.

On one sort of question, however, physicians may need the help of an advisory public commission to set or reset public and medical policy. It is an old problem, yet one that is going to become increasingly urgent in the practice of genetic medicine. By environmental treatment of diabetes and by enabling dia-

[5]Theodore Friedmann and Richard Roblin, "Gene Therapy for Human Genetic Disease," *Science*, Vol. 175 (March 3, 1972), pp. 949-955.

betic women to bring a child to birth, we have acted, no doubt, in the interests of those patients. At the same time, however, we have spread the gene for diabetes to more and more individuals—who in turn are more likely to reproduce than they once were. Preventing normal elimination in these cases is good treatment for the individual but bad for the species.

Gene therapy may have the same paradoxical result. The use of techniques to repair or replace a defective person's genes instead of corrective nongenetic procedures like insulin or low-phenylalanine diet will not necessarily alter this fact. Suppose, for example, that genetic therapy replaces the gene defective in cystic fibrosis with a normal gene in an afflicted person's cells but does not affect his reproductive cells. Under these circumstances, we could successfully treat individuals suffering from that severe disease. But, by making them genetically alive (*i.e.*, alive to reproductive age and fertile), we would introduce more genes for this disease into the human gene pool. The same result would follow from the practice of "genetic abortion" for dwarfism or upon all male fetuses of women who are carriers of hemophilia. Since the parents in such a case would probably try again for a normal child, there would be more genes for dwarfism in the population (assuming that victims of this defect are now at some disadvantage in reproduction) and more female carriers of hemophilia. So with gene therapy, unless the healing introduced is hereditary.

In general, in the practice of genetic medicine (except, *e.g.*, by preventing conception), elimination of abnormal children will enable couples who are carriers to have more normal children. Correction of the defect by gene therapy will make for more carriers of such defects. Thus, there will inexorably have to be more gene therapy employed in the future if we commence to use it today; and, it would seem, there must be an increasing number of genetic abortions for all time to come once we begin to use that procedure in "social" medicine. The only escape from that prospect is to eliminate and keep on eliminating not only the one out of four from certain unions who in a Mendelian calculation will be overtly afflicted with, for example, cystic fibrosis, but also the two out of four who will be carriers. (It has been estimated to require seventeen million abortions to eliminate that one genetic disease alone.)

A public advisory commission might help geneticists and physicians deal with this conflict between an individual's medical need and the effect which his healing may have in preventing a normal, balancing elimination of genetic defects. It is difficult for me to understand what society's proper judgment would be in these grave matters; but I suppose that would be the job for an advisory commission. It is difficult to believe that a profession which soon may undertake to conquer aging will have the courage and the wisdom to see that not even the defeat of

Beyond Morality: Fundamental Questions

We should, finally, go deeper than morality into the anthropology that governs or is fostered by genetic science and technical genetic appliances. We can say with certainty that if the doctrine of man underlying the contemporary science of genetics is profoundly antithetical to the doctrine of man in the Judeo-Christian tradition, or in the authentic humanism that has the blessing and support of that religious tradition, this will manifest itself through the behavior of men in this period. The unquestioned, silently operating ethical premises from which we reason, to which we do not reason circuitously or consecutively, and by which all other things are judged, are always expressions of man's view of himself, his nature and being. If philosophical anthropology is in disarray, morality will be so also. If the ethic seemingly required by science is in conflict with a Christian or other humanism, it is because the vision of man fostered (even if thoughtlessly) by the revolutionary biology lays down a broad challenge to every humanistic vision of man.

To this our contemporary moral confusion traces home, and here we must choose whom we shall serve. It is not enough to discuss procedures by which a society can decide the uses to which biomedical knowledge is to be put. Our fundamental decisions will be made—perhaps they have already been made—at the point where we accept a particular understanding of man.

This choice underlies many of the silently operating standards by which we measure the use and abuse of our rapidly advancing knowledge.

Anyone who remains within hailing distance of the biblical view of the life of this "flesh" knows that we are our bodies no less than we are our souls, minds, or wills. He knows that to violate this flesh is a violation of man no less than to violate man's will or freedom, and his ethical reflection will express this. By contrast, a so-called scientific ethic, an ethic which tries to base itself on the intentionality of the scientific mind alone, nearly always regards mind or will or freedom (though some deny the last) as the only thing that can be violated in man. According to this view, our bodies and our genes do not belong essentially to human nature. At least they are not part of that nature which has sanctity, which places moral claims upon us, and which should be cherished as a matter of stewardship. They are rather matter to be used for self-elected ends. These lower parts are classed among the nonhuman world over which God gave man dominion. So there is no reason why man should not become his own maker, the maker of all future generations, and the remaker of the nature of human parenthood.

Geneticists, of course, are troubled humanists. Still, piece by piece, genetic science seems to be leading to an additive view of man: Man is determined in theory yet boundlessly free in practice to change all that. He has no natural standard to guide him but needs only the advisory opinions of other equally towering "freedoms" to help decide what should be done or not done.

The underlying anthropology, the additive view of man is this: Each of us is a package of normal abnormalities or abnormal normalities, combinations of more or less weak genetic strengths and more or less strong genetic weaknesses, plus a number of defects that have arisen with us to be passed on in the species' gene pool. This scientific anthropology claims to have replaced Augustine's theological insight that ours is a "dying life" and a "living death"—but "explained" is the word, not "replaced," since the cellular secrets of aging and dying are now said to be open to us and subject to fundamental change. The creation in us, now known, is to be altered into something that never was. The most poignant sign that man begins to die the moment he lives, the genetic defects responsible for 40 percent of all non-trauma deaths in children's hospitals, should be eliminated. ". . . Mistakes in the genetic information carried in the cells are responsible for an enormous amount of human suffering and death" (p. 110). That is clear. Also clear is that human suffering and death are then "mistakes" and that at bottom we are all "mistakes," some more serious than others. It is all a question of "defective information." ". . . The knowledge necessary to decipher completely the language of the cell"

is. ". . . Techniques are now being developed," we are told, "to do extensive screening from just one drop of blood from the newborn infant" (p. 116). At this point, anyone familiar with the biblical point of view is liable to exclaim that "the blood is the life" (Deuteronomy 12:23; cf. Leviticus 17:14). That is, one drop of scrutinized blood will reveal the whole life, its entire genetic composition, its myriad defects, its end from the beginning, even behavioral propensities which will show up along the way and which are soon to be the subject of genetic research. Jehovah's Witnesses who use that verse as scriptural authority for refusing to have another's life transfused into them seem in a strange way to have been proved right, though not in their practical moral conclusions.

Dostoevsky's hope—against environmental perfectionists who would rationalize all suffering away—was that an undergroundling would come to stick out his tongue at living in a Crystal Palace or being reduced to the handle on a hurdy-gurdy or a key on the keyboard of a piano even if they played a merry social tune. Against genetic perfectionists who would rationalize human suffering away, the health of the human race may require an undergroundling who will stick out his tongue at genetic screening that aims to tell us all the mistakes we are. Who wants to know all that, or have others know it, from the blood that is his life? Who wants to know his end from the beginning?

In April, 1971, the National Academy of Science appointed a

special committee on "genetic factors in human performance."
Going forward with general studies in the field of "behavioral
genetics," the Academy at the same time rejected a proposal to
research the correlation of genetic behavioral differences with
racial differences—while still calling the latter "a proper and
socially relevant sceintific subject."[6] This was a rebuff of the
proposal by Dr. William Shockley that a high priority be given
to studies of possible racial factors in intelligence.

If in the present society more harm than good would result
from funding the research of "a proper and socially relevant
scientific subject" because of its racial overtones, we may at
least raise the question whether the individual might be endangered by the acquisition, in any society, of complete knowledge of his "behavioral genetics." Such knowledge may be too
heavy for many to bear and still remain spontaneous and free in
their personal lives. Moreover, such knowledge—so far at least—
means control and successful attempts to condition or alter the
subject. We have not raised the ethical question—the question of
the good for man, not first of all the good for scientific
knowledge—until we raise other questions: Do we want to live
in a world in which behavioral genetics is a master science? In
which the means exist to know, modify, and control all con-
querable genetic processes? In which government officials or
elite groups of scientists "can determine, through weather modification, whether and where it will rain, snow or shine; what the
temperature will be; and how the winds will blow"? In which
they can read people's minds, direct their thoughts, and control
their emotions and actions by chemical techniques?[7]

In our scientific, rationalistic, mind-body dualistic age, we are
greatly alarmed over the existence of banks of computerized
information about the things a man has freely done in his
lifetime. Even more threatening to the humanity of man is the
prospect of computerized information about just who we are in
genetic terms. It was the devil who tempted a king of Israel to
take a census; for to know a man's name was to know him
essentially, and that should be known only to God and on
record in his counsels. In an age in which blood and genes are
believed to be essential to man's life, when hundreds of tests

[6]*The New York Times*, Apr. 29, 1971, p. 24.

[7]Harold P. Green, "Public Policy for Genetic Manipulation," unpublished paper, National Law Center, George Washington University.

can be made from a single drop of blood and every man can be
screened so that his end and the inborn "errors" in him are
known from the beginning, ours is another temptation: to know
fully who a fellowman essentially is, which should be known
only to God and on record in his counsels. Before us then opens
up the dizzy, abysmal prospect that men can be present where
the foundations of the world were laid. Piece by piece of

The benefits and hazards of technology are escalating at unprecedented paces. The benefits of technological achievement, especially those related to specific products, can usually be translated into early and often predictable economic gains; any errors in such predictions economically penalize a very small segment of the population. Hazards—consumer, occupational, and environmental—associated with technological achievement are usually unpredictable, necessitate extensive evaluation, once suspected, and hence are generally viewed as impediments by the innovator. It has long been recognized as unrealistic to expect industry voluntarily to devote sufficient

*Based in part on testimony by the author at hearings on "Chemicals and the Future of Man," before the Subcommittee on Executive Reorganization and Government Research of the Committee on Government Operations, U.S. Senate, Ninety-second Congress, April 6 and 7, 1971.

Professor of pharmacology at Case Western Reserve School of Medicine and first occupant of the David and Mary Ann Swetland Chair of Environmental Health and Human Ecology, Samuel S. Epstein was born in England and received his medical education at the University of London. He studied tropical medicine and bacteriology, receiving a diploma in pathology and the M.D. degree. In 1961 he came to the United States and became interested in the field of toxicology and in problems of environmental pollution. Since 1957, Dr. Epstein has published over one hundred articles in professional journals and has been active as a consultant to time and resources for safety evaluation. Thus, legislative and regulatory mechanisms have been gradually created to improve product safety and minimize harm to humans and to the environment. The validity and utility of these mechanisms are now being critically examined.

Concern for environmental quality, consumer protection, and occupational safety is burgeoning, and some classic assumptions of industrial society are under challenge. Apparent conflicts have arisen between the needs for continued economic growth and for environmental management. The degree of polarization on these issues is reflected in divergent current attitudes to recent restrictions on such products as DDT and cyclamates. It is thus timely to review some basic problems of chemical pollution, develop methods for anticipating and detecting human and environmental hazards, and consider alternative or supplementary legislative and regulatory mechanisms for more rational and effective management.

The chemical environment consists of three primary compartments—air, water, and soil—which coexist in a state of dynamic equilibrium. Although a particular pollutant may be initially distributed predominantly in one primary compartment, generalized translocation may ensue, especially for persistent pollutants. Food—a secondary compartment—reflects possible contributions from pollutants in air, water, and soil.

Although the term pollutant is often pejoratively restricted to synthetic industrial chemicals, there is a wide range of other important chemical pollutants; these fit into four broad categories. The first group consists of natural chemicals in excess and includes nitrates, which are normal dietary components. At high concentrations in food or water, nitrates can cause acute methemoglobinemia in infants. The possible occurrence of

governmental agencies. He testifies frequently before congressional committees in matters of pollution and natural resources. A member of a number of professional committees and societies, he has served as chairman of the Committee on Biological Effects of Air Pollution of the Air Pollution Control Association and as chairman of two Health, Education, and Welfare Department Panels in 1969, one on "Mutagenicity of Pesticides" and the other on "Teratogenicity of Pesticides." Also in 1969 he served as chairman of the National Institute of Mental Health Panel on Chronic Non-psychiatric Hazards of Abuse of Drugs. He is currently Executive Secretary of the Environmental Mutagen Society.

chronic subclinical methemoglobinemia in infants following intake of moderately elevated nitrate levels in water has been recently reported.[1] Moreover, nitrites, reduction products of nitrates, may interact *in vitro* or *in vivo* with secondary amines to form nitrosamines, some of them carcinogenic (producing cancer), teratogenic (producing malformations), and mutagenic (producing hereditary changes) in microgram doses.[2] Oxides of

as well as partially defined components. Finally, there is the group of synthetic chemicals—agricultural chemicals, notably pesticides and fertilizers; food additives, which may be *intentional*, such as antioxidants and dyes, or *accidental*, such as pesticides, heavy metals, and plasticizers; fuel additives; household chemicals; industrial chemicals; and in a somewhat specialized class, therapeutic and prophylactic drugs and drugs of abuse.

Pollutants may induce a wide range of adverse biological effects in man, which are generically and collectively termed toxicity. Acute or chronic toxicity per se may be expressed in fetal, neonatal, perinatal, childhood, or adult life, in effects ranging from impairment of health and fitness to death. More specific manifestations of chronic toxicity include carcino-

[1] S. S. Epstein, Toxicological and Environmental Implications on the Use of Nitrilotriacetic Acid as a Detergent Builder: Report to Senator J. Randolph, Chairman of the U. S. Senate Committee on Public Works (Washington: Government Printing Office, December, 1970). N. Gruener and H. D. Shuval, Health Aspects of Nitrates in Drinking Water. Developments in Water Quality Research, Proceedings of the Jerusalem International Conference on Water Quality and Pollution Research (London: Ann Arbor-Humphrey Science Publishers, June, 1969).

[2] W. Lijinsky and S. S. Epstein 1970, Nitrosamines as Environmental Carcinogens, *Nature* 225:21-23.

[3] L. A. Goldblatt, ed., *Aflatoxin: Scientific Background, Control and Implications* (New York and London: Academic Press, 1969).

genicity, teratogenicity, and mutagenicity. The possibility that chronic toxicity is also manifest in immunological impairment or in psycho-behavioral disorders has yet to be explored.

Some pollutants may induce one or more of these types of toxicity. Pollutants or their chemical precursors may also interact *in vitro* and *in vivo* to produce unanticipated synergistic toxicity. Synergistic effects can also result from interactions between particular pollutants and common, otherwise harmless, environmental chemicals.

The need to use many synthetic industrial chemicals makes it essential to recognize and estimate the human and environmental hazards they pose and their acceptability with regard to the benefits they confer. The costs of one malformed child, based on remedial and custodial care alone and excluding deprivation of earnings, have been recently estimated as about $250,000.[4] Such cost estimation is clearly impossible for genetic hazards, the scope of whose effects in future generations cannot be predicted. Externalized environmental costs have until recently been ignored or discounted.

Hazards from a particular synthetic chemical need not necessarily be accepted even when matching benefits appear high, since nonhazardous, equally effective, alternatives are usually available. The mandatory criterion of efficacy, once extended from therapeutic drugs to other synthetic chemicals such as food additives and pesticides, may well simplify such equations, especially for hazards from synthetic chemicals with no demonstrable benefits for the general population.

There is now little doubt that many harmful effects hitherto regarded as spontaneous, including cancer, birth defects, and mutations, are caused by environmental pollutants. This realization is heightened by the exponential increase in human exposure to new synthetic chemicals—and their degradation and pyrolytic products in air, water, and soil—which in general are inadequately characterized toxicologically and environmentally.

Three Public Health Hazards

Recognition is now growing that the majority of human cancers are probably due to chemical carcinogens in the en-

4 M. W. Oberle 1969, Lead Poisoning: A Preventable Childhood Disease of the Slums, *Science* 165:991-992.

vironment and that they are hence ultimately preventable. There is also growing interest in the role of chemical carcinogens in activating tumor-producing viruses. Epidemiological studies have revealed wide geographical variations in the incidence of cancer of various organs in the general population; in some instances these studies have incriminated local environmental pollutants.

a potent fungal carcinogen, and to eating Cycad plants, containing azoxyglucoside carcinogens, respectively. The high incidence of gastric cancer in Japan, Iceland, and Chile has been associated with high dietary intake of fish; suggestions have been made implicating nitrosamines, formed by reactions between secondary amines in fish and nitrite preservatives. The high incidence of cancer of the esophagus in Zambians drinking Kachasu spirits may be related to its high nitrosamine contamination. A wide range of occupationally induced cancers is also well recognized. These include bladder cancer in the aniline dye and rubber industry, lung cancer in uranium miners of Colorado and in workers in nitrogen mustard factories in Japan, nasal sinus cancer in wood workers, pleural and peritoneal mesotheliomas in asbestos workers, and skin cancer in shale oil workers.

Two major classes of environmental carcinogens may be identified. First are *potent carcinogens* such as aflatoxins and nitrosamines, which can produce cancer in experimental animals even at the very low levels in which they have been found in foods. Identification of these carcinogens in foods has encouraged attempts to link their distribution with local patterns of cancer incidence. Second are *weak carcinogens*, such as atmospheric pollutants, certain pesticides, and food additives, whose effects may easily escape detection by conventional biological tests. Because such weak carcinogens are unlikely to be clearly implicated epidemiologically, they may pose as great hazards as the more obvious potent carcinogens. In spite of these difficulties, there is considerable epidemiologic support for a causal relationship between community air pollution and lung cancer. There are marked regional differences in lung cancer mortality patterns in the United States; increased mortality is clearly related to increased urbanization and to increased levels of organic pollutants in the air. The higher lung cancer rates in urban areas cannot be fully explained by factors such as smoking or occupation. In a survey some twelve years ago, lung cancer rates in the United States, standardized for smoking besides age, were found to be 39 in 100,000 in rural areas and 52 in 100,000 in cities with populations in excess of 50,000.[5] Similar surveys in England also confirmed the importance of this urban factor and stressed its interaction with smoking.[6] This urban excess, of 25 percent mortality in the United States, is generally regarded as being due to air pollution. Confirmatory evidence is also afforded by several studies on immigrants who tend to retain the incidence pattern of lung cancer of their country of origin, even though they assume the smoking and other habits of their country of adoption.

A second public health hazard is mutagenicity. The first evidence that environmental pollutants may influence the genetic constitution of future populations came some four decades ago from the discovery that high energy radiation induces mutations. The subsequent development of nuclear energy added a new dimension and enhanced awareness of the problem of genetic hazards. Safeguards have been accordingly developed to minimize radiation exposure. Once radiation-induced mutagenesis was discovered there were reasons to suspect that some chemicals would act similarly, but proof of this was delayed until World War II, when mustard gas was shown to induce mutations in fruit flies. Many and varied types of chemicals have subsequently been shown to be mutagenic. The likelihood that some highly mutagenic chemicals may come into wide use, or indeed may already be in wide use, is now causing serious concern.

[5] E. C. Hammond and D. Horn 1958, Smoking and Death Rates: Report on Forty-four Months of Follow-up of 186,763 Men, *J.A.M.A.* 166:1294-1308.

[6] P. Stocks 1960, On the Relations Between Atmospheric Pollution in Urban and Rural Localities and Mortality from Cancer, Bronchitis and Pneumonia, with Particular Reference to 3,4-Benzyprene, Beryllium, Molybdenum, Vanadium, and Arsenic, *Brit. J. Cancer* 14:397-418.

A mutation is defined as any inherited change in the genetic material. This may be a chemical transformation of an individual gene (which is designated a gene or point mutation) that causes it to have an altered function. Alternatively, the change may involve a rearrangement, or a gain or loss, of parts of a chromosome, which may be microscopically visible and is desig-

defects in somatic cells of the adult or fetus respectively. Mutations in germ cells are more serious still, as these may be transmitted to future generations. It should be emphasized that there is no single type of mutagenic effect. Since every part of the body and every metabolic process is influenced by genetic control, the range of effects produced by gene alterations includes all conceivable types of structure and process. At one extreme are lethal effects, consequences so severe that the individual cannot survive. If cell death occurs very early in embryonic development, it may never be detected; extensive cell death at a later stage may lead to abortion. Approximately one-fourth of spontaneous abortions show a detectable chromosome aberration; there is no way at present to know how many of the remainder are caused by gene mutations or by visually undetectable chromosome aberrations. If the embryo survives until birth, a variety of physical abnormalities may be manifest. There are numerous known inherited diseases and probably many more that are unknown, all of which owe their ultimate cause to mutations. While these are individually rare, collectively they are a cause for serious public health concern. At the other extreme are gene mutations with mild effects. Finally, those with still smaller effects may be imperceptible. In between these extremes is the whole gamut of genetic defects.

Mutations can produce a wide diversity of deleterious effects, many of them similar to those produced by nongenetic causes. The impact of environmental mutagens is thus statistical rather than unique. This problem is further complicated by the time distribution of mutational effects. Some mutant genes are dominant, in which case the abnormality or disease will appear in the generation immediately following occurrence of the mutation. Dominant mutations express themselves as early fetal deaths or in abnormalities, such as achondroplasia, polydactyly, retinoblastoma, and sterility. On the other hand, the mutation may be recessive, requiring the presence of abnormal genes in both homologous chromosomes—one derived from each parent—to produce the effect. Recessive mutations, such as albinism, Fanconi anemia, amaurotic idiocy, and phenylketonuria, may be unexpressed for many generations. The major effects of increased mutation rates would thus be less obvious and spread over many generations and would include ill-defined abnormalities such as premature aging, enhanced susceptibility to various diseases (notably leukemia and cancer), and alterations in sex ratios.[7]

The great majority of mutations are harmful or, at best, neutral. This has been established experimentally and is a deduction from the principle of natural selection.[8] Natural selection has previously eliminated those individuals whose mutant genes caused them to be abnormal. As a result, an approximate equilibrium has been established between the introduction of new mutant genes into the population and the elimination of old mutant genes by natural selection. With present high standards of living and health care, many mutants that in the past would have caused death or reduced fertility now persist. The equilibrium is thus out of balance, and new mutants are being added to the population faster than they can be eliminated. This, coupled with near eradication of many infectious diseases, makes it likely that future medical problems will be increasingly of genetic origin. As Lederberg has recently stated:

> If we give proper weight to the genetic component of many common diseases which have a more complex etiology than the textbook examples of Mendelian defects, we can calculate that at

[7] J. F. Crow 1968, Chemical Risk to Future Generations, *Scientist and Citizen* 10:113-117. Report of the Advisory Panel on Mutagenicity, pp. 565-654; Report of the Secretary's Commission on Pesticides and Their Relationship to Environmental Health, U. S. Department of Health, Education and Welfare, Dec. 1969.

[8] Crow 1968, *ibid.*

least 25 percent of our health burden is of genetic origin. This figure is a very conservative estimate in view of the genetic component of such griefs as schizophrenia, diabetes, atherosclerosis, mental retardation, early senility and many congenital malformations. In fact, the genetic factor in disease is bound to increase to an even larger proportion, for as we deal with infectious disease and other environmental insults, the genetic legacy of the species will compete only with traumatic accidents as the major factor in health.[9]

otherwise be dismissed as relatively unimportant. But in any overall consideration, many persons mildly affected may be considered of comparable importance to one individual severely affected. Experiments on *Drosophila* show that mildly deleterious mutations occur with much greater frequency than more severe mutants. Thus, although an increased mutation rate would cause a corresponding increase in severe abnormalities and genetic diseases, the major statistical impact of a mutational increase would be to add to the burden of mild mutation effects, which would be of major public health consequence and yet difficult to detect.

Chemical mutagens in the environment pose hazards which have not yet been quantitated, although sensitive and practical mammalian test systems are available. A report of the genetic study section of the National Institutes of Health states:

> There is reason to fear that some chemicals may constitute as important a risk as radiation, possibly a more serious one. Although knowledge of chemical mutagenesis in man is much less certain than that of radiation, a number of chemicals—some with widespread use—are known to induce genetic damage in some organisms. To consider only radiation hazards is to ignore what may be the submerged part of the iceberg.

9 J. Lederberg, in foreword to S. S. Epstein and M. Legator, ed., *The Mutagenicity of Pesticides: Concepts and Evaluation* (Cambridge, Mass.: M. I. T. Press, 1971), p. x.

The report further states:

> Recent investigations have revealed chemical compounds that are highly mutagenic in experimental organisms, in concentrations that are not toxic and that have no overt effect on fertility. . . .[10]

Ethyleneimines are good examples of highly mutagenic chemicals used for many purposes, including therapy of neoplastic and non-neoplastic diseases, chemosterilant insecticides, pigment dyeing and printing, fireproofing and creaseproofing of fabrics and textiles, ingredients in solid rocket fuels, intermediates in many industrial syntheses, and as cross linking agents in starches and shampoos. A joint United States Department of Agriculture and Dow Chemical Corporation study is currently determining whether ethyleneimine-modified flours and starches can be used as paper sizing agents. Ethyleneimines have also been proposed for rodent and plant control. Another example of a mutagen in common use is trimethylphosphate, which till recently was added to gasoline at concentrations of one-fourth gram per gallon for controlling surface ignition and spark plug fouling. It is also used as methylating agent, chemical intermediate in production of polymethyl polyphosphates, flame-retardant solvent for paints and polymers, and catalyst in preparation of polymers and resins. Trimethylphosphate is mutagenic in the dominant lethal assay in mice, and it produces chromosomal damage in bone marrow cells of rats following oral or parenteral administration at subtoxic doses.[11] It is difficult, however, to estimate mutagenic hazards to which the general population has been exposed in the absence of information on the concentration of unreacted trimethylphosphate and biologically active pyrolytic products in automobile exhaust. Similar considerations apply to recent fuel additive formulations based on triarylphosphates.

Fortunately, recent recognition of genetic hazards due to chemicals has been paralleled by the development of various tests for mutagenicity.[12] Submammalian test organisms—

[10]Crow 1968, *op. cit.*

[11]S. S. Epstein 1970, Mutagenicity of Trimethylphosphate in Mice, *Science* 168:584-586. I. D. Adler, G. Ramarao, and S. S. Epstein 1971, In Vivo Cytogenetic Effects of Trimethylphosphate and of TEPA on the bone marrow cells of male rats, *Mutation Research* 13:263-273.

[12]Report of the Advisory Panel on Mutagenicity, pp. 565-654.

bacteria, *Neurospora*, yeasts, plants, and *Drosophila*—help elucidate basic mechanisms. But in view of the wide metabolic and biochemical discrepancies between these systems and man, submammalian tests should be used to provide data ancillary to more relevant test systems. Of these, three *in vivo* mammalian tests are practical and sensitive: *in vivo* cytogenetics, the host-mediated assay, and the dominant lethal assay. Results from

iously estimated as ranging from 3 to 4 percent of total live births. Three major categories of human teratogens have so far been identified: viral infections, X- irradiation, and chemicals. Although the teratogenicity of various chemicals had been experimentally recognized for several decades, only after the thalidomide disaster of 1962 were legislative requirements for three-generation reproductive tests established. However, the adequacy of these tests for teratogenicity has been questioned.[14]

Methods for Predictive Testing and Monitoring of Adverse Human Effects

Pollutants to which man is exposed must be tested for acute and chronic toxicity per se and also for the more specific effects of carcinogenicity, teratogenicity, and mutagenicity. Historically, each of these effects has been studied and applied independently and by nonconverging disciplines. Toxicity per se has largely been the province of classical pharmacologists, generally with little interest in carcinogenesis or mutagenesis. This apparent parochialism was exemplified by the view commonly held in the mid-fifties that the chronic toxicity test is inappro-

[13] *Ibid.*

[14] Report of the Advisory Panel on Teratogenicity, H.E.W. 1969, pp. 656-677.

priate for determining carcinogenicity.[15] The belated regulatory requirement for teratogenicity evaluation—imposed somewhat indirectly, however, as a three-generation reproductive test—in response to the thalidomide disaster is further illustrative. Mutagenesis has been even more isolated than other aspects of toxicology. Indeed, publications on mutagenic hazards are still rarities in toxicological or public health journals and appear for the most part only in genetic journals. The present fragmentation of toxicological research thus appears somewhat artificial. New organizational patterns and training programs are needed to coordinate toxicological approaches and to make toxicology more responsive to current needs.

New and more sophisticated methods for toxicity testing must be developed which are more sensitive and responsive to low and even ambient levels of individual chemical pollutants and various mixtures of pollutants, reflecting more realistic patterns of environmental exposure. Illustrative is the recent demonstration that a wide range of nonspecific stresses, including temporary deprivation of food, cage crowding, parturition, and lactation, markedly increased the toxicity of ambient levels of DDT for rodents.[16]

Toxicity testing must not be confined to the test agent per se, but should extend to its chemical and metabolic derivatives, its pyrolytic and degradation products, and its contaminants and reaction products. These considerations are further accentuated when the various derivatives or degradation products are of toxicological or environmental consequence. Illustrative are the presence of polychlorophenol contaminants and their dioxin pyrolytic products in phenoxy herbicides,[17] cyclohexylamine as a contaminant and human metabolic product of cyclamates,[18] and the uncharacterized biodegradation products of the detergent nitrilotriacetic acid.[19] It is thus obvious that

[15] J. M. Barnes and F. A. Denz 1954, Experimental Methods Used in Determining Chronic Toxicity, *Pharmac. Rev.* 6:191-242.

[16] R. Dubos and G. Paulson 1971, unpublished data.

[17] S. S. Epstein, Testimony on Teratogenic Effects of 2,4,5-T Formulations; U. S. Senate Hearings before the Subcommittee on Energy, Natural Resources and the Environment of the Committee on Commerce, Apr. 15, 1970.

[18] National Academy of Sciences, National Research Council, Report on Non-nutritive Sweeteners (Nov., 1968).

[19] S. S. Epstein, Testimony on Potential Biological Hazards Due to

comprehensive safety testing requires detailed chemical and comparative metabolic data on the agent under test. The requirements for such data may necessitate carefully controlled metabolic studies in human volunteers, once safety has been established in comprehensive animal tests.

In any form of toxicity testing, agents must be administered acutely, subacutely, and chronically to reflect the role of

Routes of test administration *inter alia* should reflect human exposure. While inhalation is the obvious route for testing of air pollutants, the importance of this route for other pollutants has been generally underestimated. Respiratory exposure is of particular human significance for pesticide aerosols and vapors. Surprisingly, there are no data in the pesticide literature on chronic inhalation tests. While useful information may also be derived from tests involving inappropriate routes of administration, extrapolation from these data to human experience should be cautious. However, to demonstrate the presence of weak carcinogens in the environment, it is essential that the most sensitive test system available be used and that the factor of comparability of route of administration be subordinated to the requirement of sensitivity. Once an effect has been clearly established, the quantitative relevance of the experimental data to the human situation should be considered before limits can be reasonably proposed; only at this stage is it appropriate to weigh factors such as route of administration. To use such factors in a limiting sense, and to insist on precise comparability between test systems and human exposure before the hazard is established, may effectively limit the possibility of detecting

Nitrates in Water and Due to the Proposed Use of Nitrilotriacetic Acid Detergents, U. S. Senate Hearings before the Subcommittee on Air and Water Pollution of the Committee on Public Works, May 6, 1970. Epstein, Toxicological and Environmental Implications on the Use of Nitrilotriacetic Acid, *op. cit.*

weak environmental carcinogens. Such limitations would also challenge the human implications of all but the most recent data on experimental tobacco carcinogenesis.

Ideally and minimally, two mammalian species should be tested for toxicity per se, carcinogenicity, mutagenicity, and teratogenicity. In certain circumstances, when there is specific information that the rodent metabolism of the chemical pollutant in question is qualitatively different from that in humans, other more appropriate species such as pigs and subhuman primates may also be tested. Reliance on small numbers of pigs or primates is no substitute for conventional rodent tests and may even mislead. Special considerations may dictate the use of less common species in particular circumstances.

For carcinogenicity, teratogenicity, and mutagenicity, pollutants must be tested at higher levels than those of general human exposure;[20] regardless of route of administration, maximally tolerated doses are recommended for this purpose as the highest dose in dose-response studies. Testing at high doses is essential to the attempt to reduce the gross insensitivity imposed on animal tests by the small size of samples routinely tested, perhaps fifty rats or mice per dose level per chemical, compared with the millions of humans at presumptive risk.[21] To illustrate: Suppose man is as sensitive to a particular carcinogen or teratogen as the rat or mouse; suppose further that this particular agent will produce cancer or teratogenic effects in one out of ten thousand humans exposed. Then the chances of detecting this in groups of fifty rats or mice, tested at ambient human exposure levels, would be very low. Indeed, samples of ten thousand rats or mice would be required to yield one cancer or teratogenic event, over and above any spontaneous occurrences; for significance, perhaps thirty thousand rodents would be needed.[22]

Of course, in any particular instance, humans may be less or more sensitive than rodents to the chemical in question. There is consequently no valid basis for the prediction of the relative sensitivities of test animals and man. Meclizine, for example, an

[20]Reports of the Advisory Panels on Carcinogenicity, Mutagenicity, and Teratogenicity, H.E.W. 1969.

[21] *Ibid.*

[22] S. S. Epstein, A. Hollaender, J. Lederberg, M. Legator, H. Richardson, and A. H. Wolff 1969, Wisdom of Cyclamate Ban, *Science* 166:1575.

antihistamine drug used in treatment of morning sickness, is teratogenic in the rat but not apparently in the few women studied.[23] By contrast, for thalidomide the lowest effective human teratogenic dose is 0.5 milligrams per kilogram of body weight per day; the corresponding values for the mouse, rat, dog, and hamster are 30, 50, 100, and 350, respectively.[24] Thus man is 60 times more sensitive than mice, 100 times more sensitive

the impossibility of gauging human sensitivity from animal tests, ample data on interactions between carcinogens further confirm that it is not possible to predict safe levels of carcinogens based on an arbitrary fraction of the lowest effective animal dose in a particular experimental situation. As Health, Education, and Welfare Secretary Flemming stated ten years ago: "Scientifically, there is no way to determine a safe level for a substance known to produce cancer in animals."[26] The production of hepatomas in trout by feeding as little as 0.4 parts per billion of aflatoxin B_1 is sharply enhanced by addition of various noncarcinogenic oils to the diet.[27] Similarly, carcino-

[23] C. J. King 1965, Antihistamines and Teratogenicity in the Rat, *J. Pharm. Exp. Therap.* 147:391-398. J. Yerushalamy and L. Milkovich 1965, Evaluation of the Teratogenic Effects of Meclizine, *Amer. J. Obstet. Gynecol.* 93:553-562.

[24] H. Kalter, *Teratology of the Nervous System* (Chicago: Univ. of Chicago Press, 1968).

[25] W. C. Hueper, *Occupational and Environmental Cancers of the Urinary System* (New Haven: Yale University Press, 1969).

[26] A. Flemming, Hearings on Color Additives before the House Committee on Interstate and Foreign Commerce, 86th Congress, 2nd Session, 501, 1960.

[27] R. O. Sinhuber, J. H. Wales, J. L. Ayers, R. H. Engebrecht, and D. L. Amend 1968, Dietary Factors and Hepatoma in Rainbow Trout (*Salmo gairdneri*); 1. Aflatoxins in Vegetable Protein Feedstuffs, *J. Nat. Cancer Inst.* 41:711-718.

genesis for mouse skin of low concentrations of benzo[a]pyrene and benz[a]anthracene is increased one thousand times by the use of noncarcinogenic n-dodecane as a solvent.[28] Intratracheal instillation of benzo[a]pyrene and ferric oxide in adult hamsters elicited a high incidence of lower respiratory tract tumors only in animals pretreated at birth with a single low dose of diethylnitrosamine.[29] Such considerations underlie the 1958 Delaney Amendment to the Federal Food, Drug, and Cosmetic Act, which imposes zero tolerances for carcinogenic food additives. The amendment states, " . . . No additive shall be deemed to be safe if it is found, after tests which are appropriate for the evaluation of the safety of food additives, to induce cancer in man or animal. . . ." Zero tolerances should also be imposed for occupational carcinogens such as asbestos.

It must also be emphasized that testing at high dosages does not produce false positive carcinogenic results. There is no basis whatsoever for the contention that all chemicals are carcinogenic or mutagenic at high doses. To illustrate, in the recent bionetics study, sponsored by the National Cancer Institute, about 140 pesticides were tested orally in mice of both sexes and strains at maximally tolerated doses from the first week of life until sacrifice at eighteen months; less than 10 percent of these pesticides were found to be carcinogenic.[30]

Experimental finding of carcinogenicity, mutagenicity, and teratogenicity in synthetic industrial chemicals, such as pesticides and food additives, is unusual. Once carcinogenicity has been determined, similarly efficacious but noncarcinogenic alternatives are generally available. Methoxychlor, for instance, can replace the persistent and carcinogenic DDT; moreover, the efficacy of DDT for its major usage in the United States—cotton insect control—is now questionable, owing to the emergence of

[28] E. Bingham and H. L. Falk 1969, Environmental Carcinogens: Modifying Effect of Carcinogens on the Threshold Response, *Arch. Env. Health* 19:779-783.

[29] R. Montesano, U. Saffiotti, and P. Shubik, The Role of Topical and Systemic Factors in Experimental Respiratory Carcinogenesis, in U. S. Atomic Energy Commission, Inhalation Carcinogenesis, April, 1970, p. 353.

[30] J. R. M. Innes, B. M. Ulland, M. G. Valerio, *et al.* 1969, Bioassay of Pesticides and Industrial Chemicals for Tumorigenicity in Mice: A Preliminary Note, *J. Nat. Cancer Inst.* 43:1101-1114. Report of the Advisory Panel on Carcinogenicity, H.E.W. 1969, pp. 459-506.

insecticide resistance.[31]   Similar considerations obtain for Mirex, another persistent and carcinogenic insecticide, whose utility for the eradication of the imported fire ant (at worst a minor pest) has been recently challenged.[32] These considerations apply with even greater force to carcinogenic intentional food additives, such as the recently banned cyclamates, that were virtually useless for the general population.[33] Special pleas

tion products with known or presumed toxicological relevance need be monitored.

Even with well-planned and well-executed toxicologic testing, it is likely that unexpected adverse effects from pollutants will be seen in man, reflecting the insensitivity or inappropriateness of the test systems. Epidemiological surveys of human and animal populations may provide *post hoc* information on geographical or temporal clusters of unusual types or frequencies of adverse effects—including cancer, birth defects, and mutations—after exposure to undetected or untested pollutants in the environment. Such surveys are complicated by the long interval which may elapse between exposure and subsequent adverse effects. This may be measured in decades for cancer and in generations for mutations.

Epidemiologic techniques serve to detect trends or fluctuations in mortality, morbidity, and disease patterns. Provided that clear differentials in exposure levels to pollutants exist in the general population, epidemiology may then correlate particular toxic effects with particular pollutants; the relationship between heavy cigarette smoking and lung cancer is a classic example. However, these relationships are more difficult to

31 R. Bosch, 1970, Pesticides: Prescribing for the Ecosystem, *Environment* 12:12-15. Diminishing Returns (staff report), *Environment* 11:6-36.

32 D. W. Coon and R. R. Fleet 1970, The Ant War, *Environment* 12:28-39.

33Epstein, Hollaender, Lederberg, *et al.*, *op. cit.*

establish when exposure differentials are minimal, as with a food additive consumed by the general population at not widely dissimilar levels. Moreover, logistic considerations, quite apart from inadequate current surveillance systems, may limit the utility of epidemiological approaches even when temporal or geographical clusters of adverse effects have developed. Disquietingly, no major known human teratogen—X-rays, German measles, mercury, or thalidomide—has been formally epidemiologically identified, even in industrialized countries with good medical facilities.[34]

One of the most critical needs is for development of comprehensive national surveillance and registration systems for birth defects and mutations. This could simply operate by referral of any obvious birth defects to a specialized regional center. As the incidence of obvious birth defects in the United States is approximately 2 percent, this sample would very likely include effects induced by environmental teratogens or mutagens. Recognition of temporal or geographical clustering of such effects might permit the isolation of causal environmental influences.

In order to monitor mutation rates accurately, special indicator traits would need to be selected. These would have to be dominant, unique, present obviously and conspicuously at birth, and associated with sterility, to obviate the possibility of parental transmission. In addition to such relatively gross approaches, more refined monitoring procedures could be developed cytogenetically and biochemically, as both intrauterine and neonatal tests.

The study of spontaneous abortion has recently been recommended as a simple and practical method for monitoring mutation rates.[35] The required parameters would include the proportion of pregnancies spontaneously aborting; the proportion of abortions due to fetal failure rather than maternal malfunction; the proportion of analyzable abortuses with chromosome aberrations; and the incidence of chromosome aberrations, such as trisomy, XO, and polyploidy. The most informative single statistic for monitoring the mutation rate would be the proportion of all pregnancies with an abortus; the

---

[34]Report of the Advisory Panel on Teratogenicity, H.E.W. 1969, pp. 656-677.

[35]A. J. Bateman 1970, A personal communication.

spontaneous incidence of these is approximately one percent. The same data could be used for polyploidy, for nondisjunction (parallel increase of both trisomy and XO), and for teratogenic effects, which would also be detected among full-term pregnancies. Teratogens may produce chromosome aberrations as well, but since they act after fertilization the aberrations will be sporadic against a normal background. The action of teratogens

such as carbon monoxide, aromatic amines, dioxins, nitrosamines, asbestos, enzyme detergents, and heavy metals. It is to be hoped that adequate legislation will be developed and enforced to stop the use of workmen as unwitting guinea pigs for society. In this connection, it should be pointed out that available National Consensus Standards relate to only a small fraction of toxic chemicals to which workmen are exposed, and further that most of these standards are based on grossly inadequate and outdated information.

Current toxicological techniques are insensitive and relatively limited in their ability to detect weak carcinogens and other toxic agents individually and in various combinations or mixtures realistically reflecting low or ambient levels and patterns of environmental exposure. Similarly, epidemiological techniques are unlikely to detect weak carcinogens and other toxic agents, unless there are sharp differentials in exposure of the general population, as with cigarette smoking. For widely dispersed agents, such as intentional or accidental food additives to which the population at large is generally exposed, human experience is unlikely to provide any meaningful indication of safety or hazard.

Illustrative Current Problems with Food Additives

Diethylstilbestrol (DES) is a synthetic estrogen which is mixed with cattle feed or administered parenterally to increase the efficiency of protein conversion from feed. The efficacy of DES in improving the texture and quality of meat, however, has not been demonstrated. DES is carcinogenic to many species,[36] and produces a high incidence of mammary carcinomas when fed to mice at levels as low as 0.2 micrograms per gram.[37] For these reasons, the FDA has imposed a zero tolerance for DES in meat.

It is required that DES be removed from cattle feed forty-eight hours prior to slaughter in order to prevent the occurrence of residues in meat, which would violate the Delaney amendment. In the absence of adequate sampling and analytic programs, it is difficult to determine whether farmers and feed lot operators are voluntarily complying with this law. Recently it has been alleged that USDA inspection and sampling is inadequate in that less than five hundred out of thirty million cattle treated annually with DES are examined for residues, and further that the analytic techniques employed cannot detect residues at levels of less than two parts per billion.[38] Even so, USDA records show that DES is detected in an average of one out of every two hundred cattle tested. Thus we are ingesting levels of DES in our diet which cumulatively exceed the oral carcinogenic dose for mice. For these and other reasons, Sweden and many other European countries will not import United States beef unless it is certified as additive-free by the USDA.[39] The question of whether DES enters drinking water as a contaminant from feed lots also merits further consideration.

Nitrites are added to fish and processed meats at permissible levels of two hundred parts per million. The functions of nitrites are to improve the appearance of the meat, and also to act as a preservative, particularly to inhibit Clostridal contamination. Such levels of nitrites pose no acute hazard to adults, although under certain restricted circumstances they can produce acute methemoglobinemia in infants.

Over the last decade, however, evidence has accumulated that nitrites can combine with secondary amines—which are com-

[36] P. Shubik and J. L. Hartwell, Survey of Compounds Which Have Been Tested for Carcinogenic Activity, Supplement 2, U. S. Dept. of Health, Education, and Welfare, 1969.

[37] R. A. Huseby 1959, *Proc. Amer. Assoc. Canc. Res.* 3:29.

[38] H. Wellford 1971, A personal communication.

[39] V. Barry (Director of Meat and Poultry Inspection, USDA), oral statement, Apr. 1, 1971.

mon dietary components, besides being found in tobacco smoke and drugs—to produce a class of chemicals known as nitrosamines which are highly carcinogenic and possibly the major candidate group of human carcinogens.[40] There is a growing body of direct and indirect evidence from several laboratories that such nitrosamine synthesis occurs in food and in the gastrointestinal tract of animals. Exactly what this means in

> ... These suspicions would make it impossible under present regulations for the agency to approve the present level of nitrite if the compound had been discovered last week. But that is because you would not have the factor of human experience. Man is the most important experimental animal and nitrites have not been linked to cancer in all the years that man has been eating the chemical.[43]

Yet for reasons discussed above, it is unlikely that human experience could have established causal associations between nitrite ingestion and cancer.

Clearly, further investigation is needed on nitrosamine biosynthesis, on the efficacy of nitrites, and also on the identification of more acceptable preservatives.

Regulatory and Legislative Deficiencies and Needs

Federal regulatory agencies suffer from certain limitations and constraints. Jurisdiction over products and their applications is commonly fragmented among the sixty or so executive

[40] Lijinsky and Epstein, *op. cit.*

[41] W. Lijinsky, Testimony Before the Intergovernmental Relations Subcommittee, House Committee on Government Operations, Mar. 16, 1971.

[42] *Meat Science Review* 1971, AMI Foundation, chap. 5:1.

[43] L. L. Ramsay, quoted in *National Observer*, Mar. 22, 1971.

agencies concerned with environmental problems. Moreover, there are certain categories of products, notably industrial chemicals, for which there are only minimal regulatory controls, if any.

Agencies are generally inadequately funded and are subjected to political pressure and lobbying by vested interests. Federal agencies tend to be preoccupied with highly visible, immediate problems as they move from crisis to crisis. Anticipation and prevention of crisis situations, which should be major aims of regulatory agencies, and awareness of the need for a more systematic approach to consumer, occupational, and environmental safety are often lacking.

Legislative responsibility in environmental and related areas now extends to some twenty congressional committees. Occupational exposure to toxic chemicals and dusts and to noise and stress, exposure of the public at large to industrial effluents in air and water (such as sulfur dioxide and mercury), and consumer exposure to common industrial products (such as detergents and fuel additives) are inadequately dealt with legislatively and thus inadequately regulated. Deficiencies in establishing safety criteria and deficiencies in regulatory practice may be illustrated by reference to recent or current problems: the carcinogenicity, mutagenicity, and ecological effects of the insecticide DDT; the teratogenicity of the herbicide 2,4,5-T and its dioxin contaminants; the carcinogenicity and mutagenicity of the food additive cyclamate; and the little-known toxicology of the detergent ingredient nitrilotriacetic acid (NTA), quite apart from its questionable efficacy in the stated objective of preventing eutrophication due to the use of phosphate detergents. It should be pointed out that serious questions as to the efficacy and safety of NTA were only recently raised[44] in spite of assurances to the contrary, based on ten years' industrial research. Such questions should have been raised at an earlier stage, not after some detergent manufacturers had made irreversible and major economic commitments.

Approximately six hundred food additives, some of which have never been adequately evaluated toxicologically, are now on the FDA "Generally Recognized as Safe" (GRAS) list; both

[44] Epstein 1970, Testimony on Potential Biological Hazards Due to Nitrates in Water, *op. cit.* Epstein 1970, Toxicological and Environmental Implications on the Use of Nitrilotriacetic Acid, *op. cit.*

their toxicological and their legal status is suspect. Proper enforcement of the Food Additive Amendment of 1958 would probably bar the majority of these chemicals from the GRAS list. Before 1958, the criterion for inclusion on the GRAS list was safety, based on scientific evaluation or on experience from common usage in food; after 1958, scientific evaluation should have been the only allowable criterion. Apart from these GRAS

sponsibility for the testing of profitable food chemicals alleged to be safe, as the FDA currently proposes.

Current enforcement of the requirement to stop feeding cattle the carcinogen DES forty-eight hours prior to slaughter now appears to depend largely on the voluntary cooperation of farmers and feed lot operators. There is evidence that this requirement is not being enforced.[45] Moreover, as was mentioned above, it appears that USDA analytic techniques for DES residues in meat are insensitive and that the number of carcasses sampled is inadequate. This problem merits urgent investigation to determine the extent of the exposure of the public to this carcinogenic food additive and the degree to which the Delaney amendment is being violated. Another area where federal meat regulations are not being enforced by the USDA lies in the use of nitrites as preservatives for sliced meat products without appropriate labelling.[46]

Before a new synthetic chemical may be distributed into commerce and the environment, questions as to its efficacy, identity and safety must be posed and satisfactorily answered. Similar questions should also be asked about many existing chemical pollutants, such as the GRAS food additives; these questions should apply, too, to those chemicals for which new alternatives are proposed. Questions on safety must also be

[45] Wellford, *op. cit.*
[46] *Ibid.*

resolved prior to occupational exposure to synthetic chemicals. Does the chemical in question serve a socially and economically useful purpose for the general population? If not, why introduce it and accept potential hazards without general matching benefits? Such considerations clearly apply to the use of monosodium glutamate in baby foods and cyclamates for the public at large. The self-evident need for efficacy, now generally accepted for drugs, should be extended to all synthetic chemicals. These concepts were emphasized at a recent White House conference on nutrition, where it was recommended that food additives be excluded from products unless these conditions are met: they must either significantly improve the quality or nutritive value of the food or lower its cost, and they must be safe.[47]

Standards of safety must be particularly rigorous for persistent chemicals—or for chemicals which yield persistent degradation products—which are environmentally mobile, lipophilic, and consequently likely to accumulate in the food chain. In particular, the industrial use of chemicals in this category such as mercury and polychlorinated biphenyls should be permitted only under carefully controlled conditions, within closed systems which prevent environmental contamination and ensure almost complete chemical recovery.

Synthetic chemicals, with their concentrations and impurities, should be clearly labelled and identified in fuel, foods, pesticides, household items, and all other formulations. Arbitrary exemption of particular products from labelling requirements creates unfortunate precedents and unpredictable toxicological situations.

Besides clear identification of the chemical in question, information about its chemical and pyrolytic products, metabolites, and contaminants is essential for reasonable attempts to anticipate adverse effects. Such data should also permit realistic monitoring in the environment, in animals, and in man. For example, the pesticide Captan degrades, possibly to thiophosgene, within seconds of contact with serum; monitoring Captan in man or animals is thus inappropriate. Again, polychlorophenols, which are major industrial and agricultural chemicals,

[47] D. M. Kendall, A Summary of Panel Recommendations: Report of a Panel on Food Safety to the White House Conference on Food, Nutrition, and Health, Nov. 22, 1969, p. 19.

yield stable and persistent dibenzodioxins when heated. Some dioxins are highly toxic and teratogenic in minute amounts; most dioxins are, however, toxicologically uncharacterized. [48] NTA is already being used as an alternative detergent builder to polyphosphates in an attempt to reduce cultural eutrophication in lakes and rivers; the current annual usage of phosphates in detergents in the United States is approximately two billion

[text illegible]

genicity, and mutagenicity by appropriate routes of administration in two or more species. In addition, microcosm or model ecological studies, an approach which has barely been explored, are critical for predictions of environmental safety.

After the criteria of efficacy, identity, and safety have been satisfied, the new chemical agent may be registered for commerce or otherwise introduced into the environment. Still, the possibility of error due to insensitivity or unsuitability of toxicological and environmental testing must be recognized. Such a contingency can be minimized *post hoc* by ecological, monitoring, and epidemiological studies. Monitoring of levels of chemicals or chemical or metabolic degradation products in the environment, and in body fluids or tissues, presupposes the existence of data on the relevance of a particular chemical pollutant to a particular adverse biological effect. Epidemiological surveys should relate to populations at high risk, apart from the general population; the limited occupational data that currently exist are virtually inaccessible.

48 Epstein 1970, Testimony on Teratogenic Effects of 2,4,5-T Formulations, *op. cit.*

49 Epstein 1970, Testimony on Potential Biological Hazards Due to Nitrates in Water, *op. cit.* Epstein 1970, Toxicological and Environmental Implications on the Use of Nitrilotriacetic Acid, *op. cit.*

50 N. Chernoff and K. D. Courtney 1970, Maternal and Fetal Effects of NTA, NTA and Cadmium, NTA and Mercury, NTA and Nutritional Imbalance in Mice and Rats (unpublished data).

Registrations for synthetic chemicals should be granted on an annual basis, to be reviewed each year in the light of all further evidence that may have developed with regard to human and environmental safety. In addition, such review should examine critically any new evidence on questions relating to efficacy for established and altered patterns of usage and application.

Standards for drugs are maintained in most countries on a national level and by the World Health Organization in the *International Pharmacopoeia*. Similar national and international specifications and registers would be highly desirable for all other categories of synthetic chemicals. Data on safety should be collated and distributed nationally and then internationally. These data on efficacy, chemical identity, toxicology, monitoring, epidemiology, and environmental effects for all synthetic chemicals should be analyzed and stored in a manner suitable for rapid access. Various registries such as the Environmental Mutagen Society Information Center (EMIC) currently deal with different but fragmented aspects of these requirements.

There is a growing consensus of opinion on the need for legislation to ensure impartial and competent testing of all synthetic chemicals for which human exposure is anticipated. The present system of direct, closed-contract negotiations between manufacturing industries and commercial and other testing laboratories is open to abuse, creates obvious mutual constraints, and is thus contrary to consumer and long-term industrial interests. One possible remedy would be the introduction of a disinterested advisory group or agency to act as an intermediary between manufacturers and commercial and other testing laboratories. Various legal and other safeguards would have to be developed to avoid or minimize potential abuses and conflicts of interest in the operation of this intermediary group. Manufacturers would notify the advisory group or agency when safety evaluation was required for a particular chemical. The advisory group would then solicit contract bids on the open market. Bids would be awarded on the basis of economy, quality of protocols, and technical competence. The progress of testing would be monitored by periodic project site visits, as is routine with federal contracts. At the conclusion of the studies, the advisory group would comment on the quality of the data, make appropriate recommendations, and forward these to the regulatory agency concerned for appropriate action. This approach is certainly more consistent with general industrial practice than is the award of noncompetitive or unpublicized contracts. In addition, quality checks during testing would ensure high quality and reliability of data, minimizing the need to repeat studies and reducing pressure on the federal agencies involved to accept unsatisfactory data and *post hoc* situations. This approach would not only minimize constraints due to special client interests but would also serve to improve the

lines. The national laboratories should also represent a source of research potential, but under their existing charter they cannot be directly responsive to industrial needs. Further consideration should be directed to the possible need for an independent consumer protection agency and to the development of stronger scientific and legal representation of consumer, occupational, and environmental public interest groups in all agencies concerned directly and indirectly in these areas.

It is critical that industrial, commercial, and other laboratories be provided with unambiguous guidelines stating exactly what tests are required and supplying the necessary protocols for such tests. These protocols should relate to tests for both human and environmental safety and also delineate principles for interpretation. Concerned parties should be given ample opportunity to challenge or otherwise comment on such protocols before they are formally ratified. Such protocols should be subject to mandatory annual review.

These procedures would provide a clearer definition of the precise responsibilities of industry and regulatory agencies in safety evaluation and would thus minimize existing mutual constraints in these areas. Industry would know what tests were required and could predetermine the approximate costs of such tests before deciding whether to proceed with further product testing and development.

Further legislation concerning public access to data is critically needed. All formal discussions between agencies, industry, and expert governmental and nongovernmental committees on all issues relating to human safety and environmental quality, and all data relevant to such discussions, properly belong in the public domain and should be a matter of open record. Such records, including clear statements by all concerned of possible conflicts of interest, should be immediately available to the scientific community, to scientific and legal representatives of consumer, occupational, and environmental groups, and to other interested parties. Appropriate legal safeguards for the protection of patent rights will need to be developed.

In addition to open access to data on all issues of public health and welfare and environmental safety, it is essential that the interests of consumer, occupational, and environmental groups be adequately represented, legally and scientifically, at the earliest formal stages of such discussions. Decisions by agencies on technological innovations or on new synthetic chemicals after closed discussions on data which have been treated confidentially, are unacceptable. Consumer interest, occupational hazards, and environmental safety apart, such decisions are contrary to the long-term interests of industry, which should be protected from perforce belated objections.

My perspective on the critical issues of pollution and health comes from involvement in those issues as an industrial chemist and as vice-president of a chemical company. It is not my intention to respond point by point to Dr. Epstein's text. I will mention certain clarifications which I feel are important. I will point to some areas of agreement and also some areas of disagreement where I think the public may have been misinformed. Finally, I will touch on recommendations which I think

---

Dr. Julius E. Johnson is Director of Research and Development and a vice-president and member of the Board of Directors of the Dow Chemical Company. He is a graduate of the University of Colorado and received his Ph.D. in Biochemistry from the University of Illinois in 1943. He is active in professional circles, a member of the American Chemical Society and a former member of the Midland Board of Education. In 1969 he was appointed to the Mrak Commission on Pesticides and Their Relationship to Environmental Health. In 1943, Dr. Johnson joined Dow Biochemical Research Laboratory and developed a wartime program of testing Dow compounds used as anti-malarial and anti-infective drugs. At the war's end, he shifted his emphasis to nutrition and disease control in farm animals and poultry. Presently, he is engaged in a wide range of matters pertaining to the development and use of drugs and chemicals. He is chairman of the Dow Ecology Council, which catalyzes the company's actions in environmental improvement.

207

should be considered in enacting or implementing additional regulations.

Dr. Epstein has very properly identified three primary compartments of pollution relating to air, water and soil, these coexisting in a state of equilibrium (p. 180). Food becomes a secondary compartment which may acquire pollutants from air, water and soil. When one thinks about pollutants it is also important to think about four other factors or properties which enable classification of the degree of hazards that may result. These factors are stability, movement, bioconcentration, and toxicity.

Stability: The stability of a chemical substance is its resistance to breakdown or change in the environment. A material which degrades to harmless substances or to commonly encountered degradation products such as carbon dioxide, water and chloride ordinarily presents little, if any, hazard to the environment. On the other hand, a stable molecule, or first or second generation breakdown products from a stable molecule which in turn are stable, can cause difficulties (*e.g.*, DDT to DDE). It is very important to determine the potential stability or instability of a chemical substance early in its developmental history. This information is a useful predictor which, intelligently applied, can aid substantially in the determination of risk.

Movement: The chemical agent which "stays put" (for example, insecticide for termite control under a house) presents no substantial environmental hazard. But one which moves away from the point of application, whether via water, air, or food, deserves additional attention to its hazards.

Bioconcentration: A compound which is stable and which moves may or may not concentrate in various life forms, particularly aquatic organisms such as fish, oysters, or clams. The phenomenon of bioconcentration is usually, as Dr. Epstein has indicated, tied to solubility in fat. Such is the case with DDT and DDE. A stable, fat-soluble substance predisposes concentration by food chain organisms. In some instances this material concentrated in the food of a lower form of life ascends the food chain, a phenomenon also known as biomagnification.

Toxicity: The fourth factor of importance in predicting environmental hazard potential is toxicity. If a compound is stable and moves, and particularly if it bioconcentrates, the resulting toxicity is of extreme importance. This should include acute as well as chronic long-term toxicities, and meaningful tests of carcinogenicity, mutagenicity, and teratology should be performed as indicators of subtle toxicity. The methods by which these tests are performed is the subject of considerable debate in scientific circles today.

These four factors should be considered important determinants of hazard potential whenever you are called upon to evaluate whether reports of environmental hazards are truly

need for established protocols to define the test methods by which toxicity assessments are made (p. 204). Moreover, I agree that we need to understand better the subtler forms of toxicology with emphasis on mutagenesis, carcinogenesis, and teratogenesis. We need to reexamine materials that have long been used and hitherto recognized as safe, but this reexamination should be done calmly and without yielding to the almost irrepressible urge to publish fragmentary information.

The New National Center for Toxicological Research

It is encouraging that certain important steps have been taken to establish better understanding of the controversial questions about protocols and threshold levels. The President has approved a National Center for Toxicological Research which will be established at Pine Bluff, Arkansas, in a facility formerly used for chemical warfare research and development. This facility will be managed by the Food and Drug Administration, under the general administration of the Environmental Protection Agency, and will involve a policy board comprising government and other advisory personnel. Advice should also be sought from industrial consultants who, without conflict of interest, can bring valuable insights to bear.

Many member companies in the Manufacturing Chemists Association have supported the creation of such a facility and have recognized the need to establish protocols. An important function of this laboratory for toxicological examination will be to conduct tests in a statistically meaningful manner in order to establish more precisely whether or not a threshold does exist for weak carcinogens, weak mutagens, or weak teratogens. One of the important unanswered questions in interpretation of toxicological data is the relationship of dosage and response. At high dosages, often so high as to overload the animal's natural defense mechanism, cancers, mutagenic effects, or deformed embryos result from testing compounds to which humans may be exposed in trace amounts. This does not necessarily mean that minute traces of these materials encountered in the environment are *hazardous* to man. The toxic responses which occur at "threshold" levels are very difficult to measure in a significant way. It is hoped that the new National Center for Toxicological Research will shed more light on this particularly knotty question.

Dr. Epstein states, "It has long been recognized as unrealistic to expect industry voluntarily to devote sufficient time and resources for safety evaluation" (p. 179). With this statement I both agree and disagree. I agree in the case of commodities which have long been articles of commerce and are produced by several manufacturers; for these the burden of proof should be shared. Eventually the cost of this proof will be passed on to the user in one way or another. It is proper for government to undertake funding of such tests. In the case of new materials, however, where the supplying company has a proprietary position, the burden should be carried by the company, once meaningful protocols and meaningful definitions of expected safe limits are established by regulatory agencies. Industry needs to know where it stands and what is expected, as Dr. Epstein suggests. Moreover, the burden on industry should fall proportionally on the various competitors. The regulations should help to insure safety but should not kill the incentive to innovate in a constructive way.

Industry's Concern

The inference might be drawn from Dr. Epstein's paper that industry has done little to establish trustworthy data to quantify the hazards of its products. The Haskell Laboratory of du Pont has been in operation for many years and has guided the company not only in evaluating the safety of its products but also in helping to sustain du Pont's exceptional safety record. Carbide has used the Mellon Institute for years as a supplier of information on toxicology. Dow's toxicology laboratory was established in 1933. Virtually every material that Dow makes has been tested to identify potential hazards not only to workmen but also to the customer. Dow understood early the potential hazards of 2, 4, 5-T if the intermediate trichloro-

rials that are not hazardous to the user under normal conditions of exposure.

Many of the chemicals we first synthesize and test never reach the market.[2] Today nearly ten thousand compounds are tested for each pesticide which succeeds in the market. Lack of efficacy, toxicity, or cost rules out the many compounds which are set aside. Even in past years when the demands on pesticides were perhaps less critical, five thousand compounds, on the average, were tested before one emerged that was acceptable for registration and use.

I remember clearly a very effective and potent fungicide discovered in the mid-fifties which worked extremely well for the control of disease on apples and pears. The toxicity of the spray mist of this material was worrisome, hence the product was abandoned as a pesticide. Another investigator later became interested in the same material because of its effect in paints, especially marine paints; it prevented barnacles from attaching to ship bottoms. This created some excitement, and development was started. At this point the compound was known to be stable. Moreover, it was learned that the compound slowly

[1] Julius E. Johnson, "The Public Health Implications of Widespread Use of the Phenoxy Herbicides and Picloram," American Institute of Biological Sciences Symposium of Bloomington, Indiana, Aug. 26, 1970.

[2] Julius E. Johnson, "Safety in the Development of Herbicides," California Weed Conference, Sacramento, Calif., Jan. 19, 1971.

leached from the paint film and entered the aquatic system in extremely minute amounts. Its toxicity was known to be severe, and caution was indicated. The next piece of information discovered was that the material could be concentrated by algae in the water. It was concluded that the stable compound—which moved into the aquatic environment, possessed a wide spectrum of toxicity, and also was bioconcentrated—presented a risk greater than the value gained. The project was terminated.

The profit motive is continually under attack and the feeling is widespread that a company will do anything for a buck. I shall not engage in a defensive polemic, but I will point out a few factors to consider. A large company, research-based, has three powerful constraints. First is the constraint of the customer, who voluntarily makes the buying decision. He is free to buy or not to buy, and the ultimate decision must be good for both parties. Whether the trade is between two individuals, two companies, or two nations, this trade is an act of consent by both parties. Successful suppliers require repeat customers, which implies satisfaction with the product and with the price. The second constraint is the investor, who must be sufficiently satisfied with the performance of the company and its future potential that he is willing to invest his savings with the hope for appropriate return. A company that does not satisfy its customers will not long satisfy its investors. The third constraint is time: a successful company must conduct itself in such a way that it builds for the future in a manner satisfactory to employees, investors and customers. The time constraint is a subtle one, not easily visible to those outside the corporate structure. Nevertheless, to survive and prosper in a constructive way, we must conduct our business in a manner which accommodates long-term goals as well as short-term ambitions. We must also respond to the social needs that become evident as our society evolves.

If we do a good job, we are well paid. Nearly 15 percent of our income goes for state and local taxes. On the profit which remains after all expenses are paid, approximately one-half goes to federal income taxes. On the net profit after taxes, one-half goes to the investors in the form of dividends (on which they are subsequently taxed) and one-half is used for reinvestment to protect the future growth of the shareholders' investment. If we do well we can afford to innovate and we can afford to do a better job. If we do poorly, the ultimate price is to go out of business.

In this frame of reference, decisions on environmental diligence may vary. Speaking from an industrial viewpoint, I would welcome regulations with clearly understood standards, well-defined protocols, and clearly understood methods of information exchange, because these regulations would help to equalize

in the chemical industry. The spirit is high indeed, not only at the bench level but in management as well. For example, in November, 1969, the concept of an Ecology Council was born and discussed with the Dow Board of Directors. By January, 1970, a Director of the Ecology Council had been appointed. Quickly an organization was formed with councils and subcouncils throughout the company, and ecology and environmental concerns, like workers' safety, became everybody's business. Prior to this time a large base of capability, interest, and activity had been established to control pollution. But on January 7, 1970, everyone in Dow became part of an organizational network to identify the problems, assess their priorities, and implement better practices. This effort was divided into three primary categories: first, the effect of our manufacturing on the environment; second, the effects of our products on the environment; and third, the commercial opportunities that might result by applying our technology to environmental cleanup. Fortunately the Ecology Council was already organized when the mercury pollution question first came to our attention. This organization enabled speedy action to assess the problem throughout the company and to institute remedial steps where needed.

Dr. Epstein has suggested that a disinterested advisory group serve as a buffer between industry and government and that this

3 *Ibid.*

group place contracts for toxicological research with the qualified testing laboratory of their choice (p. 204). I agree that an agency should be shielded from inappropriate pressures. But I am not in favor of total shielding of either the agency or the laboratory, because a thorough understanding of the problem by all parties is necessary in order to consider, design, and implement tests relevant to the particular situation. Certainly I do not favor lobbying tactics, but I do favor speedy flow of information among all concerned parties so that the appropriate protocols can be selected on a rational basis rather than on a simplistic, procedural basis. Perhaps an advisory group could do this, but even so the process of gaining all the relevant facts presents a difficult human challenge. There is no such thing as a completely disinterested group. Everyone has his pet ideas. Everyone who receives a research grant from government or elsewhere is to some extent influenced by the attitudes of those who supply the grant. Political ambitions or party preferences can influence every man. Ideological preoccupations can establish a mental set sufficient to sway a critical conclusion. If an advisory group is utilized, I strongly recommend that it involve qualified technical peers from different backgrounds. Qualified individuals from industry should be included to bring valuable and necessary insights.

Laboratory Certification: A Possible Solution

I have suggested to my colleagues in the chemical industry (and this suggestion has been forwarded for legislative consideration) a somewhat different approach: the certification of laboratories.[4] I have recommended that a Board of Certification be established under federal auspices, involving people from industrial, governmental, university, and private backgrounds, to assess the capabilities, the facilities, the protocols, and the operations of laboratories destined to provide data for regulatory decisions. Once certified (with certification and qualifications to be reviewed periodically), these and only these laboratories would be acceptable as suppliers of data admissible for regulatory decision. Data from noncertified laboratories would be inadmissible. Such certification should be granted to all private contract laboratories, industrial laboratories, governmental lab-

[4] *Ibid.*

oratories, and university laboratories that wish to involve themselves and meet the requirements. Greater public confidence could be developed in the results issuing from such laboratories if certification required that a qualifying board periodically rule on the adequacy of personnel, procedures, equipment, and housing. The objective would be to improve and standardize the data used in evaluating products for environmental effects.

Once laboratories were certified, only toxicological data from certified laboratories would be admissible in relation to product registration, residue tolerances, or environmental decisions. It is further suggested that, after the original supplier's patents have expired, the second supplier of a chemical be permitted to purchase the certified data he would be required to submit. This could be purchased either from the original petitioner or from a governmental agency. The main objective would be to burden the second supplier so that he does not have an unfair competitive advantage over the one who has borne the original cost of development.

If certified data were the only type of toxicological data admissible for the support of a regulatory decision, and if the second supplier were required to pay his way, then data in the registration or the petition for tolerance in support of environmental matters could be made open for inspection, and it would be possible to encourage publication. Openness of these data would relieve many objections. Today neither the qualified investigators nor the public has access to the facts. Hence the public is suspicious. Moreover, agencies expected to help support the use of a product do not have access to certain registration information. Experiment stations and extension specialists need confidence in the validity of backup data supporting pesticides. In addition the public official charged with registration of tolerance proceedings is forbidden to make certain information available without consent of the petitioner. This whole situation promotes public distrust, because the supporting facts are not out in the open.

I also advocate greater use of experimental labels and a more aggressive pilot usage of certain materials prior to full registration so that typical, though limited, sale can be achieved under qualified supervision.[5] This practice would permit the development of valid use experience while limiting the exposure of the

[5]*Ibid.*

total population. The objective would be to discover any unexpected effects that are difficult or impossible to discover under laboratory or field test conditions.

My goals in making these suggestions are to improve the openness of handling information to protect the proprietary rights of the first supplier and place an equal burden on the second suppliers by requiring them to pay their proportionate costs, and to improve the quality of the data generated. To achieve this satisfactorily, we should worry less about conflict of interest and more about good communications and openness.

Alfred North Whitehead, although he published most prolifically in the first third of this century, developed some insights which are remarkably germane to the problems of today.[6] Whitehead found it impossible to define what a great civilization really is. In examining the great civilizations of the past, however, he concluded that the following characteristics were manifest: truth, beauty, art, adventure, and peace. Surely sensitive people and responsible leaders today are cognizant of the importance of each of these factors; in connection with this study let us look briefly at Whitehead's account of adventure and truth.

Adventure, according to Whitehead, provides zest for a civilization. This zest is essential to freshness and progress. I hope that the national desire for exploration in any form is not now inhibited, for there is grave danger in losing the spirit of adventure and the zest which results. Even though occasional mistakes are made, if they are detected early, it is better to endure these mistakes than to inhibit exploration and inquiry or to inhibit sensible trial of new practices.

Whitehead's observations on truth are particularly valid for our times. He states that truth is the confirmation of appearance and reality. Much of what we see and hear today, resulting from the discoveries of science, does not necessarily reflect reality. The appearance is distorted. The scientists themselves all too often publish prematurely. Misleading results can be picked up by a hungry press, and if these results have political implications they can be grossly misinterpreted. Somehow, in recent years, the process of internal challenge by scientists has somewhat fallen by the wayside. Vigorous discussion by scientific or

6 Alfred North Whitehead, *Adventure of Ideas* (New York: Macmillan, 1933).

interdisciplinary peers prior to publication has often been by-passed. The result has been unnecessary fear by a public which could hardly be expected to evaluate for itself the significance of these published and republished conclusions. The signals—so often conflicting in themselves and so often at conflict with apparent social values—can be grossly misread. The gap between appearance and reality is wide indeed.

I have abundant faith in the ability of the United States to endure and thrive on diversity of viewpoint; and I hope the present misreading of the influence of science will be in part self-correcting, once the scientist himself understands the need for more care both in experimentation and in voicing his con-clusions. I hope that those in authority in government, univer-sity, and industry, when considering ethical matters, will place greater reliance on peer review of projects, goals, conclusions, and products. In selecting scientists to do our work and in counseling those scientists, it is well to remember one key test that helps assure objectivity. That test is the courage to design experiments to prove one's hypothesis wrong, not experiments designed to prove oneself right. Such courage helps create the intellectual rigor necessary for the confirmation of appearance and reality.

CHAPTER XI

POLLUTION AND HEALTH
A Senate Counsel's Response
LEONARD BICKWIT, JR.

In responding to Dr. Epstein from the standpoint of my own discipline—that of a congressional committee staff member—it would seem appropriate to concentrate on the section dealing with "Regulatory and Legislative Deficiencies and Needs" (pp. 199-206). To summarize his perceptive remarks in this area, he seems primarily concerned with two basic questions: First, how can we organize our various regulatory mechanisms in the field of chemical pollution into a consistent scheme? Second, what should be the components of that scheme? Since he dwells at much greater length on the second of these questions, I will do the same. The first, however, also merits consideration by anyone involved in legislation in this area.

Organizing Regulatory Controls

Although Dr. Epstein never in fact poses the first question, it is implicit in several of his remarks. He writes, for instance:

Mr. Leonard Bickwit, Jr., a resident of Washington, D.C., took his B.A. degree at Yale and graduated magna cum laude in the field of liberal arts. He then attended Oxford University, England, where he received his M.A. in Philosophy, Politics, and Economics. In 1966 he graduated from Harvard Law School and began legal practice as an associate in a New York firm. In 1969 he was appointed Counsel to the Subcommittee on the Environment of the United States Senate Committee on Commerce.

Federal regulatory agencies suffer from certain limitations and constraints. Jurisdiction over products and their applications is commonly fragmented among the sixty or so executive agencies concerned with environmental problems. Moreover, there are certain categories of products, notably industrial chemicals, for which there are only minimal regulatory controls, if any (p. 199).

He further complains that "Legislative responsibility in environmental and related areas now extends to some twenty congressional committees" (p. 200).

As Dr. Epstein suggests, the resulting complexity is unfortunate, to say the least. On the federal level, standards for exposure to chemical pollutants in air and water are established by the Environmental Protection Agency, tolerances for exposure through food are generally set by the Food and Drug Administration, while standards in the work place are the province of the Department of Labor. It is often alleged that there is insufficient coordination between these standard-setting agencies, so that when standards are set for one source of exposure, insufficient account is taken of likely exposure from other sources.

The problem is one not merely of too many agencies but also of too many laws with inconsistent provisions. If dangerous mercuric compounds are used in pesticides, clearance by regulatory authorities is required before the products are placed on the market. However, if similar compounds go into cosmetics, no such clearance is necessary. Moreover, industrial uses of mercury are subject to no direct regulation whatever but are controlled only through regulation of the effluent or emissions of the industrial plant. One can find numerous other examples of equally dangerous chemicals receiving disparate treatment under the numerous federal laws.

While less fragmentation and increased consistency are highly desirable, it is unlikely that we will see those objectives achieved in the near future. To produce one omnibus law dealing with all forms of chemical pollution would require a tour through each of the congressional committees Dr. Epstein refers to—a tour which no bill could ever hope to complete in the course of a given Congress. The alternative is to amend each of the existing laws, making them as consistent as possible with each other, and to supplement them with new laws in areas that are not yet regulated. While this is a worthy objective, it would take a great deal of time, if indeed it could ever be achieved. This, too, requires a united effort of the various committees as well as a united resistance to lobbyists who oppose additional controls—a highly unlikely prospect.

This route, however, ought certainly to be explored. Perhaps the best way to proceed would be for Congress to attempt to enact model legislation in areas such as industrial chemicals where all agree that present controls are insufficient. Pressure might then be applied to conform existing statutes to that model, departing from it only in situations where differences in products truly justify departures. Requirements might be imposed upon existing agencies to coordinate their setting of standards and enforcement activities with each other. In addition, further thought could be given to increased consolidation of these agencies. While there are obvious limits to the extent to which consolidation is desirable, the President's establishment last year of the Environmental Protection Agency certainly seems a step in the right direction. If that agency proves adequate to meet the numerous and rather awesome responsibilities delegated to it, consideration ought to be given to further expanding its role in the field of chemical pollution.

Determining the Basic Elements of the Regulatory Scheme

Dr. Epstein makes numerous welcome suggestions on how regulatory procedures for chemicals might be reformed. Essentially they relate to the problems of when a regulatory decision regarding the use of a given chemical ought to be made and how it ought to be made so as to avoid constraints between industries and regulatory agencies (p. 205).

With regard to the timing of decisions, he is persuasive in his argument that these decisions should be made at the earliest possible time. Rather than cage the lions, it seems sensible to do all we can to control the lion population. The Food and Drug Administration now faces a mammoth task in inspecting fish and other foods for the presence of toxic materials due in part to industrial waste discharges. From the standpoint of both safety and economics, we would be much better off had the chemicals which produced these discharges been controlled at an earlier stage. Our experience with mercury and other toxic metals argues strongly for clearance before use as a mechanism for pollution control.

Given that decisions involving the manufacture and use of chemicals should be made at the earliest possible time, we are left with the central question of how to make those decisions as enlightened and objective as possible. Increased research on the efficacy and potential dangers of given chemicals is obviously necessary, and Dr. Epstein alludes to this need. He spends considerably more time on the less obvious need to eliminate "constraints" between industries and testing agencies. Here he concentrates on the need to ensure the accuracy of data, and he presents as one possible means "a disinterested advisory group or agency to act as an intermediary between manufacturers and commercial and other testing laboratories" (p. 204).

This proposal is interesting, but it may not be necessary. In terms of cost effectiveness, we might be better off by continuing to allow industries to do their own testing, spot-checking their results, and imposing stiff penalties when data are found to be inaccurate. This assumes, of course, that industry will be told what tests are required and what results must be obtained before the chemical is allowed on the market. On this point, Dr. Epstein wisely underscores the need for promulgation of exact protocols to guide industry in its testing.

The question remains, however, of how these protocols, and more importantly the criteria for safety and efficacy for new and existing chemicals, are to be determined. It goes without saying that if the data presented are perfectly accurate but the criteria they are required to meet are inadequate, we have achieved nothing. Moreover, it should be noted that if constraints are present with regard to the presentation of data, they may also be present with respect to determination of the criteria which the data are required to satisfy.

Here Dr. Epstein offers as a solution "stronger scientific and legal representation of consumer, occupational, and environmental public interest groups in all agencies concerned directly and indirectly in these areas" (p. 205). He also suggests consideration of "the possible need for an independent consumer protection agency" (p. 205). By this presumably he means something similar to the proposal introduced before Congress by Senator Abraham Ribicoff and Congressman Benjamin Rosenthal to establish an independent consumer advocate. To aid in this consumer advocacy function before agencies, Dr. Epstein further proposes increased public access to data relevant to agency determinations.

All of these suggestions are highly desirable, but they may not be sufficient. If industry pressure causes an agency to consider benefits more seriously than risks in determining safety criteria, is increased consumer representation in the administrative agency really likely to change things? If an agency is inclined not to restrict the use of a chemical because the Chairman of its Appropriations Subcommittee opposes any such restriction, is a public hearing really going to reverse that inclination? Experience teaches us that regulatory agencies frequently get chummy with the regulated and become influenced by the politics surrounding their actions. It will be a rare case in which consumer advocacy within the agency will be able to match these pressures. Moreover, if the consumer advocate is himself an agent of the federal government—as the Ribicoff-Rosenthal proposal would have it—he may be subject to the very same pressures as the agency before which he argues.

Something further is needed to ensure that decisions of such great importance will be made objectively on the merits and in the absence of the traditional biases of regulatory agencies. Several alternatives should be examined.

Alternative Approaches to Elimination of Industry-Agency Constraints

First of all, Congress might take it upon itself to make these decisions. Several have advocated this approach by introducing bills to ban DDT, other chlorinated hydrocarbons, and several additional chemicals. My reaction to this approach is critical for two reasons. First of all, it goes without saying that Congress is subject to many of the same pressures experienced by the agencies. Second, I am inclined to question the competence of Congress to reach intelligent decisions on highly technical matters such as these. True, the decisions are political. Risks and benefits must be balanced, and ultimately the problems boil down to questions of values. Yet while we traditionally look to the legislative branch of government for value judgments, it is inadvisable to do so here. It would require an inordinate amount of time for a member of Congress to understand the problems he is dealing with. In the absence of such understanding, decisions would invariably be made on the basis of uninformed constituent preference, without sufficient regard for the factors involved.

A second alternative is for Congress to tighten the guidance given to the administrative agencies that make these decisions. Congress could state specifically what considerations are to be weighed in what proportions by the agency involved.

An example of this approach may be found in S. 808, a pesticide control bill introduced in 1971 by Senator Philip A. Hart and now before the Senate Commerce Committee. The bill provides that a pesticide must be banned whenever there is reasonable doubt as to its safety for humans or the environment and there are less serious doubts as to the safety of some reasonable alternative pesticide. While this kind of guidance is desirable, there will inevitably be limits to its effectiveness. In the case of the Hart bill, the administrator is still left to determine what is a "reasonable" alternative. Thus he is still required to make the delicate kind of decision which is all too frequently influenced by irrelevant "constraints." Unless Congress is actually to decide in each case—which seems inadvisable—the agency will have to be given some room to make such decisions. We can narrow the problem by increased legislative guidance, but we certainly cannot eliminate it.

Some argue that the best way to eliminate it is to change the nature of the agencies themselves. What is needed, it is suggested, are new selection and funding processes that will help free the agencies from objectionable political pressures.

As far as selection is concerned, the traditional process has many faults. Top administrators, initially chosen by the President, quickly become identified with "the Administration." Their resulting concern to perpetuate the Administration is obviously an unhealthy factor. Agency administrators ought certainly to be responsive to public wants and needs, but the responsiveness which this orientation generates is often to the wants and needs of campaign contributors.

Efforts to "depoliticize" the selection process are thus very much to be applauded. One possible advance in this direction would be to give agency administrators increased tenure so that they could not be fired at will for unpopular, but meritorious, decisions. But beyond this point the going gets tougher. Some argue that Congress itself ought to do the appointing. Yet since Congress is also politically motivated, it is hard to see how this would achieve the desired result.

Even if an adequate selection process were devised, the problems of funding would remain. If agencies are to remain dependent upon the appropriations process, the example of pressure by that subcommittee chairman will continue to haunt us. Obviously these are among our knottiest problems, and a good deal of additional study will be needed before solutions are available. Such study should certainly be undertaken, but in view of the complexity of the issues involved we cannot expect it to produce the desired changes soon.

The Hart-McGovern Approach

Since I have been critical of all the alternatives presented thus far, it is with pleasure that I turn to one which appears to have a good deal of promise. This is a proposal to enlarge the rights of citizens to review agency determinations in court. The theory behind it is rather simple. If an agency is insensitive to the interests of citizens because of some of the factors mentioned earlier, those citizens ought to have recourse to another, perhaps more objective, forum. This is the theory implicit in a bill introduced in Congress by Senator Hart and Senator George McGovern, entitled the Environmental Protection Act of 1971, and presently under consideration by the Subcommittee on the Environment of the Senate Commerce Committee. It is also the theory of Professor Joseph Sax of the University of Michigan, who guided a similar bill into law in Michigan last year.

What the Michigan law does and what the Hart-McGovern bill would do is to create a right of all citizens to a decent environment and to allow them to enforce that right by enjoining in court all "unreasonable pollution, impairment, and destruction" of their air, water, and land. Among those who could be sued under this approach are agencies who have permitted such unreasonable activity to take place. Citizens would also be able to sue private individuals who behave unreasonably, regardless of whether the latter's behavior is countenanced by regulatory agencies concerned with the matter.

The basic argument in support of this approach is that citizens ought to be empowered to defend the environment since it is their environment that is at stake. Because of his personal interest in the outcome of environmental litigation, the citizen may well prove a better advocate than any agency of government authorized to represent him. Where the citizen and the agency conflict in their views, it is felt therefore that the citizen should be entitled to complete review of the agency activities before the judicial branch of government.

This is not to say that he has no right to review under existing law. That right, however, is severely circumscribed. In most cases the citizen will not be able to set aside an agency determination in court unless that determination is illegal, *i.e.*, violates some procedural rule, or is so horrendous as to be labelled by a court as "arbitrary and capricious." The major thrust of the Hart-McGovern bill is that it would remove that restriction on the court, thus enabling it to question agency determinations of fact and the exercise of agency discretion. Decisions which were not arbitrary but were nonetheless wrong would thereby be subject to citizen attack.

Many arguments have been advanced against this approach. The bill has been regarded as a radical—some have said dangerous—departure from traditional practice. The argument most often put forward is that the bill would open the courts to "the floodgates of litigation." Yet the Michigan experience has been otherwise. After eight months' experience with the new law, only a dozen or so cases have been brought. Virtually all of these have been responsible suits, countering the contention that the bill would lead to frequent harassment by cranks.

Another criticism of the bill frequently voiced is that it would put too great a burden on the agencies—or, put more extremely, lead to the destruction of the administrative system. The Michigan experience also seems to answer this objection. A total of twelve suits in eight months indicates that administrative agencies have hardly been paralyzed.

What accounts for the Michigan experience, it seems, is the fact of life that litigation is never undertaken lightly. It is both costly and time-consuming, and neither the Hart-McGovern bill nor the Michigan law proposes to change that. Furthermore, neither gives the plaintiff the right to monetary relief. Plaintiffs will therefore include only those who are willing to risk a substantial loss of money (as a result of legal fees, court costs, etc.) with no possibility of monetary gain. If plaintiffs join in a class action, they can minimize their risks by splitting up their costs. Yet even under these circumstances it seems safe to assume that few will go forward.

Many of the important environmental suits thus far have been brought by public interest law firms who do not charge fees for their services. Were these firms to expand significantly in number, the objection that the courts will be overloaded might indeed have some force. This does not seem likely to happen, however, since even existing public interest firms have been strapped financially. Unless there is a significant change of heart with regard to foundation funds, the "floodgates" are virtually certain to remain closed.

One cause for concern, put forward by the President's Council on Environmental Quality, is that judges are incompetent to review administrative decisions in the environmental area. This area is so technical, so the argument goes, that the judges should refrain from contesting administrators with greater technical expertise. Yet judges have been getting into technical matters for centuries. Familiar examples are nuisance cases, malpractice suits, and actions for patent infringement. While it is true that they have little expertise in environmental protection—generally even less than Congressmen—the judicial adversary process, unlike the legislative process, is conducive to responsible action in the area. The objective fact-finding capability of the judicial system, together with its capacity to clarify points of conflict, gives the courts a considerable advantage in dealing with specific environmental issues. It should further be noted that Hart-McGovern would not require courts to set aside administrative determinations when the judges themselves regard the matter as beyond their own competence. Most likely, courts will be quite reluctant to get involved in complicated factual issues where administrators have already acted. Where they are willing, however, there seems every reason to permit them to do so.

Another argument occasionally heard against this approach is that it would create uncertainty as to what must be done to comply with pollution laws. Admittedly the standard of "unreasonable pollution" is susceptible to many interpretations. Moreover, since administrative determinations may be set aside, even the individual who follows the regulators' advice may be sued by those dissatisfied with the regulators. If he chooses to comply with all environmental protection standards, he is vulnerable nonetheless if those standards are found to be inadequate.

This point would be well taken but for the fact that similar uncertainty already exists under present law. In light of prevailing concern for the environment and new technological advances, environmental protection standards are consistently being made stricter. In his environmental message to Congress at the beginning of 1971, the President suggested that this trend will continue. It follows that mere compliance with currently applicable standards gives industrial defendants at present little more security than would be allowed them under the Hart-McGovern proposal.

A final argument against the bill, and perhaps the best one, is that it will not provide much of an improvement over existing mechanisms of environmental control. Knowing that administrators often have been unresponsive and biased, why should we expect judges to do any better? One answer is that in most cases they won't have to. The theory of the bill is that the threat of suit will provide a healthy discipline for the agencies but very few cases will actually be brought to court. Secondly, it does seem safe to assume that judges on the whole will be less susceptible to outside pressure. In theory, they are wholly separate and distinct from the executive branch, even though that branch may have appointed them. In practice, it is difficult to envision long lunches and gifts flowing from regulated industries to the judiciary.

While the benefits offered by the Hart-McGovern approach may prove limited, a good case can be made for trying it out at this time. In my view, it would provide a useful supplement to Dr. Epstein's proposal for increased citizen participation in the administrative process. The prospect of citizens actively functioning in the agencies and the courts is an appealing, if somewhat uncertain, one. To frustrate this participation in deference to the arguments discussed above would be a serious misallocation of priorities—a triumph of administrative convenience over considerations far more important for society. To promote it on the other hand would be to benefit significantly both the citizens involved and the environment they are determined to protect.

CHAPTER XII

POLLUTION AND HEALTH
A Theologian's Response

CHARLES W. POWERS

Contemporary man's ability to fabricate far exceeds his ability to comprehend the meaning and impact of his fabrications. He has not only failed to regulate the deleterious impacts of his technological discoveries; he is also frequently unaware of what those impacts are. This is perhaps the central point to emerge from Dr. Epstein's study and from the burgeoning literature on ecological topics.

The American people vaguely perceive the threat and are galvanized into action when specific and obvious examples of

Charles W. Powers is assistant professor of social ethics at Yale Divinity School. Dr. Powers received his B.A. from Haverford College and was granted a diploma in theology from Oxford University in England, a B.D. from Union Theological Seminary, and a Ph.D. from Yale University in 1969. He has been granted a number of fellowships and scholarships in his academic career and has taught at Yale, Princeton, and Haverford. His most recent interest has been in the field of social investment. He has served as a member of the committee on financial investment of the United Church of Christ and with a group requested by Yale University to investigate the ethical implications of investment choices. He is a contributor to numerous church and secular magazines, and in May 1971 Abingdon Press published his book, Social Responsibility and Investments. *He is also the co-author with John G. Simm and Jon P. Gunnemann of* The Ethical Investor: Universities and Corporate Responsibility, *published by Yale University Press in 1972.*

technology run amuck, disrupting their lives. Capitalizing on both this general uneasiness and on a startled citizenry's willingness to respond when it suddenly comes face to face with the irrational consequences of supposedly rational scientific achievement, the ecological movement is fast becoming one of the most important phenomena of the 1970's. At present most of the members and supporters of this movement are long on sweeping generalizations and rhetorical comment; like converts to most popular cultural movements, they are often short on careful scrutiny of the issues and on developing effective strategies for unraveling and meeting the incredibly complex set of problems into which technology has led us. The movement has great potential, however, for reshaping the cultural ethos in ways which may lead to the development of more systematic proposals for the reshaping of public policy and the restructuring of outmoded political and economic institutions and ideologies.

Charles Reich to the contrary, this "new consciousness" is not a stable one which will inevitably take root and grow. We must not overlook the fact that an oversimplified, subtle, and deceptive counterattack has already begun in response to the environmental movement. Recent speeches by leaders of industry, media advertisers, and government spokesmen have already shown that there are those who would redefine and redirect the themes employed by proponents of ecological reform. One sees, for example, an effort to play upon the conflict in social goals which would develop if environmental defenders on the one hand and proponents of racial, social, and economic justice on the other were to obtain all they appear to propose. Indeed, the reformers often leave themselves open to such attacks, since both their programs and the language in which they are couched are susceptible to such willful confusion. For instance, it is in part because protectors of "spaceship earth" have dislodged the concept of "social cost" from its carefully articulated home in economic analysis[1] and used it indiscriminately that reactive governmental authorities have been able to make a case, persuasive to the ill-informed, that the ecological movement is itself making socially costly proposals. One hopeful sign that reformers are aware of this danger is the recent decision by public

1 K. William Kapp, *Social Costs of Business Enterprise* (New York: Asia Publishing House, 1963).

interest lawyers and others concerned for environmental defense and by their counterparts working in the area of housing discrimination to try to develop a common strategy which will thwart efforts to play these two groups off against each other.

In this response I shall concentrate on the issues of institutional responsibility for correcting the abuses and deficiencies which Dr. Epstein has elucidated. I shall be particularly concerned with how the churches might find their witness in speaking to these questions. This is not because the work of examining Dr. Epstein's implicit normative assumptions is not important. Nor is it because the task of explicating a doctrine of man or a set of ethical principles derived from either theological or nontheological sources in relation to the health problems we are discussing should go begging. But I do believe that we ethicists too often retire from the field after concepts are clarified and principles enunciated and leave unattended the issues of how our institutions should put those clarifications and normative understandings to work. Furthermore, I am relatively confident that there is sufficient agreement in society that the toxicological effects Dr. Epstein has discussed *are* socially injurious to permit us to focus on such questions as *who* is responsible for correcting or regulating pollution abuses and *how* we should cultivate an ethos which fixes that responsibility.

Let us look briefly at the economic, political, and cultural milieu in which these problems have arisen; sketch the criteria of institutional responsibility; and finally, concentrate on the responsibility of the churches.

The Economic, Political, and Cultural Milieu

Since the 1930's, Americans have realized that a technological society whose chief economic engines are giant corporations cannot rely on the invisible hand that Adam Smith envisioned to regulate the marketplace and its impact. That realization was a long time in coming, for a host of reasons,[2] and even today most Americans have grasped it only in part. But for some time we have been busy creating a visible and vigilant hand to

[2] Henry Steele Commager, "America's Heritage of Big Business," *Saturday Review,* July 4, 1970.

regulate and minimize the hazards of economic production. Our nation's history since the waning years of the last century has been a series of efforts to determine what mechanisms would work and which of them should reside in the hands of public agencies. We have tried to keep our economic institutions small and competitive (anti-trust legislation); we have tried to establish countervailing powers in the private sector (labor and consumer legislation); we have tried a host of regulatory agency structures (using advocate and judicial models for agencies which are quasi-independent or under administrative and legislative supervision). We have centralized and decentralized. We have tried placing faith in the consciences of managers of corporations[3] and industry groups (*e.g.*, National Association of Manufacturers). Mr. Bickwit has joined a growing chorus which proposes that we shift more responsibility onto the judicial system and away from the legislative branch which he, as a legislative assistant, is convinced is unequal to the task.

Quite obviously nothing has worked. Let us look, for example, at regulatory agencies. The catalogue of legislative and regulatory deficiencies in the area of chemical pollutants which Dr. Epstein offers in the final pages of his paper is not an isolated aberration, a list of administrative failures in respect to only one area of the nation's life. As long ago as 1955, John Kenneth Galbraith described the life experience of most regulatory bodies as follows:

> [they] have a marked life cycle. In youth they are vigorous, aggressive, evangelistic and even intolerant. Later, they mellow, and in old age—after a matter of ten or fifteen years—they become, with some exceptions, either an arm of the industry that they are regulating, or senile.[4]

What has changed in the intervening sixteen years? These agencies are now endowed by their creators (the executive and legislative branches) with few of the rights, perquisites, explicit powers, and economic resources necessary to their assigned tasks; their periods of infancy and youth grow shorter and their old age longer. Indeed, few of our regulatory agencies

3 Adolph Berle, "Economic Power and the Free Society," *Fund for the Republic Pamphlets*, Dec., 1967.

4 John Kenneth Galbraith, *The Great Crash* (New York: Houghton-Mifflin, 1955), p. 171.

seem to have any period of young adulthood when they are both vigorous enough to pursue their tasks zestfully and mature and knowledgeable enough to do competent work. Meanwhile technology leaps ahead, and industry, with only sporadic gestures to indicate that there may be something awry in the maxim that what is most profitable is also most socially beneficial, continues to develop inadequately researched products and production procedures. When the hazards of these products and methods are finally documented, business has become so heavily dependent upon them that the corporation spokesmen resist regulation by pointing to the consequences for the industry and the economy generally of having to abandon the product or procedure. All too often their appeals are heard, and the regulation proposals are bargained and modified, while the nation's health suffers.

As one studies the various attempts to correct or reform our administrative procedures, he can begin to understand why students of technology have been driven to the unrelieved pessimism of a Jacques Ellul or the utopian "Consciousness III" vision of a Charles Reich. The task, as I see it, is to admit the inadequacy of the social paradigms we have developed without indulging the desire to slip away *either* into utopian or doomsday fantasies *or* back into outmoded decision-making models such as are presented in the "disjointed incrementalist" strategy of Lindblom and Braybrooke.[5] Until we discover and develop new paradigms, most of our efforts will be incremental and all too disjointed. Perhaps I have proposed only such limited measures in my comments on the church's responsibility as an institutional investor. But the fallacy is to believe either that

---

[5] David Braybrooke and Charles Lindblom, *A Strategy of Decision* (New York: The Free Press, 1963). The key features of this "strategy" of decision-making are that the policy-maker should limit himself to marginal changes in existing policies, will therefore have a very restricted number of policy alternatives to choose from, and hence need consider only a restricted number and range of the consequences of his incremental policy changes. The underlying assumption of the strategy appears to be that when decision-making is limited to such marginal alterations of existing societal states, there will be other decision-makers or groups with sufficient social power to correct or compensate for any deleterious consequences of that alteration. Hence, it can be argued that the strategy presumes that the basic patterns of institutional interaction which now exist in the society are acceptable, or at any rate as satisfactory as can be devised.

such limited initiatives will be sufficient or that they are the best that can be made by contemporary man. It is when our minds are shaped by either of these basic presuppositions that we are really lost.

Toward a Definition of Institutional Responsibility

Responsibility is a concept so bandied about in our ordinary discourse that we may lose any sense that its contours can be generally charted and that its component parts can, to a degree, be specified. It is fallacious to think that this is wholly a result of linguistic imprecisions. It is in part a result of the fact that the social paradigms on the basis of which we implicitly or explicitly define personal and institutional rights, obligations, and perquisites are now in flux and are being continually redefined. As we have seen in the previous section, we are searching for functional and effective principles of social organization in this country. In such a situation it is easy to slip into a frame of mind that suggests that everyone (person, group, or institution) is responsible for everything; the unhappy result is that no one takes responsibility for anything.

I would like to suggest that responsibility is gradable—that there are degrees or levels of responsibility and, further, that we may specify four formal features of situations and contexts in which men or institutions act which can serve as guides in helping them to determine whether they have obligations and how strong their obligations are.

Responsibility accrues to an agent when: (1) a situation is one in which there is a *need* for ameliorative activity; (2) the agent has *proximity* to that need, (3) the agent is *capable* of responding in an ameliorative way to that need, and (4) other agents *cannot* or *are not* effectively ameliorating that need.[6]

All four features must be present to some degree before an agent may be held responsible, and where all four are present, responsibility in the situation becomes greater as any one or more of these features is more strongly present in the situation.

[6] The exposition which follows is largely derived from the exposition of the concept of corporate and shareholder responsibility which appears in chapter 2 of *The Ethical Investor: Universities and Corporate Responsibility*, by John G. Simm, Charles W. Powers, and Jon P. Gunnemann, which was published by Yale University Press in 1972.

(1) *Need.* What constitutes human need will be dependent upon one's explicit or implicit normative understandings. For the purposes of this study, it is assumed that the growing effect of industrial pollution on human health constitutes a need in the human community which requires amelioration—and that such a need is a serious one.

(2) *Proximity.* Proximity is a spatial concept, but the nature of the "space" differs. One is proximate to a need first of all when he has notice of it—or stands in relation to the need in such a way that we may expect him to have notice of it. So, for example, while an industrial polluter may not actually be aware that when his procedures or products are combined with those of others they will constitute a health hazard, he is still to some extent "proximate" to that need if he has failed to take the necessary precautions (*e.g.*, adequate research) to become aware of those results.[7]

Geographical relation to need, which relates to another perspective on "space," is increasingly more difficult to specify in the contemporary period. One is obviously "proximate" to a need when he witnesses a knifing in front of his apartment. But both because the effects of our actions are more distant from us in a technological society and because our ability to be cognizant of situations far removed from us is increased, immediate geographical relation to need is a less adequate guide to our proximity to it.

(3) *Capability.* There are many things which reduce or enhance our capability to act in response to need. Still, two basic features can be delineated. First, capability is intimately related to an agent's *power* to moderate or remove need. A man in Arkansas may be aware of the effects of air pollution caused by a large, New York-based corporation in that city. But unless he has some power to halt it, he is not responsible. The tendency of men and institutions to rationalize concerning their power is an increasingly serious problem in the contemporary period, but the problem is not with this aspect of the notion, "capability." Capability as it relates to power is intimately connected with proximity. If, for example, the man in Arkansas is the deposed

---

[7] Involved here is the whole question of when one is responsible for the unintended consequences of his acts or of his failure to act. This range of issues, as they arise in both law and morals, is treated at length and with sophistication in H. L. A. Hart and A. M. Honore, *Causation in the Law* (Oxford: Oxford University Press, 1959).

vice-president in charge of research of that firm and did not foresee as he should have the consequences of the production methods his researchers developed, then his responsibility for the pollution accrues from that time when he could have done something to stop it.

Second, capability is present or absent (and reduced or increased) depending upon other needs which one must meet or goals and purposes he must serve. Here the question of competing obligations arises. A corporation which gives priority to its obligations to make a profit for its stockholders rather than concentrating on research into the effects of its pesticides perceives itself as incapable of reducing the health hazards of its products. So also does the investment manager of a nonprofit hospital who seeks a maximum investment return for meeting the health service needs of that institution. Whether most of our institutions have properly ordered their responses to the competing obligations which they face, and whether they have accurately gauged their power to ameliorate needs, are the issues at the heart of much of the contemporary questioning about institutional behavior.

(4) *Absence of other sources of ameliorating activity.* It is perhaps this feature which the complexity of contemporary society has most affected. Agents who know and are capable of moderating or removing a need simply do not know when or whether some other agent will take the required action. It is, of course, precisely this ambiguity which the functionalists thought they could reduce by developing an adequate specification of the "division" of society's labors. Here we are pressed back to our earlier discussion of the inadequacy of our social paradigms and mechanisms. Whether it was Adam Smith's invisible hand, or a view of public versus private responsibilities, the basic assumption of most agents, individual or institutional, has been that meeting any need which falls outside specifically declared or assigned goals and purposes is the "responsibility" of someone else. In a period when needs of various sorts persistently are not, in fact, being met and when agents generally do not step forward to meet them, the assumption that "someone else will do it" should be discarded. Since a person or group rarely knows when he is the last resort in this period of societal confusion, perhaps the assumption should be that an institution or person having proximity and capability *is* the last resort—or at least that it or he is responsible for assuring that

someone else will in fact meet the discerned need. One constantly hears the disclaimer, "But that is the government's job," or, "That is the responsibility of the university." As the buck is being passed, needs that we all acknowledge to be real needs are simply not addressed. Many of our expectations will have to be altered if we encounter needs with the thought, "The buck should stop here, because I know about it and can do something." But it is precisely that alteration in mindset which is now required.

The Church and Pollution and Health

All this is preparatory to my primary concern: the church's responsibility in the area of pollution and health. The church as an institution has special purposes, albeit not so limited as those of most institutions. It has developed certain competencies and capabilities and not others. It knows about (is proximate to) many needs, but not all. I will not attempt to structure the discussion which follows rigidly around the four features of responsibility I have just enumerated, for that would result in a wooden treatment of a subject which must be discussed less formally if all relevant considerations and nuances are to be explored. But because those features continually crop up in other verbal costumes, and because citation of them reminds us that as the church thinks out its role in its own terms it cannot forget that it is one institution among many, I will cite one or more of them when relevant.

What is the church's mission and task in relation to the issues of pollution and health? Surely one thing it should be doing is what it is doing in the development of this book. Here the church is constituting itself as what James Gustafson would term a "community of moral discourse" or a "discursive community." It is doing what Paul Ramsey believes is nearly the entire ethical task of the church, the role of the theoretician who weighs the empirical data relevant to technical decision-making and attempts to sharpen understanding of the direction decisions should take when guided by Christian warrants or perspectives. Such ventures are absolutely necessary if the church is to escape its propensity for becoming a "piece of wood floating in the sea, its course, its destination, determined by the currents it does not try to direct."[8] It must not—though it often does—enter an argument armed with unexamined policy directives which indiscriminately bless or damn societal developments on the basis of inadequately researched data and ill-considered, often contradictory, principles.

Cooperative studies such as this one also give the church and its theologians a chance to discern and criticize the often implicit and unexamined ethical presuppositions which guide the practice of scientists, businessmen, and public policy-makers. Hence, even in its role as a community which fosters moral discourse, the church moves beyond its isolation into the world. It is peculiarly suited to recognize the need for normative clarification and to gather through diverse groups ethical expertise to respond to issues like pollution with theological acumen, moral sensitivity, and technical competence.

Quite obviously, the church has not generally been altogether successful in such efforts. Rather than helping society get a grip on its present and prepare for its difficult future, the churches in the past decade have careened wildly among a bewildering variety of theological and eschatological visions. Take your pick: Christianity has a "theology of—" prepared to put the stamp of divinity on almost every conceivable perspective or issue. This is not a distinctively contemporary phenomenon. The blame for many of our present societal dilemmas, for example, lies partially with a church which has often nurtured and even sacralized naive views of human progress and hence given impetus to uninhibited technological development. By permitting a superficial reading of such biblical statements as "By their fruits you shall know them," the church has assented to and spurred on an economic system whose most fundamental maxims depend upon the uninhibited pursuit of profit and growth. No theological formulation has more persistently guided the day-to-day practice of the average Christian than Wesley's "Earn all you can, save all you can, give all you can." That Wesley discovered at the end of his ministry that this separation of economic life from charity results in a view of Christianity which "saps its own foundation"[9] is largely ignored.

[8] James M. Gustafson, *The Church as Moral Decision-Maker* (Philadelphia: Pilgrim Press, 1970), p. 155.

[9] "The Causes of the Inefficacy of Christianity," in *The Works of the Rev. John Wesley, A.M.: Sermons* (New York: Hunt & Eaton, 1825), vol. 2, p. 441.

Whether it concentrates on promulgating Christian principles or on funding the consciousness of the moral agent, the church which attempts to shape and inform the moral ethos in which issues such as pollution are addressed must regain its balance and demonstrate to its own members and to the wider society that it neither sanctions nor excuses those seeking to escape the social and moral consequences of their actions, especially if they do so through slick theological excuses.

For many, the church's responsibility to the world is fulfilled when it has played this theoretical and ethos-forming role. In their opinion, the church oversteps its own authority, misconceives the relationship between church and state, goes beyond its competence, and fails to attend to its own distinctive mission when it moves beyond these tasks and pretends that it either can or should develop public policy directives or utilize its social power to get them implemented.

My remarks here will be limited to the responsibilities of the church as a corporate investor, but I would make analogous points concerning its role as a consumer, property owner, and employer.

Since virtually all national denominations and many local and regional church groups own common stock, each is a part owner of some or many corporations. Although in this economic and political system the law requires that the shareholders have final decision-making authority in respect to some aspects of corporate policy, the doctrine of owner control of corporations has become more a fiction than a reality. Managers have had delegated to them more and more power, and corporate and administrative law has made it increasingly difficult for the stockholders to affect policy-making.

In the last several years, however, a movement to reinstate the idea of corporate democracy has begun, and a recent Federal Court of Appeals decision has added legitimacy to this movement. Perhaps the single most important sentence in that decision is the one which criticizes "management's patently illegitimate claim of power to treat modern corporations with their vast resources as personal satrapies implementing personal, political or moral predilections."[10]

[10] Medical Committee for Human Rights vs. Securities Exchange Commission, U.S. Court of Appeals, District of Columbia Circuit, July 7, 1971 (432, Fed. 2nd, 655). (On appeal by the S.E.C. the case was declared moot by the Supreme Court as this book goes to press.)

Both the movement and the Court of Appeals decision seem to be premised on an understanding that new forms of personal and institutional interaction are necessary—and that many of these new forms will develop in the private rather than the public sector. Was it not just such an understanding which led Dr. Epstein to ask, in his concluding section on legislative and regulatory deficiencies and needs, that private persons and groups be provided with the data necessary for informed involvement and influence? Was it not this understanding which drove Robert Kennedy to increased conversation with nonpublic agencies and groups in the last years of his life? If government cannot or will not consistently function as the visible hand which protects the public interest, or if it consistently defines the "public interest" as equivalent to the maintenance of the existing balance of interests, then—as a last resort—we must search for those societal mechanisms which can most readily be erected or resurrected to step into the breach. Corporate owner decision-making (social investment) has become one of those resurrected mechanisms.

Like universities, foundations, private trust funds, mutual funds, and pension trusts, the churches innocently entered the securities market to seek the maximum return on their assets for their programs. They have suddenly found themselves heirs to a forgotten tradition and thus involved in a complex of social decision-making situations. The investing church has only two basic options in such a situation:

(1) It can get out of the common shareholding business. I agree with the comment of the treasurer of one of the nation's larger foundations: 'If you don't want the emerging responsibilities of being a common stockholder you should not expect the benefits." In other words, if you can't stand the heat, get out of the kitchen.

(2) The church can, on the other hand, affirm that as an economic entity it does have power—not dispositive power, but surely significant fractional power—either to enter its own distinctive social message directly into social policy-making or to join with other institutions in the reduction or elimination of social injury.

The churches will have distinctive views in many areas of social concern.[11] Let us admit that in the area of pollution and

11 See, for example, "Investing Church Funds for Maximum Social

health the church probably has no special competence and may not have a peculiar set of societal goals or even a special perspective. I am wary of the crash efforts now under way to resurrect or create *ex nihilo* a natural theology for the ecological movement. We have developed "instant theologies" too often in recent years—and have regretted their development a few months later. Perhaps the Christian doctrine of creation, when related to other doctrines, does make the church especially concerned about the value of human life. But the church's dominant theological interests seem to provide us only with an incentive persistently to seek health and human wholeness in ways which most non-Christians would also find compelling.

Still, without pretending to competence which it does not yet have, and without spinning out new theological dogmas, the church may find that the governmental deficiencies to which Dr. Epstein has referred call for shareholder involvement. Let me suggest several concrete examples:

(1) Since the Federal Drug Administration has not adequately enforced its regulations that all food additives be evaluated toxicologically prior to marketing, the church could support or initiate a shareholder resolution or a stockholder derivative suit to require that the corporation itself promulgate a firm corporate policy of compliance with the administrative regulation.

(2) Many corporations lobby privately and effectively to limit governmental restrictions on the pollution they cause. A church could initiate or support a shareholder proposal recommending to the corporate management that it seek an industry-wide agreement to make public all special requests of, and information given to, governmental agencies and personnel when those requests and that information are concerned with governmental activities relating to the effect of the industry's products or practices on public health.

(3) If a church holds stock in a corporation which persistently markets products later found to be injurious to health and which then pressures government not to enforce costly restrictions or require product alteration, a church could sponsor a shareholder resolution instructing management to withhold all new products pending the finding of a truly independent re-

Impact." The Report of the Committee on Financial Investment, The United Church of Christ, 1970. The guidelines developed in this report are derived from the social and moral views expressed by that church's General Synod during the past decade.

search group that the products would not create a health hazard. That proposal could be followed by another requiring the management to promote publicly the government's development of adequate protocols for the Federal Register.

(4) If a church owns stock in a corporation whose products have adversely affected the health of a geographically restricted population, a church could try to persuade management—or initiate a shareholder proposal which mandated—that a specified percentage of its corporate contributions should be made available to augment health care facilities in the affected area.

The examples just given are relatively nonaggressive ones. They are simply responses to specific deleterious consequences of past corporate activities. It is also within the province of shareholder power to initiate efforts for structural changes in the corporation which would reduce the possibility that future corporate practices might be injurious to ·health. A church might, for example, support stockholder proposals instructing management to include in all its decision-making processes representatives of constituencies whose health might be affected by its activities. Or it might propose a corporate charter amendment establishing an independent watchdog committee, with full access to all information, which would make an annual report to the stockholders on the corporation's efforts or failures in the area of pollution abatement.[12]

Let us admit that those who protest that the church has recently been promulgating superficial and airy social policy directives in recent years are not altogether wrong. But I would suggest that the reason may be not that the church is by nature incapable of more sophisticated and discriminating social analysis but that law and convention remove the church *qua* church from direct participation in public policy formation. Perhaps it is because the church has had no context of direct responsibility for making decisions that many of its decisions and statements have been vague. When word must be connected to deed, verbal expression is often more precise and thought more disciplined.

When the investing church begins to utilize the mechanisms

---

[12] A church should probably not anticipate winning majority approval of any of the above-mentioned proxy contests in the near future. The social investment movement is not yet that strong. See Charles W. Powers, *Social Responsibility and Investments* (New York: Abingdon, 1971). Public attention focused by similar proposals during the past several years, however, has apparently been an important spur to corporate reform.

for relating its moral and social views to actual practice as an investor, it will confront all the ambiguities and complexities that real social policy decision-making involves. There are costs as well as benefits in having to bring moral views into relation with action. It is possible that the church will get so mired in technicalities that it will lose its distinctive message and become a community of political and strategic discourse rather than one of moral discourse and theological proclamation. I view this as a very real danger. On the other hand, perhaps it is precisely because some of the features of responsibility we have enumerated have been absent when the church has thought about social issues that it has functioned so poorly as an ethical theoretician. Is it not true that a church which discourses on moral and social questions only in the abstract will tend to miss the salient features of real practical reasoning and hence will tend to be irrelevant to actual decision-making?

In its role as an investor, the church realizes certain real needs, knows that it is capable of meeting those needs, and has no assurance that any other agent will meet them. Active involvement in this area may help the church to gain capability and proximity with respect to other needs and issues, for it surely will involve the church in a host of new and difficult institutional interrelationships. Perhaps when individuals and institutions recognize and take on all the responsibilities which they already have we will be on our way toward discovering the new paradigms for our society's life that we so desperately need. Indeed, we may learn that some types of "incrementalism" are not at all productive of "disjointed" results.

The New Genetics and the Future of Man
Michael Hamilton, Editor

The leading architects of change and revolution in contemporary society, according to this fascinating and sometimes frightening book, no longer are the generals, or even the politicians; rather, it is the scientist-technologist who holds the key to the future. But unlike the soldier or the statesman (who speak a language that can be followed, if not always completely understood, by laymen), the scientist speaks a language so foreign to the rest of us that we have long since stopped trying to understand or to influence his activities. As a result, the scientist often works in what amounts to a vacuum of public opinion, despite the fact that he wields potentially more power over our destiny than all the Presidents and Premiers combined.

As The New Genetics and the Future of Man makes clear, society runs a grave risk by granting carte-blanche to the scientific community, particularly in the area of genetics. Test-tube babies, cloning, and gene manipulation were awesome enough merely as elements of science fiction novels. Now that they have become imminent possibilities, communication between the scientific world and the lay world is imperative.

The essays included in this volume make an important contribution to such a dialog. Three